PENGUIN BOOKS
ROMAN BRITAIN

SIR I. A. RICHMOND was educated at Ruthin School and Corpus
Christi College, Oxford, and was a Craven Fellow and Goldsmith's
Senior Student of the University, becoming a lecturer at Queen's
University, Belfast. He later became Professor of the Archaeology of
the Roman Empire at Oxford University. He was Director of the
Society of Antiquaries of London, a Vice-President of the British
Academy and a Royal Commissioner of Ancient Monuments in
England and Scotland. He excavated widely upon Hadrian's Wall
and many other Romano-British military sites. He died in 1965.

MALCOLM TODD has been Professor of Archaeology at the University
of Exeter since 1979. He has written widely on the western Roman
provinces and the early Germanic peoples; his books include *The
Walls of Rome, The South-West to AD 1000, Roman Britain, The Northern
Barbarians* and *The Early Germans*. He edited the journal *Britannia*
from 1984 to 1989. He has served as a Royal Commissioner on the
Royal Commission on Historical Monuments (England) and been a
Visiting Fellow of All Souls College and Brasenose College, Oxford.
He has also held a Senior Research Fellowship of the British Academy
and Leverhulme Trust. From 1961 to 1963 he was a pupil of I. A.
Richmond.

THE PELICAN HISTORY OF ENGLAND
Edited by J. E. Morpurgo

1. ROMAN BRITAIN
Ian Richmond, revised by Malcolm Todd

2. THE BEGINNINGS OF ENGLISH SOCIETY
(FROM THE ANGLO-SAXON INVASION)
Dorothy Whitelock

3. ENGLISH SOCIETY IN THE EARLY MIDDLE AGES
Doris Mary Stenton

4. ENGLAND IN THE LATE MIDDLE AGES
A. R. Myers

5. TUDOR ENGLAND
S. T. Bindoff

6. STUART ENGLAND
J. P. Kenyon

7. ENGLAND IN THE EIGHTEENTH CENTURY
J. H. Plumb

8. ENGLAND IN THE NINETEENTH CENTURY (1815–1914)
David Thomson

9. ENGLAND IN THE TWENTIETH CENTURY (1914–79)
David Thomson with additional material by Geoffrey Warner

I. A. RICHMOND

* * *

ROMAN BRITAIN

REVISED BY MALCOLM TODD

PENGUIN BOOKS

PENGUIN BOOKS

Published by the Penguin Group
Penguin Books Ltd, 27 Wrights Lane, London w8 5TZ, England
Penguin Books USA Inc., 375 Hudson Street, New York, New York 10014, USA
Penguin Books Australia Ltd, Ringwood, Victoria, Australia
Penguin Books Canada Ltd, 10 Alcorn Avenue, Toronto, Ontario, Canada M4V 3B2
Penguin Books (NZ) Ltd, 182–190 Wairau Road, Auckland 10, New Zealand

Penguin Books Ltd, Registered Offices: Harmondsworth, Middlesex, England

First published in Pelican Books 1955
Second edition published 1963
Third edition, revised by Malcolm Todd, published 1995
1 3 5 7 9 10 8 6 4 2

Printed in England by Clays Ltd, St Ives plc
Set in Monotype Baskerville

Contents

LIST OF ILLUSTRATIONS   vii

PREFACE TO THE 1995 EDITION   ix

1. BRITAIN BEFORE THE CONQUEST   1

2. MILITARY HISTORY   20

3. URBAN CENTRES   55

4. RURAL SETTLEMENT AND SOCIETY   87

5. ECONOMIC LIFE   125

6. RELIGIOUS LIFE   162

BIBLIOGRAPHY   191

INDEX   199

List of Illustrations

PLATES

1. Housesteads (Borcovicium); air view (Dr J. K. St Joseph; Crown copyright)
2. (a) Head of Claudius (copyright © Mrs Holland)
   (b) Cameo of a British bear (Society of Antiquaries, Newcastle)
4. (a) Hoxne spoons (copyright © British Museum)
   (b) Hoxne bangle, necklace and bust (copyright ©) British Museum)
5. (a) Corbridge Granary (copyright © Malcolm Todd)
   (b) Corbridge Strongroom (copyright © Malcolm Todd)
6. Hinton St Mary Mosaic (copyright © W. J. White)
7. Coin showing Claudius and his Triumphal Arch (copyright © S. Goddard)
8. Relief of Mithras

FIGURES

1. Inscription from Wroxeter (copyright © Oxford University Press) (p. 63)
2. Gadebridge Park villa (copyright © Society of Antiquaries, London) (p. 97)
3. Woodchester villa (p. 105)
4. Lydney religious site (p. 182)

MAPS

1. *Civitates* of Roman Britain and Roman *coloniae* (p. 14)
2. The Invasion (p. 22)

3. The northern frontier *c.* AD 85 (p. 33)
4. The northern frontier *c.* AD 100 (p. 37)
5. The northern frontier *c.* AD 125 (p. 39)
6. The northern frontier *c.* AD 140 (p. 42)
7. Germanic material AD 400–452 (p. 104)
8. Mineral resources (p. 127)

Preface to the 1995 Edition

The second edition of this book appeared in 1963, immediately before a major explosion of work on Roman Britain and only two years before Ian Richmond's untimely death. The continuing popularity of his little book has long underlined the need for a revised edition, though it is now a virtually impossible task to provide anything more than a general guide to the history and culture of Roman Britain in a work of this modest size. Moreover, a work written by Richmond poses particular difficulties in revision. He was a scholar with a distinguished cast of mind who wrote in elegant, somewhat mannered prose which is not to be imitated. Several chapters have thus been virtually completely rewritten, especially those on urban life, rural settlement and economics. That on military history has been heavily revised, though I have ventured to preserve parts of Richmond's original treatment of religious life. The introductory section on Britain before the conquest is new. It was decided at an early stage to adhere to the original division of chapters, although an entirely new work on the province would certainly be differently ordered. The divisions between urban and rural settlement and between economic life and almost everything else seem increasingly dated. But then it is now nearly thirty years since Richmond's death. Those who were privileged to be taught by this remarkable man will best understand why this revised edition of his book has been prepared.

January 1993

CHAPTER ONE

Britain before the Conquest

Britain may have been known to the merchant-adventurers of
Massalia (Marseilles) as early as 500 BC. A people known as the
Albiones, of the land of Albion, are reported on the far western
shores of Europe from about that date, and they were thought
worthy of mention by a Roman writer nearly a thousand years
later. But Britain entered the reliably recorded history of Europe
with the voyage of Pytheas, also of Massalia, late in the fourth
century BC, the sea-route via the Strait of Gibraltar having been
closed by the Carthaginians for the preceding two centuries.
Pytheas' achievement was to demonstrate that Britain was an
island by circumnavigating its northern end, and he was also able
to make some exploration of its mineral wealth. His account of
this voyage, however, was deemed by many to be fantastic and
much of it has perished as a consequence. After him, there was
virtual silence about the island for another two hundred years.
When we next hear of Britain, the focus of interest was its
minerals, notably the tin of the south-west. When taken together,
the brief accounts of Caesar, Strabo and Pomponius Mela do not
indicate that much had been learnt about the interior of Britain.
Roman public opinion felt distant Britain as almost legendary,
the source of mineral wealth, its very size and definition as an
island in doubt, a new world of awesome isolation and uncharted
risk.

Compared with the peoples of Gaul described by Caesar, the
British tribes had made only modest advances beyond primitive
government. While some of the Gaulish tribes had abolished
kingship in favour of government by magistrates supported by a
tribal council, the Britons by and large retained tribal kings
down to the Roman conquest. In some cases, a unified kingship
may have emerged late in the first century BC. Caesar encountered four kings in Kent, so that a single monarchy among the
Cantiaci must have post-dated 54 BC. Still later, there are signs of

dual kingship among the Iceni and Corieltauvi. Some of the tribes encountered by the armies of Claudius may have emerged as separate entities only in the previous century, or less. It is at least a strong possibility that some had come into existence as a consequence of contact with Rome. Whether, and to what extent, the political structure of the southern British tribes was influenced by Gaulish institutions is not clear, but it is worthy of note that the British tribes had not made any move to replace their kings with elected magistrates by the time of the Roman invasion. Dynastic kings are what the coinage reveals and Roman reference is exclusively to such rulers and never to tribal councils and magistrates. But our evidence for such matters relates only to the south-eastern peoples. To the North and West, less centralized forms of power may have prevailed. Caratacus was able to impose his will upon the Silures and other tribes after his cause was lost in the South-east. We hear of no Silurian king who made way for him, nor later of any single ruler of the Ordovices. In the north, the Brigantes formed no closely unified power and were, apparently uniquely in the Celtic world, ruled by a woman in the mid first century AD. In her relations with Rome, there is no mention of nobles or elders forming any consultative body, although Cartimandua herself came from noble stock. Further north still, tribal kings are not referred to by our sources. When the Roman armies confronted the Caledonians late in the first century, the northerners had many leaders and the man who led them into battle, Calgacus, was presumably elected for that purpose. Whatever the precise status of Calgacus, Tacitus revealingly does not refer to him as a king.

The nobles of the Celts in Britain, like their Gaulish kinsmen, were a warrior-aristocracy, devoted to war and the panoply of war. Single combat between warriors still played a large part in warfare between Celts, though increasing contact with the well-equipped and highly trained armies of Rome from the third century BC had begun to compel the development of a more orderly approach to set-piece battles. There is no sign that such tactics were applied in Britain, even after the Roman invasion. The emphasis was still upon the ambush or the rapid strike and withdrawal before Roman infantry could come to grips. The wealthier British warriors were equipped with the long sword, designed for slashing and used by the foot-soldier and horseman alike. The rank and file were more often armed with spears, jabbing and thrusting weapons, though javelins were also in use. The main means of defence was the shield, usually an elongated oval or rectangle in form, generally of wood, with or without a boss, though a few fine examples in sheet bronze are known; these were clearly parade weapons. Body armour of any kind was very rare and confined to leading warriors. Roman stone reliefs of British warriors show them either naked or wearing no more than breeches. Helmets, too, were possessions of only the wealthier chieftains. The proportions of infantry to horsemen cannot be estimated, but the main body of Iron Age warriors fought on foot. The war-chariot, however, continued in use in Britain until well into the Roman period and was to disconcert Roman troops on several occasions. The rapid onrush of massed chariots could disrupt infantry formations and it is clear that they were used as fighting vehicles, not merely as means of transport to the battle-line. Parts of chariots have been found in votive deposits over much of south-eastern Britain, while most of one vehicle was consigned to a peat-bog deposit at Llyn Cerrig Bach in Anglesey.

The agricultural economy practised by the inhabitants of south-ern Britain was a great deal more sophisticated than Caesar's account suggests. Mixed farming prevailed over most of the island, not merely in the lowland south. Arable agriculture was well established in South Wales, North-east England and eastern Scotland. Climatic conditions markedly improved after 450 BC, permitting settlement in areas that had earlier been inhospitable and encouraging exploitation of marginal ground. By the begin-ning of the first millennium AD, the climate may have been broadly similar to that of today or perhaps a little warmer and drier. These more amenable conditions seem to have stimulated greater specialization in the crops grown by certain communities, for instance on the chalk downland. The wider use of iron tools also improved agricultural practice, though major innovation in such implements as the plough does not seem to have occurred until very late in the Iron Age at the earliest. Sites in valleys and on lowlands tended to raise more cattle and pigs, chalkland and upland settlements to devote more attention to sheep. The great expansion of settlement from the fourth century BC brought under occupation the heavier claylands of the Midlands and damp soils in many other parts of the island. Field-systems that display a high degree of planning in their layout are evident in East Anglia, Wessex and elsewhere, while boundaries marking out large areas of landscape are known in Yorkshire, the Midland plain and Wessex. All this is clearly to be related to a rising population and one in which social structures of some complexity had taken shape before 200 BC. Most of what was to become Roman Britain was well peopled at least two centuries before the Roman invasion and the main lineaments of rural settlement for the next five hundred years already existed by 100 BC.

Economic change on this scale was inevitably accompanied by major developments in related fields, including metalworking, pottery-making, quern production, the manufacture of salt from brine and a wide range of secondary crafts. All of these activities were pursued on a localized basis, but increasingly also as central-ized industries. The growing importance of iron for tools and implements led to large-scale extraction and smelting of the deposits of ironstone in Northamptonshire, Lincolnshire and the Weald. Salt-making developed on the coasts of Essex and Lincoln-shire and the mineral was also extracted from the ground at Droitwich in Worcestershire. Fine pottery was produced at a variety of centres, including the Malvern hills, the Somerset lowlands and south Dorset, and distributed in quantity from them. Textiles, rotary querns and even glass beads were all produced by specialist craftsmen. Such specialization is unlikely to have been generated solely by economic needs, though an enlarged population will have provided its own stimulus. At least as influential will have been the efforts of Iron Age leaders to strengthen their own power-base by promoting and controlling the production of specialized goods and commodities. This marked an important stage in the emergence of political units in southern Britain; these would develop in the first century BC into the tribal kingdoms revealed by the coinage.

The forms of Iron Age settlement were dominated by single farms and small nucleated sites, often enclosed by a bank and ditch, sometimes by a more defensive barrier such as a timber palisade. In all areas of Britain, the *Einzelhof* or single family homestead is so well represented that earlier scholars were persuaded that it was virtually the only settlement type apart from the hill-fort. Small community settlements do, in fact, occur, though in no region do they seem to have been the norm. Larger-scale lowland settlement developed from the second century BC in southern and eastern Britain and by the first century the extensive *oppida* at Verulamium, Calleva and Camulodunum were well established. Hill-forts, in their heyday from the middle of the first millennium to 200 BC, were being progressively abandoned thereafter as leaders sought to dominate larger expanses of lowland territory. The more advanced began to carve out petty kingdoms and mark their power by issuing coinage. Socially and economically, these rulers may have drawn some of their authority from their external contacts, particularly with Gaulish merchants seeking to exploit the raw materials and other products of Britain. In order to satisfy the commercial demands from the Continent, British leaders may have extended their power, either by conquest or by forceful development of the exchange network. They may also have been influenced in their ideas of leadership by Roman recognition of some rulers as friendly kings. One mark of this may be the appearance of the word *rex* on the coinage of Eppillus, Verica and Cunobelin.

The trade links that the Roman world operated with Britain clearly reflect a variety of economic structures and may not be given a single interpretation. An early attraction was the tin of Devon and Cornwall, known to Pytheas in the later fourth century BC, and a regular target for continental traders by the first century. The main centre of exchange in this metal was the island of Ictis, close to shore and linked to the mainland at low tide. Several candidates for this place have been proposed, including the Isle of Wight, Hengistbury Head and Mount Batten on Plymouth sound, but identification is as yet beyond us. By the early first century BC, continental imports were arriving at several points on the southern coast, notably Hengistbury Head, Mount Batten, Poole Harbour and possibly Portland Bill. Amphorae of wine were to the fore in this trade, followed by fine pottery from northern Gaul and other Gaulish imports such as silver coins. Inland, Hengistbury drew upon the raw materials of the Mendips, Wessex and the south-western peninsula, while at the site itself craftsmen were working in silver, bronze, iron and shale. There is no direct evidence for the involvement of Italian traders. Gauls are much more likely to have been the principal intermediaries, exploiting the ties of kin and clientship. Other imports arrived as gifts and diplomatic offerings rather than goods of trade. Bronze vessels found in a burial at Aylesford in Kent came from Italy and may represent gift-exchange. Leading members of the Trino-vantes and Catuvellauni were buried in elaborate grave-vaults along with amphorae and fine imported drinking sets. At Welwyn a chieftain was the possessor of a pair of silver drinking goblets, a gift emanating from a high level in Roman society.

The developing economic connections with the adjacent Conti-nent are most fully documented by the coinage, a vital source of information on political and economic conditions. The earliest coins arrived from northern Gaul in the late second century BC. These were high-value gold issues and are thus to be related to rewards for service and the storage of wealth rather than to the functions of a true currency. These early coins may well have been brought back to Britain by warriors who had given military service to Gaulish leaders. They were soon followed by issues struck in Britain to both sides of the Thames valley and in East Anglia. A further spurt of coinage was imported from Gaul about the time of Caesar's conquest there, reasonably to be linked with the flight of the leaders of tribes like the Bellovaci, who fled to Britain in 57 BC, and with individuals such as Commius, who had his private reasons for quitting Gaul. Commius was one of the first rulers in Britain to sign his coins. Thereafter, the practice was taken up by the leading houses of most of the southern peoples. A significant development of the later first century was the spread of bronze coinage, a token currency indicating the growth towards a market economy and the lesser transactions that gold and silver coins could not service. Interestingly, Roman coinage was not imported, though Roman coin-types and motifs were added to certain series of British coins after 20 BC. Overall, the use of coinage spread north to the Trent and Humber and west to the Severn basin, but not to the peoples beyond. In the North and West older economic systems were to continue down to the Roman conquest and beyond.

The technical and artistic achievements of the later Iron Age population of southern Britain are spectacularly revealed by the fine metalwork of the second and first centuries. British rulers and their leading warriors increasingly displayed their wealth and status in magnificent weaponry and ornaments, many of which have been recovered from votive deposits in streams and rivers. The skill of the metal-smiths who produced the gold torcs found at Snettisham and Ipswich was not to be surpassed in Britain until the Anglo-Saxon centuries. Bronze-working was carried to as high a pitch as anywhere in Europe in such pieces as the Battersea and Witham shields, the chamfrein (frontlet for a horse) from Torrs and the mirrors from Birdlip and Desborough. The achievement was by no means merely technical. There is a sureness of touch in the designs and decorative treatment of the finest objects that is breathtaking. These are aristocratic posses- sions, but by the later stages of the Iron Age fine brooches, bronze bowls, belt- and harness-fittings and pottery were widely distrib- uted on humble settlement sites. Even the superb and lavish gold torcs had their modest counterparts in bronze.

THE PEOPLES OF BRITAIN

The tribes best known to Rome before the conquest were the three peoples Trinovantes, Catuvellauni and Atrebates. The Tri- novantes, on the northern shore of the Thames, were known to Caesar and gained, at least briefly, from his protection. At the heart of their territory lay the great *oppidum* of Camulodunum, the seat of Trinovantian kingly power from at least the earlier first century BC. Their coinage had begun by that time and from the later first century reveals a continuous dynasty of rulers from Addedomarus to Cunobelin, the greatest of British kings. One or more of the lords of Camulodunum rose to the rank of king from a power-base elsewhere. Dubnovellaunus had earlier held sway in

Kent and took possession of Camulodunum, and presumably of all the tribal territory, before fleeing to Rome as a suppliant, along with Tincommius, about AD 5. He was succeeded by Cunobelin, the scion of the Catuvellaunian house, who was to reign for at least the next thirty years and dominate the south-eastern tribes during that time. Connections both cultural and political between the British tribal nobility and the Roman world developed apace during the reign of Augustus. Some rulers almost certainly achieved recognition as kings by Rome, no mere empty form in a society in which kingship was not inviolable, and they proclaim the fact on their coinage in Latin. A leader buried in the Lexden tumulus at Camulodunum included among his grave-goods a portrait-medallion of Augustus, quite clearly a diplomatic gift. The burials of other nobles reveal more material accessions from the Roman provinces: silver drinking cups, bronze vessels and amphorae of wine provided either through the channels of trade or as tokens of friendship and alliance. The coinage of the later dynasties also bears the impress of these contacts. Several series of coins not only bore designs that came from the imagery of the Roman world but also were struck from dies that were probably engraved by Roman craftsmen. Further stimulus to-wards the development of a market economy was provided by the growth of commerce with the Roman provinces. Wine came in from Italy and Spain, fine pottery from Italy and Gaul, more workaday vessels from northern Gaul and the Rhineland. The development of these commercial links may have played a part in the 'hands-off' policy that Augustus pursued towards Britain, along with his generally relaxed view of the British kingdoms, which in any case constituted no great threat to the security of the north-western provinces. Strabo may well be repeating an official view when he remarks that tolls on cross-Channel traffic yielded as much as would the conquest of Britain.

The other major centre of power in the later Iron Age lay between the middle Thames and the Channel: the kingdom of the Atrebates. This may have been the creation of Commius after his dramatic flight from his erstwhile ally Caesar in 50 BC. At all events coins bearing his name appear as the first inscribed group in his region and his successors describe themselves as sons of

Commius. Commius' contacts in Gaul may have enabled him to establish his new power-base with ease and despatch. His capital was most probably Silchester (Calleva), which made important strides in urban development late in the first century BC, though another substantial *oppidum*, about which little is known, existed around Chichester. Tincommius succeeded his father by 20 BC and shortly afterwards his coinage began to reveal designs so close to those of Roman currency that Roman craftsmen must be seen as their authors. It is thus not a complete surprise to find Tincommius appearing in the *Res Gestae* of Augustus as a refugee and suppliant to the emperor, along with Dubnovellaunus, about AD 5. He was succeeded by his brother Eppillus and he in turn by Verica, both of whom proudly proclaim their status as *rex* on their coins. Verica seems to have enjoyed a long reign, but was forced to flee to the emperor Claudius shortly before AD 43, thereby providing a convenient (though scarcely needed) pretext for invasion.

One of the most shadowy of the peoples of Britain was, ironically, the Belgae. The *civitas Belgarum* in the Roman period included both Winchester (its capital) and Bath, so that the territory of the tribe should have reached from southern Hampshire to the Somerset Avon. But modern discussion of the Belgae in Britain has centred on the vexed question of 'Belgic' (northern Gaulish) cultural and political influence in the island, some writers arguing that several of the leading tribes of the south-east were 'Belgic' or strongly affected by Belgic culture. These included the Catuvellauni, Trinovantes, Atrebates and Cantiaci. That there were political and cultural links with northern Gaul is undeniable, but archaeological evidence alone does not permit assessment of how deep this influence ran. After Caesar, the only Belgae mentioned in Britain are those included in the *civitas Belgarum*, and it is worth considering that the main Belgic group in the island was situated in this territory and not further to the south-east. This may help to explain why Commius fled to, or through, this area of Britain: it was a region with which he already had connections. A major centre of power may have lain at Winchester, where an extensive settlement bounded in part by earthworks is known.

The south-western peninsula of Devon and Cornwall was occupied by the Dumnonii, of whom literary sources say virtually nothing except in connection with the trade in tin in the later first millennium BC. The geography of the peninsula did not encourage unity and the record of settlement indicates a dispersed and apparently numerous population. Large hill-forts were few and they lay mainly east of the river Exe. Large numbers of hill-slope enclosures rather than strongly fortified hill-forts are a marked characteristic of the region in the pre-Roman Iron Age and some of these may have remained in occupation into the Roman period. The dominant settlement type was the 'round', a small enclosed site usually comprising a single homestead. No central focus of tribal authority is known and the tribe may well have been an agglomeration of several *pagi* or sub-units. It is even possible that two tribal units were brought together by Rome to form the *civitas Dumnoniorum*. The Dumnonii themselves may have been centred on what is now Devon, while Cornwall could have been the seat of the Cornovii, whose name figures in the place-name Durocornoviorum ('fort of the Cornovii'). So much is speculation, but it would at least help to explain why the Roman administrative centre of this people was sited at Exeter, far to the eastern side of the *civitas*. The Dumnonii struck no coinage and no names of tribal rulers are otherwise recorded. Their territory, however, was rich in mineral deposits, especially of tin both in Devon and Cornwall, but including also copper, iron and a little silver and gold.

The Durotriges of Dorset, south Somerset and west Hampshire seem not to have maintained close cultural connections with the peoples to the east of them, but were certainly in contact with the peoples of Gaul, two or three days' sail away. Trade with Armorica was well developed by the early first century BC, and commercial activity widened its scope and importance as Roman merchants came upon the scene thereafter. The Durotrigian clans maintained some of the largest hill-forts in Britain, including Ham Hill (the largest of all), Maiden Castle, Hambledon, Hod Hill and South Cadbury, and several of these had developed into substantial town-like communities by the late Iron Age. Apart from these strongholds with their forbidding defences, at least one major lowland *oppidum* existed, at Ilchester in Somerset, but the tribe remained politically fragmented. Their coinage, which never bore inscriptions, was ultimately derived from the British B series but soon deteriorated in fineness of metal and design. The later base pieces did, however, circulate as a token currency into the Roman period. Some of the cultural traditions of the tribe were markedly conservative. They continued to inhume their dead, resisting the introduction of cremation from further east, until well after the Roman conquest. Their contacts with the Continent did not then wholly destroy their individuality nor their tribal integrity.

The lower Severn basin and the Cotswolds were the preserve of the large tribe of the Dobunni. Here, too, lay large hill-forts but many had been abandoned in favour of lowland settlement in the later phases of the Iron Age. A large *oppidum* existed at Minchinhampton near Stroud and another at Bagendon, north of Cirencester, both of these developing in the first century BC. Culturally, the Dobunni made great advances after 100 BC, perhaps under stimulus from tribes to the east, and they may have extended their territory to the south to include the Mendips and their mineral wealth. They struck coins from the middle of the first century BC and the names of rulers began to appear after about AD 10: Anted, Eisu, Catti, Comux, Corio and Bodvoc. Some of these, including Corio and Bodvoc, were apparently contemporaries, ruling over different parts of the tribal territory. Dobunnic lands were wide and rich and could easily have supported several petty kingdoms. One of these, at least, would later find it politic to submit at an early date to the advancing Roman armies.

West of the Severn, in the Glamorgan and Gwent plain and the broken hill-country behind, lay the Silures. Their heartland was the fertile coastal plain but they also occupied the much less hospitable valleys and the bare plateaus between them, a terrain which will have naturally turned their eyes towards the rich land to the east, well within the range of plundering bands. No nucleus of Silurian power is known and probably none existed. Their leading families were able to import, or loot, fine metalwork from their neighbours, but other contacts were strictly limited. West of the Silures, in Pembrokeshire, were the Demetae, whose territory was dotted with a myriad small defended homesteads. Hill-forts were rare and no tribal centre is evident. The hills and coastal plain of North and central Wales and the fertile island of Anglesey were the domain of the Ordovices, probably the largest of the Welsh tribes and, like the others, very scattered in their settlement pattern. Their settlements are best known on the Caernarvonshire hills, taking the form of isolated hut-groups set within their own fields. Centralized forms of settlement were unknown and the tribe may have been no more than a loose assembly of clans. Smaller and more unified was the tribe of the Deceangli, which inhabited Flint and Denbighshire. They controlled important deposits of silver, lead and copper and were thus to be an early target of Roman attention. South and east of them lay the Cornovii of the Cheshire plain and the upper valley of the Severn, a people scarcely known to history but occupying a strategically vital area of the Marches through which routes led into the central hills of Wales. Several hill-forts dominated their territory, that on the Wrekin being perhaps a major political centre towards the end of the Iron Age. The Roman seat of the *civitas Cornoviorum* was later founded over the site of an abandoned legionary base in the valley below. Nothing is known of their ruling house, though the fact that their land was early used by Roman armies as a springboard for attack on central Wales has been seen as an indication of a pro-Roman leaning among the leading group.

The Midlands from the Trent basin to the Nene was the territory of the Coritani or Corieltauvi, a very large tribe with close links with the South-east of Britain. Several large settlements are known from the later Iron Age, including Leicester, Old Sleaford, Ancaster and Dragonby, all in low-lying positions and all apparently undefended. There was a mint at Old Sleaford, but the distribution of the other sizeable settlements seems to suggest a fragmentation of political power. The fact that later coins of the tribe bear the names of two rulers or magistrates adds substance to the case. Political division may have allowed the Romans a quick success against them after AD 43, for the tribe is not mentioned as one that was involved in the early campaigns, and yet Roman forts were quickly established on their territory. The natural resources of this region were great: there was abundance of iron and salt as well as excellent farming land. Such wealth might well have attracted the attention of dynasties to the south.

Wealth in portable form had also been accumulated by the Iceni of Norfolk and north Suffolk. Although a small tribe, its leading members had access to surprisingly large quantities of gold and electrum, as is revealed by a number of hoards dating mainly from the first century BC. The most remarkable concentration of these lay at Snettisham, where as many as seventy separate caches of gold objects have recently been found. The Icenian coinage names a series of rulers from about AD 25 onward: Anted, Ecen, Aesu and Saenu, but there is no reference to the king whose death in AD 59 was to lead to disaster for the tribe: Prasutagus (below, p. 25). As an allied tribe, the Iceni may have been permitted to continue their coinage after the Roman invasion. Major settlements are not well known, though obviously one existed in the Snettisham area. An intriguing site, either a palatial residence or a religious centre, lay near Thetford and continued in use into the early Roman period, perhaps down to the Boudiccan revolt.

A highly distinctive Iron Age culture had emerged in south-east Yorkshire by the third century BC, which may cautiously be identified as ancestral to the historical Parisi, placed by Ptolemy between the Humber and Bridlington Bay. The very name of the Parisi is a strong hint of an ultimate derivation from northern Gaul, though the archaeological connections seem to point to Champagne or the middle Rhine rather than the Seine basin around Paris. The most striking element linking East Yorkshire with northern Gaul is the square-ditched burial monument, in some cases surrounding the graves of warriors who were accompanied into the next world by carts as well as sword and shield. The settlements of the Parisi are less well recorded and no central *oppidum* is known. They did not strike coinage but there are signs that they engaged in a lively trade with merchants based in south-eastern Britain and possibly directly with Roman entrepreneurs. Their largely lowland territory may have attracted the jealous interest of their neighbours to the north, the Brigantes,

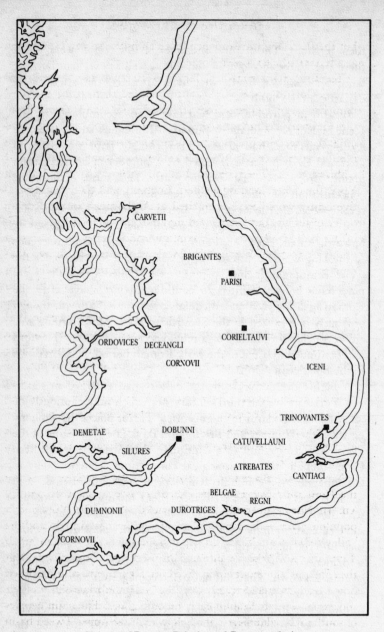

1. *Civitates* of Roman Britain and Roman *coloniae*

but they retained their independence and were to win recognition as a separate *civitas* under Rome.

The Brigantes covered the largest territory of any of the British tribes, which may be why Tacitus believed them to be the most numerous people. Their lands stretched from sea to sea and from the southern Pennines to the Tyne–Solway gap. So large and upland a terrain did not promote unity and the names of a number of septs or sub-tribes are known, for example Carvetii and Gabrantovices. The heartland of the tribe was the Vale of York, the richest land in northern England, and their administrative centre would have been sited at Aldborough in the Roman order of things. But there is no sign of a major Iron Age nucleus in the Vale, the nearest approximation to it being the *oppidum* at Stanwick in the valley of the Swale. Large hill-forts were not numerous among the Brigantes, the common settlement-form being smaller enclosed sites on valley-sides and floors. Although often seen in the past as a largely pastoral society, the Brigantes had access to good agricultural land and it is fairly certain that their economic life was varied. They did not strike or use coinage and no Brigantian rulers are recorded before Cartimandua, whose relations with Rome were to prove such a source of trouble for her people (below, p. 27). But any ruler would have had difficulty in maintaining unity among so extensive a tribe, comprising so many warlike clans with little or nothing in common. The leading nobility of the Brigantes had access to wealth, as is seen in their fine metalwork, found in hoards from Yorkshire to southern Scotland.

North of the Brigantes lay peoples unknown to history before the Roman advance into their territory late in the first century AD. In Northumberland and Berwickshire lay the Votadini, a populous tribe with many settlements in the coastal plain and the valleys of Cheviot. Their principal *oppidum* was the isolated hill of Traprain Law, which continued in use under Roman rule. But the bulk of the population lived in settlements and enclosed homesteads scattered widely over the Northumbrian hills, as their successors were to do until early modern times. The main peoples of southern Scotland were the Selgovae of the upper Tweed basin and the Novantae to the south-west. Neither had any obvious focus: the tribesmen lived apart in homesteads, crannogs and small hill-forts, though they were capable of concerted action on occasion, as when they were called on to oppose the Roman advance. The most densely settled regions of Scotland were the lowland between the Forth and the Clyde, and the coastal plain of Fife and Strathmore on the eastern flank of the highlands. There were many fortified places in both areas, ranging from forts to small enclosed fastnesses or duns, eloquent testimony to the warrior-society that held sway here. Extending northward were the imposing stone-built towers or brochs, some of which were still occupied in the first century AD.

JULIUS CAESAR AND BRITAIN

The remoteness of Britain from Roman experience is clear enough from the writings of Diodorus and Strabo, and from the immense fame that Julius Caesar was to enjoy merely by invading the island. What his military and political intentions were in doing so is virtually impossible to divine: possibly Caesar himself had not defined them closely. He had encountered British warriors fighting against him in Gaul, as he reports, and that provided him with the occasion for punitive action; this may indeed have been the sole pretext for the invasion of 55 BC. The much larger expedition of the following year looks more like an attempt at permanent conquest. Even that of 55 was formidable enough to impel several British tribes to offer submission to Caesar before he sailed from Gaul.

Late in August, a force of two legions and a cavalry unit was assembled for the Channel crossing. The cavalry transports, however, were late in starting and were then blown back to Gaul by adverse winds. They attempted a crossing a few days later but this time were scattered by a storm. The main force made its landfall, probably in the area of Dover and Walmer, in the face of an opposing force of Britons. Caesar had sent ahead an officer to reconnoitre the coast for useful harbours, but neither in 55 nor in 54 was a secure anchorage found or used. In both campaigns the deficiency was to prove very dangerous. In 55 the storm that scattered the cavalry transports in the Channel also badly damaged Caesar's fleet on the beach. His forces on land achieved little beyond a landing; one of his units, the VII legion, had to be rescued from a British ambush. Caesar had been much closer to disaster than to success, and he must have been relieved to return to Gaul without serious loss. But his aim to return to Britain was fixed.

The preparations undertaken in the following winter reveal the serious intent with which Caesar viewed the campaign in 54. No less than 600 transport vessels were made ready, in addition to twenty-eight warships. The transports were built to a design that was broad in the beam and shallow in draught, navigable by oar as well as sail. Caesar intended to get his men ashore quickly, by beaching the troop carriers. The force to be conveyed comprised five legions and 2,000 cavalry, an army that might well aim to overrun a large part of south-east Britain. In all, with the inclusion of the vessels of private individuals, more than 800 ships made a difficult crossing in early July. This time the landing was not opposed. The Britons had moved back to more commanding ground inland, and Caesar's forces got ashore with ease and established a base camp. The sudden and rapidly executed strike was a favourite tactic of Caesar's and he used it now, thrusting inland to a river (perhaps the Stour) where the Britons had assembled in strength. Caesar had no difficulty in pushing them back from their position on the river-crossing and then in capturing a stronghold on the north side, using the classic manoeuvre of the *testudo*, in which legionaries of the VII legion locked shields together over their heads and broke into the hill-fort after constructing a causeway across its ditch.

Hardly had this success been gained than Caesar heard of a major loss to his ships through a storm on the previous night. The damaged vessels were promptly repaired, but time was lost and the Britons regrouped under the war-leadership of Cassivellaunus, a chieftain or king elected by his peers to perform the specific task of opposing the invaders. He was well aware that the Britons could not hope to prevail in pitched battles against Roman troops. Instead, he based his strategy upon sudden attacks on forces on the move or constructing fortifications, using his large force of charioteers to good effect. Caesar's soldiers had no experience of chariots in war, for they had been abandoned in western Europe earlier in the first century, and time was needed to devise effective tactics to deal with them. But Caesar pushed on to the Thames, fording it a few miles upstream of the later site of London, and moved into the territory of the Trinovantes, one of whose princes, Mandubracius, had earlier fled to Caesar in Gaul when his father had been murdered by Cassivellaunus. At Caesar's approach the Trinovantes sued for peace; they were soon followed by other tribes. But Cassivellaunus retained the loyalty of many warriors and continued his effective guerrilla campaign. When Caesar began to close in on his stronghold, the British leader commanded the kings of the tribes in Kent to attack the Roman naval camp. It was a bold and skilful ploy but it failed, and shortly afterwards Cassivellaunus submitted to Caesar. The summer was well advanced and Caesar may have received disturbing news from Gaul. At any rate, he was ready to depart. Hostages were taken from the defeated tribes, tribute was arranged and the Trinovantes were given sureties against attack from their neighbours. Caesar's expedition had been a qualified success but it led to no lasting results. Britain was not drawn into the orbit of Roman power and influence. Caesar may have felt that the decisive first step had been taken towards the creation of a Roman province in Britannia, but, if he did, there was to be no follow-up. The arrangements made by Caesar in 54 may have been observed for a time, but they were to lapse and gave rise to no closer relationship between Britain and Rome. Tacitus' summary on Caesar's achievement was fair: he had revealed Britain but not delivered it to Rome.

There was to be no return to Britain for a century. Although Augustus left open the possibility of an invasion of Britain, and may have seriously mooted that project from time to time, it is unlikely that such an intervention was ever seen as a pressing matter of imperial policy. Even when there were signs of evident planning towards a campaign against the Britons, as in 34 and 28 BC, we cannot be certain that this was not Augustan propaganda, designed to conceal a real intention in some other direction, or a ruse by an emperor who was always sensitive on the matter of military success and its benefit in popular support. When a poet like Horace writes that Augustus was about to attack the Britons, the most remote people in the world, it is rash to see this as a reflection of determined policy. A theme which might evoke echoes of Caesar would have had resonance early in Augustus' reign. But after 16 BC and the beginning of the great enterprise in Germany, such references lost their meaning and could be quietly dropped.

CHAPTER TWO

Military History

Towards the end of the long reign of Cunobelin came the first of a number of events that focused Roman attention on Britain once more. About AD 40 Cunobelin expelled his son Adminius, who fled to the Continent and submitted himself to the emperor Gaius. At the time that unstable prince was engaged in directing an expeditionary force in northern Gaul, which halted at the Channel coast about Boulogne but which, uniformly hostile sources report, had been assembled in order to carry out an invasion of Britain. We cannot now hope to fathom the true intentions of Gaius, a capricious young man, but it is at least plausible that he did plan to invade the island and was prevented by indiscipline among his troops. The matter of Britain did not fall back into obscurity when he was assassinated and Claudius was propelled into office. Another British leader, Verica, who may have been pro-Roman in inclination, was expelled by the sons and successors of Cunobelin and British demands for his return were turned down. The changed scene in Britain coincided with a new age in Rome. The new *princeps* stood in need of early military success, for which two possible theatres presented themselves: Mauretania (Morocco and western Algeria) and Britain. The latter promised a far greater share of glory, not least because it had been invaded by the great Caesar but not subdued by him. Other considerations, such as the mineral wealth of Britain, may have been weighed, but they were secondary to Claudius' quest for military renown.

The expeditionary force that assembled early in the summer of AD 43 comprised four legions: the II Augusta from the Upper Rhine, the IX Hispana from Pannonia, the XIV Gemina from the middle Rhine and the XXth from the lower Rhine, and an unknown but very sizeable contingent of auxiliary units, under the command of Aulus Plautius, a distant relative of Claudius by marriage and governor of Pannonia. The high importance of the expedition is reflected in the calibre of the senior officers who took part, including two men destined to be emperors, Vespasian and Galba, and two who would be governors of Britain, Ostorius Scapula and Didius Gallus. The start was inauspicious. The army at first refused to embark, disturbed by the prospect of sailing beyond the limits of the world, and had to be persuaded to their duty by one of the emperor's close advisers, the freedman Narcissus. The delay thus caused may have convinced the Britons that the expedition had been put off: at all events they made no attempt to oppose the landing of the great fleet. Our only source on the early course of the invasion, Cassius Dio, reports that the Roman forces sailed in three divisions, and thus possibly made separate landfalls, a reasonable strategy in ancient sailing conditions. Dio does not specify where the forces went ashore, but east Kent is the most likely area, for here were several good harbours and short communications with the Thames valley. The anchorages sheltered by the Isle of Thanet are unlikely to have been ignored and Richborough was certainly quickly in use as a stores-base. Dover and Lympne might also come into the reckoning but no evidence has yet been recovered for Claudian use here. The fleet, or part of it, may have been sent on ahead to reconnoitre the coast and gather intelligence. The main force was soon on the move towards the Thames and did not encounter resistance until the Britons, led by the two sons of Cunobelin, Caratacus and Togodumnus, made a stand at a river crossing, probably the Medway, and held up the advance for two days. But Roman troops forced the crossing and were soon advancing to the Thames, to which the Britons fell back. Again the training of Roman auxiliaries enabled them to cross the stream and inflict heavy casualties on their opponents. Some time later Togodumnus was killed and Caratacus was left to continue British resistance on his own. In order to do so effectively, he retired far to the West, to the Welsh hills, and there sustained a guerrilla campaign for the next nine years. Having crossed the Thames, Aulus Plautius halted his advance to enable the emperor to join his army for the final push on the British capital of Camulodunum, no doubt by prior arrangement. Claudius had his victory, and he celebrated his formal triumph in Rome in 44. The Imperial

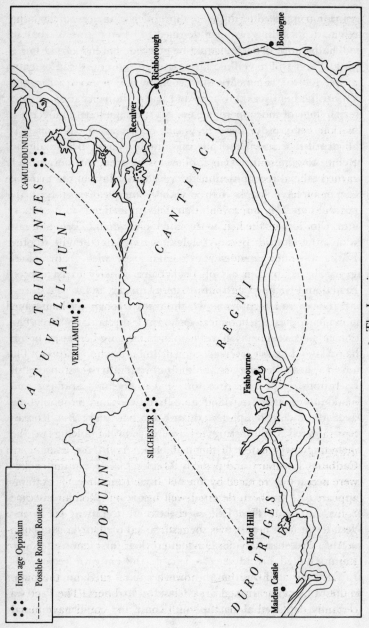

2. The Invasion

coinage trumpeted forth the fact for much of the rest of Claudius' reign.

The capture of Camulodunum marked the end of the beginning. There will have been little time left for serious campaigning in 43, for the summer was well advanced or even at an end. Probably as early as this, some of the British tribes began to seek terms for surrender or alliance with the invaders. The Iceni of Norfolk were one of these, their king achieving recognition as an allied ruler. The origin of the most famous of the British allies of Rome, Cogidumnus or Cogidubnus, is obscure, but he probably earned official recognition in the very early days of the province and may have sought refuge with Rome before AD 43. It is possible, though unproven, that he was related to Verica or otherwise seen as the heir to the latter's kingdom. The realm over which Cogidubnus presided, later enlarged by the gift of other lands, no doubt provided the Roman army with an invaluable springboard for their assault on Wessex, which clearly followed hard upon seizure of the south-eastern *civitates*.

Wessex was a territory in which hilltop strongholds had played a major role in the political geography of the later Iron Age. Some, like Danebury, had been abandoned long before 43; others, like Maiden Castle, were occupied down to the conquest. This landscape studded with strongholds is probably the setting for the operations of the II legion, for some two years under the command of Vespasian, in which more than twenty native strongholds were seized, thirty battles fought and two powerful tribes defeated. Several Wessex hill-forts reveal use by units of the Roman army, including the greatest of them all, Ham Hill, Hod Hill, South Cadbury, Hembury and possibly Maiden Castle. Not all of these were necessarily reduced by force of arms: Hembury, for example, appears to have been deserted well before the Roman invasion. Some, including Hod Hill, were held by the army for over a decade, perhaps nearer two, suggesting that the Durotriges continued to cause anxiety for long after their first encounter with Rome.

The main military bases, however, were sited on the major routes and in the coastal areas close to harbours. The fleet was certainly deployed along the south coast and could have moved men and supplies with decisive speed. A stores-base was established at Fishbourne, at the head of a navigable creek, and the many advantages offered by the Solent will not have been missed. Further west, the large and inviting expanse of Poole Harbour would have exerted its attraction and early Roman material is recorded from here at Hamworthy. A large fort, probably for a legionary force, was established a short way inland at Lake Farm near Wimborne. No full-scale legionary fortress is yet known in Wessex and it is a strong possibility that legionaries were being deployed in small battle groups for a decade or more after the invasion. But by the early fifties a legionary base was founded at Exeter and probably occupied by Legion II Augusta. The conquest of the peninsula of Devon and Cornwall was not finally completed until the late fifties or sixties, but this was a far less urgent task than the subjection or control of the peoples of eastern Wales. This was to engage a succession of governors for a decade after AD 49 and was to prove no light undertaking, despite the scornful judgement passed on the achievement of the commanders by Tacitus.

Censure might with greater justice have been cast upon Roman strategy in Wales rather than upon the activity of individual governors. The first thrust, by Ostorius Scapula in 49, was against the Deceangli in the north-east. It was called off when a disturbance among the Brigantes required the intervention of Roman arms. Next, Ostorius turned upon the Silures, whose native spirit of resistance had been stiffened by the arrival among them of Caratacus some years before. Realizing that it was only a matter of time before the net closed on the Silures, Caratacus switched his base to the Ordovices of North Wales. His elusive tactics were effective for a time but at length he decided to stand and fight in a last throw. The desperate courage of the tribesmen was not enough and defeat was total. Although Caratacus was able to flee to the Brigantes, Cartimandua honoured her undertaking to Rome and handed him over. He was later despatched to Rome where he was to put on a dignified performance in a public show.

By the mid fifties Roman forces were in control of the Midlands, the Welsh borderland and the Trent basin. No campaigns are recorded in eastern Britain after AD 43, though the allied Iceni rose in protest in AD 47 and had to be restrained. The realities of Roman rule must by now have been evident to the other *civitates* of lowland Britain. Considerable change was made to military dispositions between AD 50 and 60. A legionary base was established at Kingsholm, Gloucester, in about 50, and this was held for at least fifteen years. Substantial Roman forces were already deployed in south-east Wales by the mid fifties and a large supply-depot was sited at Usk by AD 55, implying the presence of a sizeable number of units by that date. Occupation of the country between the upper Trent and Severn had begun by 55, if not earlier, with large forts positioned at Wall (Staffordshire) and Kinvaston (Warwickshire), and the upper Severn may have been seized about the same date, as a fort at Leighton near Wroxeter suggests. It follows that there was no thought of establishing a frontier line across the Midlands from the lower Severn to the lower Trent, with the Fosse Way as its line of lateral communication. Such a concept had not yet been developed in mainland Europe and in any case would have run counter to the strategy which had been applied in Britain from the beginning: to conquer the rest, or as much as possible.

North Wales and Anglesey formed the target for the next major campaign in the West. The governor appointed in AD 58 was Suetonius Paullinus, a commander of distinction who had earlier operated in Mauretania, bringing under control the warlike peoples of the Atlas mountains by seizing the fertile plains on which they relied for supplies. He decided upon a similar policy in Wales, aiming first at the fertile island of Anglesey (Mona: Mam Cymru) and reserving the hill-country to a later stage. Much care was given to preparations for the expedition, and shallow landing-craft were built to navigate the Menai Strait. Initially appalled by the defenders on the far bank, whose fighting spirit had been whipped up by druids and black-clad women running among the lines of warriors, the Roman forces gathered themselves and pushed forward to a decisive victory. What should have been a great success, crowned by the conquest of the rest of North Wales, was cut short by news of a massive and terrifying rebellion in the South-east, one of the most serious threats to Roman authority ever made in the western provinces.

The seat of the revolt lay among the Iceni, whose king Prasutagus, long friendly towards Rome, died in or shortly before AD 60.
He left half of his estate to the emperor and the remainder was
divided between his two daughters. There was to be no continuance of allied status for the Iceni. The days of client rulers were
over. Claudian policy had suited well the early days of the
province, but the advisers of Nero knew well that a fully developed
Britannia had no need of allied rulers within its bounds. Prasutagus' legacy was rapidly absorbed, but much worse was the brutal
treatment meted out to his widow Boudicca and her daughters:
Boudicca committed suicide by poison. The tribal aristocracy
had its own grievances. Grants of money paid by Claudius to
leading Britons were now being called in as if they had been
loans. Roman financiers, chief among them Seneca, the philo-
sopher and tutor to Nero, had also been at work in Britain, and
they too were beginning to claw back what they had laid out.
The Trinovantes had also felt the weight of Roman exactions and
the insolence of the colonists at Camulodunum. Much of their
land had been allotted to the newcomers, who were easily able to
seize more than was due to them. The cost of providing buildings
for the *colonia*, especially the great temple of the deified Claudius,
had also been an immense burden to the tribe, and there seemed
to be no relief in sight. The governor and his army were far away
and the veteran colonists who would bear arms were few in
number. An attack on Camulodunum, as the seat of Roman
oppression, opened the revolt and the first and most hated target
of the rebels was soon destroyed and its defenders massacred. An
attempt by the commander of the IX legion, Q. Petilius Cerealis,
to intervene came to naught when the column was ambushed
and heavy losses sustained by the infantry. The Roman hold on
southern Britain was all but lost. The procurator fled to Gaul,
despairing of the situation. Word of impending disaster reached
Suetonius Paullinus before the rebels could advance from Camulodunum to London and Verulamium, but these cities too could
not be saved. Paullinus made a cool assessment of the military
options and decided to leave the two cities to their fate, electing
to concentrate his forces outside the area that the rebels controlled. He sought reinforcements from the II legion, but its

acting commander refused to move, perhaps fearful of an attack from the Silures. Paullinus chose his battlefield with care, in the face of overwhelmingly superior numbers. He had a legion, a legionary detachment and a force of auxiliaries at his disposal, but he was faced by a motley army many times greater. The British force, however, was poorly equipped and lacking in discipline. It was also fuelled by over-confidence after its recent, easy successes. They expected victory and greatly underestimated Roman powers of recovery.

The battle that ensued was a victory for Roman training and equipment over massed and disorderly forces. The British were forced back on to their own wagon-lines and there slaughtered in great numbers. Roman losses were only 400 men. The aftermath for tribes which had taken part was severe. To the bitterness of defeat were added savage reprisals which Paullinus prolonged into the following year. The governor's policy was opposed by the newly appointed procurator Julius Alpinus Classicianus, whose provincial origins may have given him a broader vision and a deeper sympathy for people who had been provoked to rebel by intolerable treatment. Nero was persuaded to send one of his freedmen to investigate, and not long afterwards Paullinus was recalled from Britain, though without disgrace.

The following seven years were the least eventful in Britain since the invasion. There were no extensions to the province, priority being given to consolidation and regrouping of military forces. There were major changes to the disposition of legions in the east, where a new fortress was built for the IX legion at Lincoln after the revolt, and in the west, where a new base at Gloucester replaced those at Kingsholm and Usk in the late sixties. The XIV legion left Wroxeter, and Britain, in 66 and must have been replaced, perhaps by the XXth, as North Wales had still not been pacified. The fortress at Exeter continued under garrison for the time being. In the north, beyond the Trent, there may have been occupation of new ground in the sixties, if not before. The large fort at Osmanthorpe on the southern edge of Sherwood Forest may have been more than a campaign-base, and the fort at Templeborough, near Rotherham, indicates a secure hold on the South Yorkshire lowland by the early sixties. Another large fort at Rossington Bridge, near Doncaster, is likely to be of similar date and might have been connected with Roman efforts to support Cartimandua after the breach with Venutius.

The civil war that broke out after the death of Nero in 68 did not directly involve Britain, but the province was not immune to its malign effects. The XIV legion was acting in support of Otho, as was Paullinus the former governor, while the other three legions sent vexillations to the forces of Vitellius. In accord with the spirit of the time, the governor of Britain, Trebellius Maximus, was forced from his post by the legate of the XX legion. He was replaced by Vettius Bolanus, who may have made some attempt at resolving the problem of the Brigantes, however unsuccessfully.

After the years of drift and civil strife, the Flavian emperors were able to appoint three highly effective governors in succession and the next fifteen years saw the virtual completion of the conquest of Britain. The first of the three was Q. Petilius Cerealis, who had served through the Boudiccan revolt as legate of the IX legion and had later been a stalwart supporter of the Flavian cause in the civil war. He was a courageous and occasionally impetuous commander. He was followed by S. Julius Frontinus, an efficient soldier and Imperial servant, who was later to write works on land-surveying, military science and aqueducts, the last following his service as *curator aquarum* in Rome. The third was Gnaeus Julius Agricola, the best-known governor of Britannia, a newcomer to the ranks of senators and a man of provincial origin, from Frejus in Gallia Narbonensis. The fame bestowed upon him by the account of his life and works by his son-in-law Tacitus makes him more vulnerable to critical assessment than any other Roman commander in the western provinces, and some modern critics have not stayed their hand.

In AD 71, Cerealis was faced with two fronts that demanded attention: Wales and the Pennines. The latter presented the most pressing and urgent problem, for only a few years earlier a long-established treaty-relationship had collapsed. The Brigantian queen Cartimandua had maintained her loyalty to Roman interests over the eighteen years that had elapsed since she had handed over Caratacus to Ostorius Scapula (above, p. 23). But in the midst of the civil war of 68–70, she set aside her husband

Venutius and replaced him with his armour-bearer Vellocatus. Venutius then raised the standard of revolt against his former spouse and the Brigantian warriors swung behind him. Vettius Bolanus had earlier tried to intervene but was able only to rescue Cartimandua. Venutius remained in control and the northern marches of Roman Britain were far from secure. The only solution was the conquest of Brigantian territory.

The campaigns of Cerealis between 71 and 74 are reported to have been wide-ranging, but sites that can be firmly associated with his armies are few. He did, however, advance the northern legionary base from Lincoln to York, placing his old unit, the IXth, in garrison there and sending the newly arrived II Adiutrix to Lincoln. The Vale of York was thus securely held and it may be assumed that Cerealis' strategy was to secure the main routes leading west and north, possibly as far as the Tyne–Solway line. He may not, however, have garrisoned the area in strength, knowing well that the tribes of Wales had still not been finally subdued. A number of forts in South and East Yorkshire, at Brough-on-Humber, Castleford and Doncaster, may have been established to cover the approaches to the Vale from the west, and a large fort at Malton may have been designed to hold a legionary detachment to guard the eastern flank. We would expect the existence of garrisons at the northern end, but these have not yet been identified.

The conquest of Wales fell to the lot of Julius Frontinus from 74. The Silures of the South had not been eliminated as opponents, and Frontinus first moved to take control of the Glamorgan plain by planting forts at the mouths of the main valleys, at Cardiff, Neath, Carmarthen and possibly Bridgend. The II Augusta was now moved forward to a new fortress at Caerleon on the lower Usk. These dispositions suggest strongly that Frontinus was using his fleet to move men and supplies along the South Wales coast, thus enabling him to occupy the land without first entering the broken country of the valleys. That phase came later and was probably also largely achieved by Frontinus, who was, in addition, able to turn his attention to the peoples of North Wales. The choice of Chester as a legionary base was almost certainly his, and the advance into the lands of the Ordovices had begun by 75 at the latest; occupation may have been largely complete by 77 when Frontinus left Britain. Both Cerealis and Frontinus must have drawn troops from garrison posts in the East and South of the island and this in turn occasioned significant changes to the *civitates* that had been under military jurisdiction for thirty years.

Agricola had already seen service in Britain and will have had an excellent knowledge of the military problems posed by the province. He had been a tribune on the staff of Suetonius Paullinus and may well have accompanied that governor on his expedition to North Wales and Anglesey in AD 59/60. Eight years later he returned to Britain, to take command of the XX legion, relieving Roscius Coelius of the post after a period of indiscipline in the unit. Under the governor Vettius Bolanus he may have taken part in the first operations against the Brigantes; and certainly under Petilius Cerealis he had experience of campaigning in the North, at first commanding the XXth, and later larger forces. He did well and was later appointed governor of Gallia Aquitania and then elected to the consulship. Either late in 77 or in 78, he was given the command in Britain, for which there can have been no better candidate. Although it is impossible to arrive at a wholly objective judgement of Agricola's achievements in Britain, modern assessments of his generalship that rank him as no more than competent seem unsatisfactory. The conquest of northern Britain, the virtual completion of what Claudian generals had begun, was one of the signal achievements of Roman arms in the early Empire, a triumph over both inhospitable terrain and an enemy who could not be underestimated. The mere fact that three emperors as different as Vespasian, Titus and Domitian could approve or endorse Agricola's command says much for the qualities of the man and his success in the enterprise.

The new governor was immediately faced with the need to complete the subjection of North Wales, where the Ordovices had destroyed a cavalry regiment based in their territory. Agricola's action was prompt. Late in the campaigning season he pushed into the Ordovician hill-country, presumably from the recently founded legionary base at Chester, almost annihilated the tribe and then thrust across the Menai Strait to take Anglesey.

The strategic routes of North Wales were now secured by forts at the main river crossings and the whole region organized under military control. Agricola was now fully prepared for his main task, the subjection of the northern peoples. The army at his disposal was huge – four legions and perhaps about ninety auxiliary regiments. Of the latter, at least twenty were probably still required in Wales, but most of the units in the Midlands and the Welsh borders could be released for active service, now that the machinery for civilian administration in those regions was in place.

The conquest of the Brigantes, already begun by Cerealis five years earlier, was probably completed within a single campaign, either in 78 or 79. Given the positions of legionary bases at York and Chester, and the natural North–South routes through the Vale of York and the Lancashire plain, Agricola's forces probably operated in two main battle groups, one to either side of the Pennines, though connections between the two must have been maintained *via* the main passes. The first season presumably took the armies to at least the Tyne–Solway line, for in the next year new tribes were met with (this can only mean the peoples of southern Scotland) and the Tay estuary reached. A large tract of wild terrain had been swiftly overrun, and the following year (80 or 81) saw the building of forts and control-points after a campaign bedevilled by severe weather. The narrows between Forth and Clyde were, according to Tacitus, garrisoned by a line of forts, and although this has been questioned by modern scholars there is growing evidence that this was indeed done, perhaps from Barochan in the west to the southern shore of the Forth. But there may have been a zone of control across the isthmus rather than a single line of forts. A fort at Doune suggests that the northern flank may also have been covered by a chain of forts, fortlets and possibly watch-towers. The lowlands of southern Scotland were now traversed by a network of forts and roads. The main routes of the advance had probably been through the Northumberland plain towards the Tweed valley and across the Cheviots along the line of the modern A68 to the Eildon Hills, where a large fort was now, or soon afterwards, established at Newstead (Trimontium).

The next objective, in 82 or 83, was the peoples of the south-western peninsula of Scotland, principally the Novantae. A westward thrust along the southern shore may have been combined with operations in the interior. Eventually, from the western coast of the Rhinns of Galloway, Ireland was seen, and a fugitive Irish princeling was to hand who might be of service if an invasion of the island was in serious prospect. Fortunately for Agricola's reputation, his estimate that Ireland could have been conquered by a legion and a few auxiliaries was not put to the test. The conquest of northern Britain was to be pursued with continued vigour, possibly at the direct behest of the new emperor, Domitian.

The following two years witnessed the high point of Roman control in the North. Reconnaissance by sea had already revealed the scale of the problem posed by the geography of northern Scotland. The western coasts and islands had been explored by the fleet, to which the Greek schoolmaster Demetrius of Tarsus had been attached. That expedition demonstrated that the Highland massif could not be outflanked to the west. The invasion of the lands north of the isthmus had to proceed through the eastern coastal plain, the route followed by later invaders of Scotland from the south. This strategy had the further advantage of bringing the most fertile part of Scotland, Perthshire and Strathmore, quickly into Roman control, thus providing an excellent springboard for the northward push. Thus far, we hear of no major set-piece battle fought by Agricola's armies in the North. But beyond the Tay lay peoples whose capacity for at least brief communal resistance was markedly greater than that of their neighbours to the south. The Caledonian tribes mobilized themselves more effectively than the Selgovae and Novantae and in Calgacus they had a warrior who earned recognition as the paramount leader for the supreme test against the legions. But Agricola still had to force the enemy to come to battle; his strategy was to send ahead the fleet to pillage and burn, thus denying the Caledonians vital supplies. Finally, in the summer of 84 or 85, the Caledonians mustered to face the invaders, who by now were in control of much of the coastal plain as far north as the area of Aberdeen.

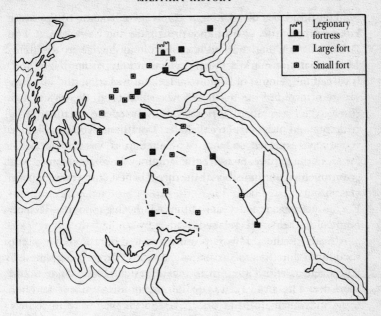

3. The northern frontier *c*. AD 85

The Roman advance is marked by the existence of distinctive types of marching camps, archaeologically dated to the mid-Flavian period and capable of housing either three legions or two legions with associated auxiliaries. The largest of these camps, at fifty-eight hectares, lies at Durno, below the mountain of Bennachie; this was easily able to house at least three legions. The geographical setting fits reasonably well with the slight, but specific, details of Tacitus' description of the battlefield of Mons Graupius. This does not amount to proof, which only a remarkable find could provide, but for the present the plain below Bennachie is the best candidate yet known for the scene of the decisive engagement. Once the Caledonians had been tempted to descend from the higher ground above the Roman camp, the issue was not long in doubt. Agricola had kept four cavalry regiments in reserve for the moment of the Caledonian onrush and these units quickly routed the northerners as they tried to swing behind the Roman rear. Only 360 Roman troops were killed in the battle, against an estimated 10,000 Caledonians. The Roman legions had not been called on to engage in the fight. Mons Graupius marked the end of the northern campaigns and, it turned out, almost of Roman control in the far North. The fleet was sent to round the north of Britain and on to the Orkneys to receive their surrender. Agricola was awarded the ornaments of a triumph and was then recalled by Domitian. Realistically, he could have expected no more, for his tenure of Britain had lasted for more than six years, twice the length of the average provincial governorship. If there was bitterness, as Tacitus records there was, this will have been due to the fate of his northern conquests. For only three or four years after Mons Graupius the Roman hold on the North was relaxed.

Already, before Mons Graupius was fought, the shape of the military occupation of Scotland had been largely determined. There had been no attempt to invade the Highlands: nor would there be. The strategy was to be one of containment and the main instruments of that design were forts that were to control movement down the major glens. Thus, the fort at Fendoch guarded the southern end of the Sma' Glen, Dalginross the upper Earn, Malling the pass of Aberfoyle and Bochastle the pass of Leny. These were all defensive positions, as is underlined by the use of only a fortlet at Inverquharity to keep watch on Glen Cova, and they were held by auxiliary units. The hub of the entire system of control was to be a new legionary fortress at Inchtuthil on the left bank of the Tay. It is not known (and may never be known) whether it was Agricola or his unnamed successor who was responsible for the decision to locate a legionary base here. If it was Agricola, it must have been one of his final acts in Britain. The base was planned for a single legion, possibly Agricola's old unit, the XXth. Surrounded by a stone-revetted rampart, the buildings of the base were of timber, though a fine stone bathhouse, intended presumably for the regimental officers, was provided to the south-east of the fortress. The troops responsible for the work of construction were housed in labour camps to the south-west. If work began in 84 or 85, it proceeded for two or three years and was then abruptly terminated. The legate's residence and several of the tribunes' houses had not been built: the baths had never been used. Abandonment was accompanied by deliberate demolition, destruction of what could be consumed by fire and concealment of what might be of use to the enemy. The date at which work was broken off and demolition completed is fixed by the evidence of coinage at 86/7 and no later.

What occurred at Inchtuthil is echoed at the auxiliary forts north of the Firth of Forth. Most of those that have been extensively examined, such as Fendoch, Cardean and Strageath, also reveal deliberate dismantling of buildings and disposal of unwanted material. The withdrawal from the northern conquests was orderly and not enforced by any Caledonian threat. The pressure came from elsewhere, from the middle Danube, where there had been reverses for Rome in 86/7. A legion was withdrawn from Britain, the II Adiutrix, leaving a vacancy at Chester. This was filled by the XXth, withdrawn from Scotland, possibly first to Carlisle. We can only speculate about why the decision was taken to evacuate eastern Scotland, leaving Inchtuthil unfinished, rather than, for example, leaving either Chester or Caerleon empty. Insecurity in western Britain can hardly have been so great as to demand the presence of two legions. Caerleon, in particular, seems hardly worth retaining after AD 90. But this was obviously not the perception at that time. The decision to withdraw from the North will not have been taken lightly. A decisive factor may have been the elongated lines of supply that the occupation of eastern Scotland demanded.

In any event, lowland Scotland south of the isthmus was still firmly held, with consequent modification to the pattern of garrisons. Several large forts were built, or rebuilt, to serve as nodal points in the occupation of the lands of the Selgovae and Novantae. These included Newstead at the foot of the Eildons, where a legionary vexillation and a cavalry squadron may have been based, Dalswinton and Glenlochar. This hold on the Lowlands was maintained for some fifteen years. About 105, several forts, including Newstead, Dalswinton, Glenlochar, High Rochester and even Corbridge, were destroyed or badly damaged by fire and it is highly likely (though not proven) that this was the result of hostile action. Another possibility is that a planned withdrawal was followed by a venting of native rage upon Roman military positions. The system of control that was created to meet the new situation in the North is not yet clearly defined, but it was based on the Tyne–Solway line. The new arrangement was not conceived as a linear frontier, such as was now emerging in Upper Germany and Raetia, but as a zone about the Stanegate, the road which ran from the lower Tyne valley to Carlisle. Along the Stanegate several existing forts, at Carlisle, Chesterholm and Corbridge, were added to by new bases at Carvoran, Brampton and possibly Newbrough, and the intervals between these forts were covered by fortlets resembling those on the Upper German frontier. The dating of most of these sites is far from secure and some could have been founded at the beginning of Hadrian's reign in connection with a different concept in frontier design.

At this same time, elements of the legionary garrison of Britain were in service on the lower Rhine between 104 and 120, as is revealed by the evidence for a *vexillatio Britannica* at Nijmegen.

The stark record of military history is now enlivened by an astonishing series of documents, preserved on wooden writing tablets found in waterlogged deposits at Vindolanda (Chesterholm), in the central sector of the northern frontier. These texts relate to the years between AD 92 and 120, a time that is covered by no narrative source. But the exceptional character of their interest resides in the detailed information they provide for the day-to-day working of the Roman army in a frontier region, and for the vivid and intimate flashes of human feeling offered by no other source. One group of documents is an archive of the prefect who commanded a cohort of Batavians in residence at Vindolanda early in the second century, Flavius Cerealis, and of his wife Sulpicia Lepidina; others are archives of later commanders of other regiments. Several texts are fragments of military reports, dealing with the supply of goods to the fort-garrison. These include parts of wagons, goatskins, supplies of meat, beer, wine, fish-sauce. Private gifts are also recorded, of clothing, shoes and oysters, as are acts of patronage, achieved or hoped for. A memorandum is briskly dismissive of the fighting qualities and

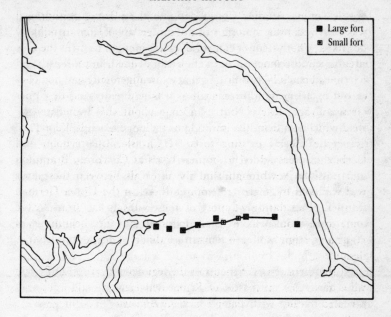

Large fort
Small fort

4. The northern frontier *c.* AD 100

military equipment of the Britons ('wretched little Britons'). The most informative of the official documents is a strength report of a cohort of Tungrians, revealing that of an actual strength of 752 men, more than half were on duty elsewhere (on the governor's staff, at London and at Corbridge), while thirty-one were ill or wounded. Only 265 fit men were in station at Vindolanda. Less predictable records are private letters between women, specifically an invitation to the wife of the commandant at Vindolanda, Sulpicia Lepidina, from the wife of a commander in a neighbouring fort for a birthday celebration. The warmth of this letter and the glimpse of family life on an inhospitable frontier are as welcome as they are unexpected.

It was now high time to reconstruct the legionary bases in more permanent form. This programme of work is marked by inscriptions, of AD 100 at Caerleon, after 102 at Chester and of 107/8 at York, though rebuilding in stone had begun at Caerleon by AD 90 or even earlier. Consolidation of the military dispositions in Britain was thus the order of the day, while Roman attention was fixed on the lower Danube. That policy was to receive indelible endorsement early in the reign of Hadrian, after a war or serious disturbance in Britain that caused heavy Roman casualties but is otherwise unknown to us. It must be assumed that this war was fought in the North, and it was followed by what was intended to be a definitive solution to the northern problem. The frontier built early in the reign of Hadrian, and in which the emperor may have played a formative part, was the most imposing linear barrier to be built in any part of the Roman world. A great wall was to be erected from Pons Aelius (Newcastle) in the east to Bowness on Solway in the west, a distance of seventy-six Roman miles. From Newcastle to the river Irthing, the barrier was to be a stone wall, ten Roman feet wide and probably about fifteen feet high. In front was to lie a large ditch, where the terrain required a forward obstacle. Every Roman mile along the wall, a fortlet, or milecastle, was to provide accommodation for a garrison charged with patrol duties, and between each pair of milecastles would be an evenly spaced pair of towers, or turrets, for observation purposes. This was to be the frontier in its original design. But while construction was proceeding there came a radical change. Auxiliary garrisons, under the original scheme to be positioned south of the wall, were now added to its line at intervals ranging from three to five miles. At the same time, the stone wall was extended eastward from Newcastle to Wallsend. When the forts were in place, the rear of the frontier zone was marked off by a broad, flat-bottomed ditch accompanied by a mound to either side, known since Bede's description of it as the vallum. This was a work of demarcation, indicating to all the proximity of a zone under the strictest military control. Later, but still within Hadrian's reign, the turf rampart west of the Irthing was replaced by a stone wall; and by about AD 135 the frontier work was complete. Measures to protect the Cumbrian coast had probably already begun before Hadrian's accession and were now amplified. A series of fortlets and towers was extended down the coast to St Bee's Head. North of the western end of the Wall outpost forts were maintained at Bewcastle,

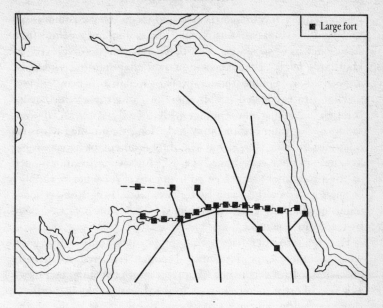

5. The northern frontier *c.* AD 125

Birrens and Netherby, as though hostile forces might be expected to approach from that quarter. The garrisoning of the Wall in Hadrian's reign was entrusted exclusively to auxiliary troops. The sixteen forts housed full units of infantry and cavalry, a total of about 10,000 men. In the hinterland of the Pennines another fifteen units were within a few days' march. On the frontier line, the senior officer *de facto* was the commander of the *ala Petriana* based at Stanwix, just east of Carlisle, the only miliary *ala* (cavalry squadron, 850 strong) in the province; another indication, perhaps, that the main threat to security lay in the western sector.

The purpose of this elaborate frontier work has provoked much discussion. The only ancient source that bears upon the point seems to spring from the fundamental intention of its creator, Hadrian. It was to divide Romans from barbarians, to demarcate the limits of Empire in this wild land. But it was also a frontier on

39

which fighting was to be expected and its military function is not to be underestimated. But Roman forces did not operate from static, defensive positions and they were not so deployed on Hadrian's Wall. The expectation was that fighting would be done in advance of the frontier, perhaps well in advance.

That strategy relied heavily on the gathering of intelligence through patrolling and contact with friendly natives. The Votadini of Northumberland may have long maintained a treaty-relationship with Rome, but the establishment of a permanent frontier will have encouraged the search for wider contacts. Such relationships might be cemented by means of subsidies, of supplies of one sort or another, and by money. Not all the Roman goods found beyond the northern frontier need have been carried there by trade or exchange.

Hadrian's frontier had been completed for only a few years when another swing in Imperial policy rendered it virtually obsolete, at least for a time. The accession of Antoninus Pius in 138 was shortly followed by a forward movement in northern Britain, resulting in the restoration of Roman arms to the Forth–Clyde isthmus and the building of a new frontier work across the narrows. The reasons for this volte-face were probably various. Hadrian's Wall may have proved so effective that the forces based upon it were now remote from the main seat of Caledonian power and thus unable to combat it. There may also have been pressure from some of the new emperor's commanders for a more adventurous approach to external policy, following a twenty-year peace in the western provinces. Cautious advance in Britain may have seemed a safe and inexpensive way of satisfying that demand.

Campaigning in southern Scotland began in 139, under the direction of the governor Lollius Urbicus; only three years later work had commenced on the new frontier. The Antonine Wall ran for fifty-nine kilometres from Bridgeness on the Forth to Old Kilpatrick on the Clyde. It was a great rampart of turf, earth and clay over a stone foundation four metres wide, rising to a height of at least 2.75 metres, fronted by a wide ditch. At first, six large forts at intervals of about fifteen kilometres were sited on the Wall and the gaps between these were covered by fortlets of which nine are known and others presumed to lie undetected. But while the Wall was still under construction, other, smaller, forts were added to it; nine of these are known for certain and another four are suspected. The fortlets are now seen to have formed a significant element in the frontier scheme, probably standing, like the milecastles on Hadrian's Wall, at mile-intervals along the entire length of the Antonine Wall. Thus the Antonine frontier was much closer to Hadrian's Wall in design than was earlier suspected. The salient modification was the omission of the vallum to the rear. A new feature was the provision of turf platforms over stone footings against the rear face of the Wall, the so-called 'expansions'. Six of these are known in three pairs and are usually seen as installations for signalling to north and south of the frontier line. The strategically and economically significant area of Strathearn and Strathallan north of the Wall was controlled by garrisons at Ardoch, Strageath and Bertha, thereby also protecting the exposed eastern flank of the frontier. The garrisons on the frontier itself were a mixed bag. Several of the forts were so small that only part-units could have been housed; these were mainly infantry. In some cases, legionary detachments were in garrison, which should imply at least the likelihood of serious campaigning. Most units moved forward from the Pennines and from Hadrian's Wall, now effectively redundant. The gates of the milecastles were removed, thus throwing open the old frontier-work, and the vallum was at least partially breached. Some of the forts, however, remained under garrison, though the military *Schwerpunkt* now lay far to the north.

The history of the Antonine occupation of Scotland was brief and apparently turbulent. Only a decade after the Antonine Wall was built there were severe disturbances in northern Britain, clearly referred to on the Imperial coinage for AD 154/5, which shows a reverse type of Britannia in a subject posture or even in mourning. The events that lie behind this image cannot be reconstructed, but they may have involved an attack on the province from without rather than a rebellion within. The Roman response was firm; an experienced governor, Julius Verus, was sent to Britain, along with vexillations from both the German

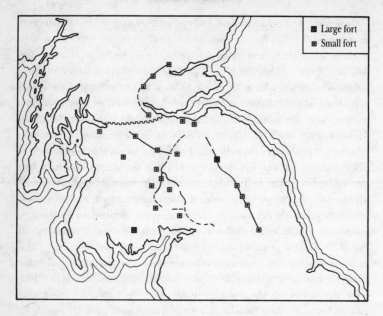

Large fort

Small fort

6. The northern frontier *c.* AD 140

provinces. About 158, the Antonine frontier was itself evacuated
and the forts dismantled to render them useless to the northerners.
Far to the rear in the Pennines, there were reoccupation and
rebuilding of several forts, including Brough-on-Noe and Birrens.
At least some work of restoration was carried out on Hadrian's
Wall itself in 158, and it is thus probable that the intention was
to reoccupy that frontier permanently. But the abandonment of
Scotland was brief. Shortly after 158 the Antonine Wall was
restored, as were the garrisons to south and north of it, in some
cases after a very short break. This second very sudden change of
plan is inexplicable on present evidence. It is possible that the
situation was retrieved after 155 more quickly than was first
expected, encouraging a return to Scotland after a short interval.
But the renewed occupation in the late 150s was also cut short.
About 165 the Antonine frontier was again abandoned, this time
for good, perhaps after a military assessment by the governor

Calpurnius Agricola, and a return was made to the Hadrianic frontier-line.

Even after these toings and froings, the northern frontier was still not secure. Shortly after 180, the northern peoples crossed a frontier wall – which must be that of Hadrian – and defeated a Roman force, killing its commander. The new emperor, Commodus, sent the stern disciplinarian Ulpius Marcellus to retrieve the situation and by 184 a victory had been won and peace restored. The wider convulsions that followed on the assassination of Commodus in 193 involved the army of Britain as a whole, but probably left little or no mark on the northern frontier. Three provincial governors with substantial armies at their backs contested the throne: Pescennius Niger of Syria, Septimius Severus of Pannonia and Clodius Albinus of Britain. The most powerful of the three was Septimius Severus, who enjoyed the support of the Rhine and Danube legions. He overcame Pescennius Niger early in 194 and then turned his attention to Clodius Albinus. The governor of Britain clearly had to attack Severus in the West and in 196 he took the army of Britain, or as much of it as could be deployed, into Gaul, hoping to win over the Rhine legions. That element in the plan came to naught and Albinus had to face Severus with his British forces and whatever troops he was able to raise in Gaul. The decision was reached in a great battle near Lyons early in 197. The army of Albinus was defeated after almost snatching victory through the work of its slingers; their leader took his own life. Severus' first governor of Britain, Virius Lupus, had work to do in the North and set in train restoration of those forts that stood in need of it, though this may have been due mainly to the age of those bases rather than to enemy action. Nevertheless, the Maeatae of eastern Scotland had to be bought off and this may have been the beginning of subsidy payments, which became a common instrument on Roman frontiers in the third century. Hadrian's Wall itself came in for repair, although not until the years 205–8. By that time a plan for renewed conquest in northern Britain had already been formed. Acting on a report from the governor Alfenus Senecio that the military state of Britain was still precarious, Severus determined on a major expedition that would take Roman forces back into Scotland.

In 208, the emperor arrived in Britain, accompanied by his sons Caracalla and Geta and his empress Julia Domna. With him came an expeditionary force which included legionary detachments and newly levied troops from the western provinces. Headquarters were established at York and campaigning began immediately. For the next five or six years, operations of the most difficult and frustrating kind were pursued, the problems being graphically portrayed in the pages of Cassius Dio. Progress was made at first and the territory of the Caledonians was seized. But in 210, the Maeatae revolted and had to be subdued by Caracalla, the emperor himself being incapacitated by illness. Further campaigns were planned for 211, but early in that year Severus died at York, leaving Caracalla to complete the task, probably with far greater success than the sources admit.

This invasion of Scotland involved such massive support operations that it must be concluded that it was intended to lead to a permanent occupation of territory north of the Firth of Forth, or at the very least to enable Roman forces to strike at the northern peoples from prepared bases. A force of legionaries was based in a new fort at Carpow on the south bank of the Tay estuary. This contained principal buildings in stone and was clearly intended to serve as more than a campaign base. Marching-camps north of the Tay suggest that campaigns were pursued at least to the river North Esk. But if Severus intended to reoccupy eastern Scotland, it is curious that no effort was made to establish a network of forts in the Lowlands. Nor is there any sign that Severus intended to abandon Hadrian's Wall and again revive a linear frontier in central Scotland. It is possible that full development of his plan was frustrated by his death in 211, and that Caracalla took a very different view of what was possible and needful in Scotland. Although at least one campaign followed the death of Severus, Caracalla arranged peace terms with the northerners and returned to Rome. It was the last Roman attempt to exercise any hold over Central Scotland. But, at long last, the northern frontier of Britain was secure and the North was not to be seriously threatened again for a century.

The dispositions of Caracalla deserve more credit than they have often received. They guaranteed peace in northern Britain for longer than the action of any other Roman general ever did, and they seem to have achieved this despite the worsening political and economic conditions that afflicted the Empire during the frequent collapses of central authority in the middle and later years of the third century. During this tumultuous period Britain was the most tranquil of the western provinces. In the military sphere it became something of a backwater; and the men appointed to govern the two provinces – Britannia Superior and Inferior, after the administrative division by Severus – were no longer the leading generals of the day. It had taken Rome a century and a half to pacify Britain, but there can be no doubt about the measure of her final success. The rural economy of Britain flourished in the third and early fourth centuries, revealing for the first time the true wealth of the island in a prolonged time of peace.

Early in the third century, all the same, anxieties about the security of the eastern and southern coasts (the Saxon Shore) manifested themselves. Coastal forts were built at Brancaster (Norfolk) and Reculver (Kent), and at Richborough the lofty triumphal monument commemorating the conquest of the island in the first century was girt by triple ditches and converted into a lookout post. Other coastal installations may owe their origin to the growing danger from seaborne raiders, especially Franks and Saxons from the northern coastlands of Europe. Their purpose seems to have been related to warning the *classis Britannica* of approaching hostile craft, with a view to their interception. That such raids might penetrate far inland is underlined by the presence of a watch-tower on the Thames at Wapping, close to Londinium itself. After about 260, the fortification of the vulnerable coasts was extended in response to the increase in barbarian power, which had been made terrifyingly plain by the devastating invasions of Gaul. From the Wash to the inlets sheltered by the Isle of Wight, forts were built to a pattern already established in urban defences, incorporating massive external towers, high walls and powerfully protected gates. Most lie close to important harbours, as at Dover, Richborough, Lympne and Portchester, and most were designed both for intercepting raiders from the sea by means of seaborne patrols and for cutting off raiders after they had landed. Similar fortifications were provided on the northern coast of Gaul from the Scheldt to Brittany, though these are less well known in detail than those in Britain. Such foundations were not confined to the south-east coast of the island. Examples occur on the west at Cardiff and Lancaster and these cannot have stood alone. Not all the coastal forts were built in a single programme of work, planned by a single mind. Some were added in the early fourth century as the security of Britain began to depend more and more upon its defences against seaborne raiders.

The enhanced importance of the fleet and its control of the sea are illustrated by the career of Carausius, the commander of the *classis Britannica* charged with the task of ridding the Channel of pirates in 286. He set about the task with a will, but he was accused of waiting too often for the return journey of the pirates and sharing the booty with them. Rather than face a trial, Carausius seized Britain and the adjacent parts of Lower Germany and proclaimed himself Augustus in 286. His island Empire, recognized for a while by central authority, lasted for six years, when he was assassinated by his chief finance officer, Allectus, who maintained his position for another three years. He was only defeated by an invasion of a sizeable expeditionary force led by Constantius Chlorus, the western Caesar, whose recovery of London is superbly commemorated on a gold medallion found at Arras in northern France. There was work for Constantius to do in Britain. There had been long stagnation on the northern frontier, where new enemies were making themselves felt. The Picts are first mentioned in 297, though their raids had probably begun well before this. For the first time Irish raiders appear as a threat to the western shores, which may help to explain the relatively large number of Carausian coin hoards in Wales. Repair or rebuilding was required on Hadrian's Wall, the result of long inaction rather than enemy assault. There was reconstruction in the Pennine forts also; and at York a grandiose renovation of the river-front defences was undertaken. New, large forts were erected at Newton Kyme, Piercebridge and possibly Elslack, covering approaches to the Vale of York, an area hitherto accounted to be safe. This activity in the northern forts is impressive, as is the major expedition that was launched and led by Constantius against the Picts in 306. That Constantius, having become the senior emperor, found such a task essential is a clear indication of the threat posed by the northerners. It was to be his last campaign. In midsummer he returned to York after winning a decisive victory, and there he died.

The garrisons on the Wall and elsewhere were units of different type from those of the early Empire. The auxiliary units were now probably less than 200 strong (an Egyptian source of Diocletian's reign records an infantry cohort of 160 men and a cavalry squadron of 120), and there was appropriate reorganization of the barrack accommodation. The fourth-century barracks at Housesteads, Greatchesters, Chesters and Wallsend comprised rows of separate apartments or chalets, perhaps designed with the needs of families in mind. This is in no way to be taken as indicating a lapse from the high standards of Roman discipline. The army was still an ordered and efficient force. But the circumstances in which it now had to operate were altered. As elsewhere on the Imperial frontiers, keeping the peace had more to do with diplomacy and recognition of selected barbarian leaders than ever before. Some of the native dynasties of Bernicia and Strathclyde may have owed their foundation to this phase of frontier history, with its striking resemblances to modern British experience in India and Africa.

Britain in the first half of the fourth century was at the apogee of its prosperity, as was evident in the countryside, in particular, and in the growth of many minor townships. It was not, however, entirely free from warfare, in some cases requiring the presence of an Emperor. After 315 Constantine took the title Britannicus Maximus, perhaps after a successful campaign by one of his western subordinates. More serious was an emergency in 342, which brought the western Augustus Constans to the island in mid-winter. The details are lost to us, but the position was grave and may have led to a change in the northern frontier arrangements, scouts known as *areani* now being deployed north of the Wall in succession to the *exploratores* of the third century. In 350, Constans was overthrown by the usurper Magnentius, a man of humble origins from Gaul, or, as some alleged, from Britain. Magnentius was soon defeated at Mursa in Pannonia in 351, but

Britain did not escape the repercussions of his actions. Some, at least, of the army in Britain must have been removed to support Magnentius' claims to power and it is not certain that they all returned. After the end of the adventure, many prominent figures in Britain suffered heavily at the hands of the Imperial agent Paul, whose soubriquet 'the Chain' is eloquent of his cruel and relentless dragging down of his victims. Even the *vicarius* (supreme governor) of Britain was compelled to desperate action and then to suicide. The propensity of Britain to produce usurpers, later to provide the leitmotif of the final phase of the provinces, was further signalled in the late 350s by a series of locally produced coins bearing the name Carausius. This man is otherwise unrecorded so that we can only speculate over a short-lived and probably localized insurgence.

After half a century of successful defence against external enemies, barbarian attacks posed serious threats to Britain from 360 onward. In 367, the Saxons, Picts and Scots made a synchronized assault upon the provinces, killing the commander of the Saxon Shore (head of coastal defence), and immobilizing the *dux Britanniarum*, commander-in-chief of the land forces. The Wall was overrun, and it is recorded that this was at least partly due to the treachery of the *areani*, who had been bought over by promises of a share in the loot. There were also many cases of desertion from the ranks of the army. Such indiscipline was a new and sinister development, illustrating the narrowing of the gulf between frontier defenders and barbarians without. Much more than the northern frontier was affected by the attacks; bands of raiders were also active in the region around London and presumably elsewhere near the coasts. The two commanders sent in turn by Valentinian were unable to restore order. In 368 the elder Theodosius was despatched to Britain with a field army, and he made directly for London from the port of Richborough, dealing with marauders as soon as he had reached the capital. There was work to be done elsewhere; the cities and other strongholds required reinforcement. Some repair work was called for on Hadrian's Wall, though this may not have been extensive. Barracks were restored at Housesteads and Birdoswald, while at Rudchester and Halton Chesters rebuilding on a larger scale was undertaken. Some of the larger buildings within forts were converted to different use: the headquarters of Housesteads was partly used as an armoury, that of Chesterholm turned into accommodation. There may also have been repairs to sectors of the Wall-curtain at this time, and certainly some of the milecastles and turrets were still in use late in the fourth century. The outpost-forts, however, seem to have been abandoned by Theodosius, some of them perhaps even before his time, and there is probably a connection here with his disbanding of the *areani*, whose disloyalty had proved so costly in 367. As to the garrisons in the Wall forts after 369, virtually nothing is known for certain, but there is no reason to think that they now consisted of soldier-cultivators or a localized militia tied to their place of service by the duties of the farmer as well as by loyalty to their Emperor. Nor is there likelihood that the forts now housed civilians in numbers, the extramural *vici* (villages) having been deserted. The frontier was still held in as firm a state of military preparedness as the exigencies of the day would allow. The creation of a new province, Valentia, probably by division of Britannia Secunda (itself a division of Britannia Inferior), located in the North and including York as its capital, underlined the continued concern for the security of the region, even though now the main threat to Britain was posed by sea-raiders from northern Europe.

The latter years of the fourth century saw further action against the Picts and other northern peoples. In 382, Magnus Maximus led an army against them, but in the following year he was diverted into taking an army from Britain to pursue his own Imperial aims on the Continent. This can only have further reduced the effectiveness of the forces in Britain and it is uncertain what troops were returned to the island when Maximus was overthrown in 388. Elsewhere than in the furthest North new measures continued to be taken that reveal concern for coastal defence. The best example known is on the Yorkshire coast, which was equipped with fortlets containing tall towers to espy and to signal the approach of sea-raiders, and to set naval operations in train for their interception. Several forts in the Pennines were still held, and in Wales at Caernarvon, Forden Gaer and Leintwardine. At Caer Gybi (Holyhead, on Anglesey) a fortified beaching-point was built for warships, matching those for the contemporary flotillas on the Rhine and Danube. There is every indication that a firm hold was kept on the nerve-centre of the North at York and upon the large inland forts connected therewith, such as Malton and Piercebridge. These and the naval ports were the bases from which the long arm of Rome could still strike. The last offensive measures mentioned in Britain, ascribed by a Roman writer to Stilicho, were naval raids following the usurpation of Magnus Maximus. Whether these actually took place or not, the fruits of comparable action on the part of the Roman government may be recognized in the regiments of Scotti and Atecotti which formed part of the continental army of the Emperor Honorius. These represent levies from overseas outside the British provinces, either exacted after offensive action or bought by Roman gold, but in any case relieving pressure upon the coasts of Britain. The Scotti came from Northern Ireland, the Atecotti from the western coasts of Scotland.

Hadrian's Wall was held to the end of the fourth century, at least, and probably into the early years of the fifth. But after the collapse of central authority about 409/10, the maintenance of a frontier garrison must have been impossible. Troops who were no longer receiving payment will not have remained at their posts. Localized settlement could well have continued, and there are signs that it did so, at Corbridge, Vindolanda and at Carlisle, where a community still existed in the late seventh century. Local dynasts may have taken on the diminished and divided mantle of Rome as best they could, but their fame did not reach the ears of anyone who could commit it to writing and to history.

Stilicho's work in Britain, as described by the poet Claudian, may be little more than a list of responsibilities rather than a catalogue of achievements. In the final years of the century, some semblance of order was restored, but by 402 troops were being removed from Britain to face Alaric and the Visigoths in Italy. What this left of an effective fighting force in Britain is not known, but defence of the island must thereafter have been increasingly precarious. Matters were not improved by a break-down in the orderly government of Britain. In 406/7 a succession of usurpers was thrown up by contending forces within the island.

The first two, Marcus and Gratian, each lasted only a few months before being killed by their own armies. Constantine III, another choice of the military, had a sharper grasp of the strategic realities. He saw that Gaul and Britain must be defended together, and quickly crossed to Gaul, no doubt taking an army with him. The Gallic prefecture was soon in his control, but he overreached himself by attempting to intervene in Italy, where he was defeated and killed by the troops of Honorius. Britain in the meantime was lost to Rome. It no longer had an army adequate for its defence, and there was no one to organize what remained. Barbarian attacks continued and in 410 an exceptionally severe invasion of Saxons brought at least part of the island into barbarian control. A few years before this the Britons had expressed their exasperation at the lack of protection now afforded by Rome and had ejected Roman administrators, living thereafter 'according to their own laws', as Zosimus expresses it. Such action was entirely understandable and was also resorted to in north-western Gaul and later in Noricum. Thus, if Honorius did indeed write to the British *civitates* in 410 with instructions that they should take measures for their own defence, he was some years late with his advice.

The final decades of Roman Britain were a time of slow decline rather than sudden cataclysm. The tale of fire and slaughter related by Gildas has never found any echo in the archaeology of fifth-century Britain. Many regions of the old provinces, especially in the West and North, will not have been visited by barbarian raids or settlement until long after AD 400, if at all. Even in the South and East the impact of Anglo-Saxon intrusion will have been localized before 500; Romano-British institutions and way of life will hardly have collapsed headlong as soon as Roman administration ended. Nevertheless, within the space of only a few decades Britain was transformed, and by the end of the fifth century large tracts of the Roman diocese were under the control of increasingly ambitious Germanic powers.

The chronology of Anglo-Saxon attacks on Britain and subsequent settlement is sketchy and incomplete. A major assault by Saxons in 408 is recorded by the compiler of the *Gallic Chronicle*, a well-informed source, and it is possible that some of the invaders established themselves in eastern Britain at this time. After the removal of the remaining military forces by Constantine III, it would have been easier for such lodgements to be made. Germanic material, chiefly pottery and a little metalwork of the earlier fifth century, is found in small quantity at a number of sites in East Anglia, Lincolnshire, around the Thames estuary and in Kent, though the circumstances under which it arrived in Britain are not clearly defined. The settlement and cemetery at Mucking on the north shore of the Thames estuary began in the early decades of the fifth century, possibly as a plantation of a Germanic group from the north German coastlands, the role of the migrants being to keep watch on seaborne traffic moving up the Thames. The Germans who were buried outside the walls of Caister-by-Norwich in the same period may also have been under supervision from a surviving Romano-British authority based on that small city. Other early settlers from the Elbe–Weser region have been detected near Leicester, Ancaster and West Stow in Suffolk. None of these communities is likely to have been very large and in other areas there are signs that Romano-British authorities were able to retain their hold on cities like Verulamium, Silchester and Lincoln for long after 400. Even as late as the seventh century, there may have been officials in Lincoln exercising powers remotely descended from those of late Roman *curiales*.

Within the old cities, the programmes of urban excavation over the past thirty years have revealed much about the fate of those cities and their communities after 400. There are few signs, if any at all, of the survival of a highly ordered urban society. At the more fully excavated cities, such as Silchester, Canterbury, London and Verulamium, the picture is one of slow decline, in some cases beginning in the fourth century and accelerating after the early decades of the fifth. Major new building generally was not attempted after the late fourth century and many earlier structures were by that date in an advanced state of ruin.

One of the clearest indices of the collapse of Roman Britain lies in the suddenness with which the larger industries disintegrated and disappeared. Although several of the large pottery centres continued working into the later fourth century, including those of the Nene valley, East Yorkshire, Oxfordshire and the New

Forest, by the early years of the fifth those industries were either defunct or confined to small-scale local activity. Other industries and crafts ran down with equal or greater speed from after about AD 380. Not the least surprising aspect of the end of Roman Britain is the way in which the mass production of a wide range of consumer goods was extinguished in a matter of twenty or thirty years. Not all crafts came to an end. It is easy to imagine that work in textiles, leather and wood continued on at least a local basis, and there is compelling evidence for the survival of the manufacture of bronze vessels into the fifth and sixth centuries. In several areas of southern and eastern Britain, bronze bowls, platters and other utensils occur in hoards buried about 400 or later in the fifth century. Many of these were spun on a lathe, not produced by beating out sheet metal, and thus derive from a Roman provincial tradition of craftsmanship. Later, they were to provide prototypes for the Anglo-Saxon hanging bowls of the sixth and seventh centuries. Other large-scale industries disappeared with astonishing suddenness in the late fourth and early fifth centuries; local craftsmen were unable to make good the resultant deficit. Utensils and ornaments that had once been commonplace now became rarities, making the archaeological study of the fifth century a demanding and hazardous art. In terms of its material products, Roman Britain perished in the first decades of the fifth century.

The final phase of the occupation of Hadrian's Wall is shadowy, but in sum the scene is of disintegration rather than abrupt collapse. Whatever Stilicho did in Britain in 400/401, it did not include any fortification of the northern frontier. In the following year he moved at least some forces from the island and these are likely to have included units of the mobile field army; these would have been of far greater use in Italy than *limitanei* (frontier-troops). Whether any of the field army was left in Britain after 402 is unknown. Quite possibly the sole defence of the island was in the hands of the stationary units on the frontier and the Saxon Shore, and even these may not have long remained in place after about 406. The coin series from some of the forts on Hadrian's Wall continue down to the first decade of the fifth century, but in sharply declining numbers. It is inconceivable that an organized military presence was maintained on the frontier after 410 at the latest, though individual forts and townships could still offer bases for settlement and a measure of local control. Such bases appear to have survived at Vindolanda, Birdoswald, Corbridge and Carlisle. In the excavated forts, the final stages are nowhere attended by signs of destruction or disorder. Nor is there any indication of a southward movement by Picts or others to settle behind the old frontier. The population of the forts and *vici*, by and large, faded back into the land that had nourished them for three centuries. Many no doubt remained on the land, but their dwelling-sites are not known to us. On the wider stage of politics Rome may have looked to native dynasties in southern Scotland to maintain some semblance of order, following old precedent, and rulers like Cinhil on the Clyde and Padern Pesrut in the Lowlands may have obtained, or claimed, a mandate from Rome. But even such arrangements will not have long remained in being.

CHAPTER THREE

Urban Centres

The military history of Roman Britain derives not a little of its interest from the variety and ingenuity of its pattern, which stamps it as a lively and vigorous reaction to Imperial problems, now external and now internal. But the basic assumption behind all such action was that there was a province worth protection, a land that paid dividends in either taxation, or troops, or raw materials; these yields were sufficient, singly or in combination, to justify an occupation on grounds of expense, quite apart from the overriding strategic considerations that originally and continually made the occupation desirable. Occupation, furthermore, by conferring peace and order brought about the conditions in which population and productivity might be substantially increased. The tribute yield of the Three Gauls was doubled in fifty years, and while the expansion cannot have continued at so prodigious a rate, it remains a valuable indication of what might happen in the first tide of peace and prosperity among people who did not welcome the new order with unanimity.

The instrument of civilization used by Rome in achieving such results was the city and the many-sided attainments of amenity and social grace that successful civic organization involves. No false modesty or feeling for others inhibited the Roman belief in their own hybrid civilization, though they enjoyed analysing its shams and pretences. The normal method of introducing civic structure in the Celtic lands, where the most important political unit was the council of tribal notables, was through the aristocratic families. These were encouraged to adopt Roman ways and to give their sons a Roman education, absorbing these things as the inward stamp of a new civilization whose outward habits and equipment possessed the magnetism of novelty and the prestige of success. Once this movement got under way the rest would follow. Tribal revenues, private generosity and family pride or emulation could be devoted to creating an urban centre for tribal government, tribal festivals and tribal markets, which had meanwhile been left undisturbed by the Roman provincial administration as far as this was compatible with its needs. At this stage the Roman government might lend a hand. The construction of the civic buildings was not permitted until the soundness of the proposal had been examined and approved. Then a surveyor or architect might be made available, frequently from a military source, and a new town or local government centre would begin to rise, its lands duly apportioned and its streets laid out in Roman manner. The timetable varied according to the wealth and disposition of the communities responsible for bringing the town into being. But the underlying impulse and purpose were the same.

Six years after the invasion the governor Ostorius Scapula founded a colony on the site of the capital of Cunobelin at Camulodunum (Colchester), immediately over the demolished remains of the legionary base constructed by the expeditionary army. The primary object of the foundation was to provide a chartered city for legionaries now discharged from military service, who would receive a house-plot in the city and an amount of cultivable land outside it appropriate to their rank. But in such foundations local inhabitants might also share within defined limits, and it is certain that the Trinovantes had a place at Camulodunum. Cities of this kind, even with help from official sources, were not erected quickly. The regular street-plan, public buildings and private dwellings might well take twenty years or more to complete, and the order of building the several elements might vary. At Camulodunum, after eleven years, a senate house, theatre and some private houses existed, but defences for the place had not been provided. After the death of the emperor Claudius the temple dedicated to the cult of the deified ruler, which was to serve as the centre for emperor-worship for the province, was constructed, no doubt absorbing a substantial part of the tribal resources. Roman historians remarked, looking back upon these events, how amenities had come first: and this is comprehensible, when the political and cultural education of the native aristocracy was the first and fundamental condition of civilizing the province as a whole. The city that was the first demonstration of this civilizing process in action had no more than a decade of life before it perished in flames and its inhabitants in massacre or torture at the hands of the rebels of AD 60/61.

Two new *coloniae* were founded in the final decade of the first century, at Lincoln and Gloucester. The conquest of most of Britain was achieved and there were veterans to release from service. Both of these cities were established on the sites of evacuated legionary bases, of the IX legion at Lincoln and of the IInd at Gloucester. The lands of both communities were presumably the old legionary *territoria*, carved out of the holdings of native tribes. A generous interpretation might be that the Romans had duly noted the feelings aroused by harsh expropriations at Camulodunum and now avoided new confiscations. Perhaps more realistically, official inertia determined the sites of the new cities and their territories. At both Lincoln and Gloucester the defences of the earlier legionary fortresses provided bounds for the cities in their early phases, and in both cases the military street-plan left its mark on the urban layout. More striking still, in modified form the troop accommodation at Gloucester continued in use in the early phase of the colony, a mark of official economy in an age in which colonial foundations were finding less favour with legionary veterans.

The British native communities, by and large, had to find their own way towards an urban culture that attracted them at first by its convenience and then by its inherent qualities. The start was made in a variety of ways and with varying degrees of enthusiasm, the nucleus being, in most cases, a major native settlement to which had been added a military fort or fortress in the years shortly after the invasion.

Even away from the military *coloniae*, the impact of the Roman army on the early development of cities was very great. Although there had been progress towards urbanism in south-eastern Britain in the century before the conquest, recognizably urban centres did not exist over much of the island in AD 43. The rapid creation of a military infrastructure of forts and roads immediately after the invasion had enormous repercussions on social and economic demography. The foundation of Roman forts at strategic positions such as road junctions and river crossings instantly brought into being a large number of focal points for the local population and for traders and others who would benefit from an affluent and free-spending clientele. Extramural settlements burgeoned around the sites of many forts in the first twenty years of the province and many of these villages were strong enough to survive when the forts were abandoned and the troops withdrawn. In many cases, however, the origins of towns were not so simple. Roman forts might also be sited at or close to sizeable Iron Age settlements, as certainly occurred at Verulamium, Lincoln, Winchester and Leicester, so that a nucleus of native population already existed. All the above proved to be the foundations of major cities, but a number of minor towns also sprang from these dual origins, including Ancaster, Cambridge, Irchester and Dorchester-on-Thames. Relatively few of the principal cities of the province seem to have had no Iron Age antecedents at all. Exeter, Gloucester and Wroxeter are the most notable cases, but even here absolute certainty has not yet been attained.

The sites of at least two legionary fortresses (Exeter and Wroxeter) were made over to infant *civitates*. Most of the other native cities had seen a phase of occupation by an army unit and it is an interesting question: by what legal mechanism was land transferred from the army to native authorities? Who was the original owner of the land under Roman law? The army could exercise no corporate ownership of land, so that the choice must lie between the emperor and the Roman people, between Imperial land and *ager publicus*. Roman lawyers themselves seem to have been unsure of the precise legal status of provincial land and might fall back on the principle that *Caesar omnia habet* (the emperor owns everything). In a province like Britain, it is most unlikely that there was close and detailed questioning of Roman administrators on the point.

There was one city that introduced a different political gradation: namely the capital of a kingdom which was left to itself as an independent unit within the province and even granted sovereignty over other tribes. This was the realm of Cogidubnus, the kingdom of the Regni (or possibly Regini), with its centre at Noviomagus (Chichester). The territory, with its core in Sussex and Hampshire, perhaps extending northward to the Thames, lay in a significant position, commanding good harbours behind the Isle of Wight and providing bases for aggressive action against the less amenable peoples further to the west. The area may formerly have belonged to Verica, who had taken refuge with Rome not long before the invasion (above, p. 20). Whether Cogidubnus was a descendant of Verica is unknown and in any case unimportant. What is certain is that he became a Roman client-king in the early organization of the province and his territory, enlarged by the gift of other tribal lands, may have been the springboard for the legate Vespasian's operations, in which he captured the Isle of Wight and subdued two great tribes. Noviomagus has yielded two remarkable inscriptions, one of them lost, the other preserved, which attest the early Romanization of the region. The lost piece was a dedication in honour of the emperor Nero, dated to AD 58–60, presumably a statue base bearing an elaborate statement of Nero's imperial ancestry. The second stone, which is not dated, is a dedication of a temple to Neptune and Minerva by a guild (*collegium*) of ironworkers on the authority of Cogidubnus, who is described as Tiberius Claudius Cogidubnus, great King in Britain. The King had been endowed with Roman citizenship by Claudius, and the text of the inscription indicates his efforts to foster, as became a client-king, the Romanization of his realm. This is demonstrated by the dedication of a temple to Roman deities, first the god of the sea over which the iron of the Weald was brought to Chichester, and then the goddess of the craft which fashioned it; by the guild of the craftsmen organized in Roman style; and, above all, by the wording of the text in Roman legal diction. The inscriptions are for Britain a valuable documentation of the activities of its principal philo-Roman ruler. Outside the city there are further indications of the early progress of Romanization. The palatial villa of Fishbourne, a little to the west, is the most notable of these; it was begun in the reign of Nero, abandoned before completion, and arose in the reign of Vespasian as a stately and richly furnished residence. It is seen by some as the seat of the ruling house. Other villas were founded within the territory at an early date, as at Angmering and Southwick, though they did not rival Fishbourne in scale and significance.

By the last quarter of the century, ambitions were growing larger among the *civitates* of the South as the material benefits of the Roman peace began to accumulate. Credit for their physical development is given by Tacitus to Agricola, though he also knew that this intelligent governor was not the first to take advantage of the current conditions. From the reign of Vespasian onward, there is a quickening of pace in the growth and embellishment of cities. Most, if not quite all, of the native *civitates* took shape over the following forty or fifty years, some in more orderly fashion than others.

This expansive prosperity was in evidence elsewhere. At Calleva Atrebatum (Silchester) there had already been development in Nero's reign, probably because the town lay within the territories under the charge of Cogidubnus. A network of streets had been laid out and a public bath constructed. Under the Flavians, other urban amenities were added, chiefly a forum and basilica at the heart of the town, over the site of a substantial timber structure, possibly one of the principal buildings in an earlier military base. Corinium Dobunnorum (Cirencester) greatly expanded in the later first century, attracting to its site inhabitants of the Iron Age *oppidum* at Bagendon nearby, as well as the usual traders and suppliers of services. Here, too, public buildings were going up in the last quarter of the century and probably into the next. At Canterbury, Winchester, Exeter and Leicester, a broadly similar picture emerges of public and administrative buildings, commercial quarters on the main street-frontages, a temple perhaps, private houses generally modest in scale and normally in timber. This considerable expansion, with all that it implies for the development of industries and crafts associated with building, must have placed a large burden upon the leading families in the native communities. It is not therefore surprising that progress towards full urban dignity was uneven from place to place. Whereas Verulamium and Silchester saw fairly rapid progress towards the completion of the major buildings, at Exeter, Leicester and Wroxeter principal elements were still being added to the plan in the reigns of Hadrian and Antoninus Pius. The forum at Wroxeter was not completed until 129/130, while the public baths at both Exeter and Leicester belong to the mid second century. At Canterbury, a theatre was provided later still, by no means a common urban amenity in Britain. Outside the category of native administrative centres was Aquae Sulis (Bath). Here it was the curative hot springs that attracted attention, and as early as the sixties or early seventies the first stone buildings at this religious complex and spa were going up. Everywhere the native aristocracy was in the best position to profit by the settled peace and evidently could now attend to the development of public amenities.

Different from any of the towns hitherto considered was Londinium (London). Nature here contained the tidal Thames and made possible the construction of a bridge, where land and sea-traffic for the whole island met. Sea-lanes converged upon it from the Rhine, the Gallic ports or by the Channel route from Bordeaux, Spain and the Mediterranean. There is as yet no certain sign that the Roman army chose London as one of its bases in the aftermath of the invasion, highly likely as that may seem. No question of status could prevent Londinium from becoming the natural centre for trade and administration in Britain. If the first intention was to govern the province from Camulodunum, it is clear that within a generation the provincial administration was based in London; while in the fourth century, it was not only the seat of the provincial treasury but the residence of the civil governor who presided over the entire diocese of Britain. The tomb of Alpinus Classicianus, procurator of Britain at the time of the great revolt of 60/61, was set up in London and it may well be that after that cataclysm the administration of the province was based here. Certainly by AD 100 the town was garrisoned like a provincial capital, a fort at Cripplegate in the north-western part of Londinium housing troops charged with official and ceremonial duties. And in the later first century a well-appointed *praetorium* for the governor and his staff had been built not far from the frontage of the Thames. As a trading centre, London was already well known when it was reduced to ashes in the rebellion of 60/61, and its advantageous position for a wide range of commerce was fully exploited in the following century and a half. A succession of river harbours lined the north shore of the Thames and to this port were brought both mundane and luxury items from the neighbouring provinces, some for consumption in London, others for transshipment to other parts of Britain. What passed through London as exports is not directly attested, but we may guess that a major part was played by agricultural products such as grain and leather, and some of the minerals, including iron, which Britain had long been known to contain. It is not surprising, then, that London furnishes mercantile documents on wooden writing tablets, fine imported artistic works in bronze and marble, and a temple to Mithras, a god honoured by traders in the major ports of the Empire. From the later first century, the town was growing rapidly, like a boom town, and was ravaged by a great fire, dating to the 120s, only to emerge phoenix-like from its ashes. Many of its buildings were no doubt built of timber and the fire-fighting appliances of the Roman world were helpless against major conflagrations. The legal status of Londinium in its early days has been much debated and is still unclear. It was not the centre of a native tribe nor a *colonia*. It may have ranked merely as a *vicus*, or village, or possibly as a *municipium*, like many contemporary towns in Spain.

There can be no doubt that the visit of Hadrian to the province in 122, when he is recorded to have 'set much in order', had a no less powerful effect in the civilian area than on the northern frontier. The most striking evidence comes from Viroconium (Wroxeter) on the upper Severn, capital of the Cornovii, where the great inscription, dedicating the basilica and forum of the town to Hadrian in AD 129–30, still excites the admiration evoked by fine Roman monumental lettering. The planned street-system is contemporary with this great building, dividing some 180 acres into spacious rectangular building-blocks, many of which were in due course occupied by the large residences of tribal magnates. The town was thus a defended centre for the wealth and enterprise of the leading families of the community. The site had been occupied by a legionary base from the reign of Nero until about AD 90, so that a fully urban development could not begin until Trajan's reign at the earliest. The Hadrianic forum was followed by a large public bath about the middle of the second century, equipped with a spacious *palaestra*, or

Inscription as found

Inscription completed

Fig. 1. Inscription from Wroxeter

exercise-hall, and a swimming-bath. The same complex also contained a public latrine and a *macellum* or market-hall, the whole comprising a compact instance of urban planning. About AD 165, the centre of Wroxeter was destroyed by fire and the forum had to be rebuilt. Over the site of burnt shops there went up a temple of partly classical design.

Public amenities were also provided at Ratae Corieltauvorum (Leicester) from Hadrian's reign onward. In the 120s the Fosse Way, approaching the city from Lincoln, was realigned and equipped with milestones, no doubt at the expense of the Corieltauvi, both in money and in compulsory labour, as was customary. The forum and basilica, begun perhaps some twenty years earlier, were completed under Hadrian, and a fine suite of public baths, of which part of the *palaestra* survives in the Jewry Wall, was added in mid-century. Further space for a market was provided in a *macellum* (market) to the north of the forum, on a site earlier occupied by a substantial private house. The

importance of markets and craftsmen's quarters in the cities of
Roman Britain is in evidence in most of the places that have been
extensively examined, offering an important reminder of the close
links between cities and their rural territories. This raises the
interesting question of the relationship of the tribal aristocracy to
trade and to incoming settlers from outside Britain. In other parts
of the Roman world landowning and trading often went together,
in the sense that a landowner would invest spare capital in a
business run by his freedmen and slaves. Intelligent, business-
trained slaves in the service of Roman citizens, as the wealthy
members of the tribal council might become by serving in magis-
tracies, graduated into freedmen, where enterprise and ambitions
lay mainly in the direction of trade. How many such men did a
Romano-British tribal capital contain? No answer is available,
just as no estimate can be made of the number of Roman citizens
in the form of retired soliders or traders who settled there for
business. Such people undoubtedly existed. There was a guild of
'non-Roman citizens settled at Calleva' (Silchester), which was
the hub of the Roman road-system to the west and south-west of
London. How did these men link with the Tammonii, one of the
leading families of the tribe, worshippers of Hercules Segomo?
What was the relationship between the tribal aristocracy of
Venta Silurum (Caerwent) and Nonius Romanus, who was important enough to be excused his guild obligations and signalled his
gratitude by a dedication to a native Mars whom he equated
with Lenus, the god of his native land on the Moselle? Such
questions cannot be answered, but the fact that they can be put
demonstrates the variety of the social scene and the many problems which cannot be solved because of a dearth of
documentation.

A community in which the impulse towards urbanization has
been revealed with exceptional clarity is Verulamium (St Albans),
where the Roman centre was developed on the valley floor below
the Iron Age stronghold of Prae Wood but still within the outer
defences of the pre-Roman *oppidum*. An early military fort at the
river-crossing may have provided the focus for early civilian
settlement, in which traders played a significant part. A remarkable block of timber shops-cum-workshops had been built within

ten years of the conquest, and from an early date the core of the settlement had been laid out on a planned grid of streets. The growing town was slow to recover from the destruction of AD 60/61, but from the early Flavian period the tempo of development quickened. The forum was completed by 79, or 81 at latest, and other public structures were provided in the late first or early second centuries. The street-plan was extended as the community steadily grew. A theatre of recognizably Gaulish type was added in Hadrian's reign, close to a Romano-Celtic temple, and two Classical temples were constructed within the forum. A thriving and well-appointed provincial city thus existed by the middle of the second century, at which time its central area was badly damaged by another major fire. Private houses in the early town were far from elaborate or richly adorned. The earliest spacious and luxurious residences seem to date from after about AD 130, but even these are few in number. The tribal aristocracy did not, then, quickly convert to urban life, preferring their landed estates where their social dominance was unquestioned. The status of Verulamium, in Roman constitutional terms, has been much discussed. The place was once described by Tacitus as a *municipium*, a chartered city, but it is far from clear that he was using the term in any strict legal sense. The legal status of other tribal capitals is similarly ill-defined. It may be that these native towns remained unchartered, *oppida* or *vici*, where status was defined in the treaty governing relations between the tribe and the provincial administration. It would have been very uncharacteristic of Roman government to assign the same constitutional status to all the native *civitates* of the south. Some of the more Romanized may have been elected to the dignity of chartered cities at a later date.

The development of Verulamium from the second to the fourth centuries is particularly instructive, though it must not be taken as a paradigm for all cities of the province. The second century was a time of expansion, especially in commercial premises and domestic properties. The first-century defences were by now entirely outmoded and were being built over by the 150s. By 170 they were systematically levelled. Buildings also went up across the river Ver, including a substantial bath-building. This bath lay over 360 metres outside the defences and its siting is therefore puzzling. The economic life of Verulamium was obviously boom-ing and there was every sign that this would continue. But about 155, a huge fire struck the central part of the city, destroying an area over twenty hectares in extent, including part of the forum. The fire not only halted the development of the city: it appears also to have impaired its economic basis, for recovery after the fire was slow. Several of the domestic buildings which replaced those destroyed in 155 were not built until after 200, perhaps not until well after, while some plots of ground remained empty for over a century. Shops and other commercial concerns were rebuilt on the main frontages but there seem to have been fewer of them after 155. Not all efforts at monumental building were suspended. A monumental arch was erected on the old city boundary about 270. But major building projects do not seem to have been undertaken by the community after the construction of the de-fences about this same date.

The fourth-century city shows the same stable and relatively prosperous conditions, though with no indication of economic advance. Several of the larger urban houses reached their peak between 280 and 350, with mosaics still being installed and bath-suites maintained. The theatre was still in use and received structural alterations after 350. It was not finally abandoned until at least the end of the fourth century. No sign of any sudden end of urban life is evident at Verulamium in the final decades of Roman Britain, nor indeed for some time afterwards (above, p. 51)

In other cities there are clearer signs of decay and dilapidation in major structures by the end of the third and the early fourth centuries. The forum at Wroxeter was in a semi-ruinous condition by about 300 and was further dismantled later. The public baths fell into disuse by the mid fourth century and subsequently, in the fifth century, provided the framework for a remarkable series of timber buildings. The great forum-basilica at London was deliber-ately demolished during the fourth century and other structures in the city were wholly or partly in ruins by 350. At Silchester the basilica housed craftsmen in metal during the fourth century, though the building survived until after 400.

In several other cities there is clear evidence for large open spaces in the late Empire. These have long been evident on the plan of Silchester. They are now also known at Exeter, Leicester, Chichester and London. At a number of cities, including London, Winchester, Canterbury, Gloucester and Cirencester, deep deposits of black earth have been observed, and this is most reasonably seen as the result of agricultural activity over a considerable period, beginning in some cases in the later second century. All this may seem to point to a radical change in the character of Romano-British urbanism. That cities in the fourth century were markedly different from those of the early Empire is certain, but the emphasis should be placed on change rather than on decline.

Still the most extensively excavated of Romano-British cities is Calleva Atrebatum (Silchester), though much of the work was carried out in the nineteenth century to poor standards. More recent excavation has added invaluable precision to the general chronology of the place as well as important information on individual structures. The plan of Silchester provides us with an unrivalled overall impression of a medium-sized Romano-British city as it existed in the third and fourth centuries. Pre-Roman Calleva, a known mint-centre of Atrebatic kings and thus presumably a royal residence, was a developed town by the late first century BC, boasting a plan of streets and an orderly layout of buildings covering over thirty hectares. The inscribed coinages of Tincommius, son of Caesar's former ally Commius, and Eppillus were struck at Silchester during this phase; imports from the Continent point to wide-ranging trade-contacts half a century before the Roman conquest. Craftsmen were also at work here, in metal and perhaps in glass, so that the major political and economic characteristics of an urban nucleus were well developed long before the Roman arrival. The early Roman city was to grow at the centre of the Iron Age *oppidum*, within the enclosure known as the Inner Earthwork. It is plausible, though not yet quite certain, that a unit of the Roman army was in garrison at Silchester shortly after AD 43. A large timber structure beneath the later forum may have formed part of a military base, or alternatively was an early timber forum. Such an amenity was unusual, but Silchester was a community that was quickly provided with a variety of urban structures. A timber amphitheatre was built in the reign of Nero, as was a substantial bath-building. The street-plan also developed shortly after AD 60 and the urban plan continued to expand over the next two decades. This unusually strong early growth was most probably stimulated by the position of Calleva either within the kingdom ruled by Cogidubnus or within the territories assigned to that realm after the conquest. Strategically, the site was not of great significance, but it lay on desirable land between the Thames valley and the chalk uplands.

The city developed steadily from the late first century, its stone forum and basilica being built about AD 100 and several temples later in the second century. No Classical temple appears on the plan and the other public buildings were modest in their architectural design. The forum was reminiscent of the plan of the headquarters building (*principia*) of a legionary fortress and may have derived from it, although it has also been suggested that the process of imitation worked in reverse. Military architects were frequently relied on in the early stages of urban planning in the provinces. In Britain, it is difficult to identify other specialists who could have fulfilled this role in the first century. As time went on, interchange between military and civilian architects is likely to have occurred, but the results in Britain were not strikingly innovative. Sadly, most of the decorative detail of the forum has been lost, though it is known that there was substantial use of Italian marble in the basilica, allied no doubt with painting, and its sculptures included a stone statue of Tutela, the guardian deity of the community, and a large bronze figure, probably of an emperor clad in armour. The original purpose of this solid and dignified building may not have been maintained throughout its life. In the later Roman period, at least part of it was given over to craftsmen in metal and other media.

The overall urban plan is of particular interest because of its completeness. The main streets were fronted by the familiar shops and workshops. Substantial private houses were far from numerous. About twenty-five large dwellings are evident, along with another twenty smaller houses. In almost all parts of the city what catches the eye are the open spaces, in which timber structures not observed by the early excavators may have existed, but which alternatively may have been occupied by gardens or orchards. A crude estimate suggests that about thirty leading families of the Atrebates maintained town houses in Calleva and that the urban population was no more than 3,000 in total. This is about the size of a small country town today, with which Calleva may be fairly compared. It must also be remembered that it is not out of scale with the medium-sized towns of pre-industrial Europe. The small number of substantial town houses might suggest that not all the families that provided members of the local *curia* or senate had residence in the capital. But it is known from North African evidence that a provincial *curia* need not always have a full complement of 100 decurions, and this could also have been true of Romano-British *civitates*.

Two individual structures are of particular note at Calleva. The first is a very large courtyard house, complete with its own suite of baths, sited near the south gate. This seems to be too large for a private dwelling and is better interpreted as a *mansio* or station for officials using the Imperial posting-service (*cursus publicus*) or engaged in other State business. The other is a small basilican building erected late in the Roman period near the forum. This is often identified as a small Christian church of the fourth century, though this is not beyond all question (below, p. 179).

There are a number of social and political matters upon which the size and disposition of the tribal capitals throw some light. Certain tribal centres in Britain are exceptionally small when compared with those in Gaul. Two of them, Venta Silurum (Caerwent) and Venta Icenorum (Caister-by-Norwich), were the centres of tribes whose resistance to Rome, in differing circumstances, had been fierce and, in the former case, prolonged. The Iceni had begun relations with Rome as an allied kingdom, whose royal house and nobility reacted strenuously when the kingdom was annexed (above, p. 26). The defeat that followed crippled the tribal nobility so that the development of Venta Icenorum was slow, and the town did not fill out the space allotted by the original planners. At Venta Silurum the tribe lost less by early stubborn resistance than the Iceni by rebellion. At all events, urban life began sooner and the town reflected on a smaller scale what was happening in the larger *civitates*, though Venta Silurum remained unpretentious in its structures. Considering the struggle between the Silures and Rome in the mid first century, the very existence of this self-governing *civitas* is astounding enough. We can only guess at the date of its creation. By the early third century the local senate were dedicating a statue to a benefactor in regular Roman fashion. This man, Tiberius Claudius Paulinus, had been the commander of the II Augusta at nearby Caerleon and later returned to the governorship of Lower Britain (Britannia Inferior) in 220. Presumably the leaders of the Silures were returning a favour shown to their community when Paulinus was legate at Caerleon; and they may have looked for more when he returned to Britain. Such connections between military and civilian government cannot have been isolated cases.

One tribe at least may have had two centres. The Durotriges of Dorset, whose initial resistance to Rome had to be broken by the storming of hill-forts (Suetonius' *Life of Vespasian* mentions twenty), seem to have been divided between Durnovaria (Dorchester) and Lindinis (Ilchester), though the former was the larger and more prosperous place. This could have been due to the natural separation of the two areas by Blackmore Forest, just as in Gaul the Vocontii of the Vaucluse were governed from different centres in their two main valleys. But the division of a tribal area (if this did indeed occur) is so exceptional for Britain that it is more easily regarded as an early arrangement intended to break the unity of the tribe and possibly to facilitate its inclusion within the realm of Cogidubnus.

Uniformity, however, was not a Roman constitutional fetish. Indeed, nothing is more characteristic of Roman Imperial development than readiness to work within existing arrangements, provided these could be assimilated to Roman form. The history of the northern tribes of Britain is an object-lesson in the handling of this principle. Those presumably included within the province were three: the numerous and far-flung Brigantes, whose lands extended from sea to sea; the Parisi, settled in east Yorkshire, thickly populated from an early time; and the Carvetii of the Eden valley, perhaps earlier a sept of the Brigantes. The Parisi had welcomed Roman merchants for a generation before they became part of the province from AD 71; and it was possibly through their territory that the army of Cerealis carried out its main advance upon the Brigantes. This move may have been peacefully received, if not welcomed, for the tribal territory was subsequently not heavily garrisoned by Roman troops. Only one such garrison was long maintained, at Derventio (Malton), on the north-western border against the Brigantes. The Humber crossing at Petuaria (Brough) was garrisoned until late in the first century and then later became the seat of the tribal capital, described in a mid-second-century inscription as a *vicus*, or village community.

The broad territory occupied by the Brigantes exhibits wider variation in urban development. At York a sizeable settlement grew up outside the legionary fortress and, later, across the river to the southwest a much larger township developed during the second century. By AD 237, and most probably early in the third century, this had received the dignity of a *colonia* and had become the capital of the new province of Britannia Inferior. York, like Lincoln, was well placed to serve seaborne commerce and probably became a major inland port. The city also stood at the centre of the plain of York, the richest agricultural region of the tribe and, indeed, of northern England. Within the plain, at the crossing of the river Ure, lay the tribal capital of Isurium Brigantum (Aldborough). No certain trace of an Iron Age settlement has yet been found here and the nucleus of early occupation may thus have been a Flavian fort at the river-crossing. The focus was never more than a modest growth, covering eventually about twenty-five hectares within its defences, but a grid-plan of streets was provided for the centre and the attempt was made to provide public structures appropriate to an administrative *chef-lieu*. Among the private structures, too, there are evident signs of aspiration towards civility, a surprising number of mosaics being recorded in the town houses of the late Roman phase. In the Vale of York outside the town a scatter of fairly modest villas dotted the landscape, but in many parts of the canton villas and minor towns are unknown or sparse. Calderdale, for example, which has produced inscriptions suggestive of the settlement of veterans from the legion based at York, has no known urban centre.

At the northern end of the Vale of York a sizeable town grew up at Catterick on the river Swale, a site early adopted by the army; this *vicus*, later walled, continued as a local centre to at least the end of the Roman period. In the sixth century it was to be the scene of one of the major battles between the Britons of the north and the expanding power of the Angles. Further north, small townships were rare and usually developed as villages outside the walls of long-established Roman forts or other bases, as happened at Corbridge, Piercebridge and Carlisle. On and near Hadrian's Wall, the *vici* at Chesters, Chesterholm and House-steads were extensive and all are likely to have enjoyed a corporate existence, as is attested by an inscription from Chesterholm. The development of the *vicus* at the supply depot at Corbridge made it a virtual town. Air photography at Piercebridge and Old Carlisle and field-work at Old Penrith indicate very large settlements there, where a military road-centre supplied the routes to markets. The substantial shops and taverns excavated in the nineteenth century at Binchester attest a similar development on the same basis. These *vici*, which developed outside forts, had an important part to play in the economic development of northern Britain. They formed the centre for a local market as well as ministering to the recreation of the soldiers, and their economic development might be so promising as to tempt the soldier into business on retirement from active service. A boost to their growth was provided early in the third century, when soldiers were permitted legal marriage, encouraging the provision of more substantial living quarters and other facilities.

In addition to their administrative functions several towns and cities were of major significance as ports, though this aspect of their history has generally not received the attention it deserves, with the exception of London. The siting of several major cities on navigable rivers or estuary-heads, often on sites originally chosen for military purposes, marks them out as probable ports, serving the same combination of official and commercial needs as inland ports such as Cologne and Lyons. Gloucester, Exeter and Lincoln, the last-named being much closer to the coast in Roman times than it is now, probably all had connections with seaborne traffic. The same is certainly true of the fortress and *colonia* at York. The legionary bases at Caerleon and Chester, and their associated townships, were easily reached from the sea and at both there is structural evidence for quays. Smaller places, such as Brough-on-Humber and Caister-by-Yarmouth, may have been more significant as ports than anything else, and a further range of minor sites with access to the sea may have served as harbours. These include Hengistbury Head in Dorset, Mount Batten on Plymouth Sound, Poole on its magnificent harbour, Seaton in Devon and Sea Mills near Bristol. There were harbours on the south-east coast that served a variety of purposes, among which military concerns may have predominated. Richborough was an important port of entry in the fourth century, as it had been in the first. The fine harbour at Dover, with its lighthouse or lighthouses, could have been used by commercial vessels as well as the ships of the *classis Britannica*, and other smaller harbours in Kent may have been used by vessels following the shortest routes from Gaul.

The most impressive structural evidence for an inland port has come from the river-frontage of Roman London. From the later first century, timber quays and contemporary store-buildings were built along the shore in the area of present-day Thames Street. Later quays and revetments were pushed out into the river, the dates of these being determined by dendrochronology. At St Magnus House, a second-century embankment was superseded by a more ambitious quay after about 225, to be followed in turn by the city wall after the mid third century, thus ending the functioning of the harbour at this point. The entire frontage of quays, however, may have been over 600 metres in length, providing ample space for later commerce. The scale of the London waterfront is itself indicative of the fact that long-distance maritime commerce was far more important here than localized traffic using the Thames. This is further borne out by the evidence of imports. Wine came in from southern Gaul, North Africa and the Aegean, and olive oil from Spain. Pottery from Gaul and the Rhineland was a major import, along with vessels from Dorset and other parts of southern Britain. From northern Britain came jet and coal, and from North Wales roofing slates. As in other great ports, craft-working was pursued close to the harbour front-age, especially in leather, bronze, bone and wood. The shipment of leather from a centre like this could have been of great importance, though this is unlikely to be revealed fully by archaeo-logical evidence.

The province contained two spas, Aquae Sulis (Bath) and Aquae Arnemetiae (Buxton), the former graced with magnificent baths which were among the finest in the western provinces and of surprisingly early date. The literal *fons et origo* of Bath was the deep mineral spring from which the healing waters issue at a temperature of 120 °F. The curative properties of the place were appreciated in the later Iron Age, as offerings to the presiding deity, Sulis, reveal. Sulis was a healing god in the Celtic religious order, whose cult was associated with that of Minerva at Bath. The great bath-complex is among the finest survivals from Roman Britain, but this was only a part, albeit a most imposing part, of the entire sanctuary. The god was honoured by a fine classical tetrastyle temple, its columns surmounted by Corinthian capitals and its pediment richly adorned with conventionally classical Tritons and Victories, but with a formidable, glowering relief of a Celtic water-god in the central roundel. This has a claim to be regarded as the finest piece of stone sculpture yet found from Roman Britain. The temple lay within its own *temenos* or sacred precinct and fronted a smaller inner precinct, within which lay an altar. If this site were in Gaul, we would expect a theatre to confront the temple, but that part of the complex is now covered by Bath Abbey. The sacred spring and the reservoir that received its waters lay in one corner of the precinct, close to the altar, the water being fed into the Great Bath at the focus of the baths. From the beginning, the baths were a monumental construction comparable in overall design and in the detail of their execution with the best work of the adjacent continent from the early Empire. The focus of the building was the Great Bath, set within an aisled hall over thirty metres long by twenty metres wide. The basin itself was over twenty metres in length and one and a half metres deep, entered from steep steps along all its sides. It had been entirely lined with lead to prevent leakage and to keep out water from minor springs that come to the surface in the vicinity. The bath was fed by a rectangular box-pipe of lead connected to the reservoir. Separated from the Great Bath by an entrance-hall lay a compact suite of baths comprising warm and hot rooms and a small swimming-pool. At the other end of the complex a smaller basin (the Lucas Bath) and another swimming-pool offered further space to those using the establishment. Not the least surprising feature of this astonishing building is its early date. Its architectural details suggest that it went up in the later reign of Nero or early in the Flavian period. In later phases the bath-suites to either side of the Great Bath were considerably enlarged, and a barrel-vault was erected over the whole structure. Thus, by the early third century, if not earlier, the Great Bath and the Lucas Bath were flanked by substantial bath-suites, that at the west end being especially elaborate. It is scarcely surprising that good sculpture was provided to embellish a building of this quality, and it is highly likely that skilled workmen came from Gaul for this purpose. At least one sculptor from the area of Chartres is attested at Bath. The entire architectural design is likely to have been the work of an *architectus* from Gaul or Italy. It is more difficult to discover who employed such a man, and who provided the funds for the work.

The supply of water to cities is attested, in the main, by simple systems, the elaborate and often grand aqueducts that served cities such as Lyons and Nîmes being unknown in Britain. Even the less imposing pipeline that carried water to Cologne from the Eifel is not matched by any recorded aqueduct in Britain. In many cities and towns there was still a general reliance upon wells and springs for everyday purposes, though the installation of public baths clearly called for a constant, or at least reliable, flow of water. One of the most ambitious systems of supply was that which led water into Lincoln from springs to the north-east of the city, through a line composed of tile pipes jacketed in thick concrete. The pipeline led to a water tank, or *castellum aquae*, sited behind the defences, from which water was distributed to points within the city, presumably by gravity feed. Wroxeter was served by a water-leat eight kilometres in length, which delivered water into timber-and-lead pipes running across the city, the surplus being carried off by an overflow that fed a duct running along a major street. This was in turn tapped for domestic purposes, including the flushing of latrines. Other cities relied upon a water-supply conducted underground in timber pipes joined and held by iron collars. This type of supply is widely known, at Verulamium, Silchester, Cirencester, Caerwent and Caister-by-Norwich, so that it may be regarded as the norm for cities. It is also well attested in forts and fortresses, and was probably introduced to Britain by military engineers. Efficient use of this means of distribution required pumps or water-wheels to raise the water to an appropriate level in the main tanks or *castella aquae*. Remains of a force-pump of a kind which could have been used in this way have been found at Silchester. Some towns and cities had open leats or channels, like that which ran along a contoured course of fourteen kilometres to Durnovaria (Dorchester, Dorset). Shorter lengths of such channels may have been much commoner than our evidence at present suggests. In general, the cities of Britain were not equipped with water supplies to the standards of the Mediterranean world. But the systems of supply were broadly comparable with those of other European frontier provinces.

The private houses in cities are a revealing source of information on the character of urban communities, though the best evidence comes from only five cities: Verulamium, Silchester, Wroxeter, Caerwent and Cirencester. In all cases, the impact of Mediterranean styles of housing was not marked at any phase of urban development – which is not entirely surprising, given the building traditions that prevailed in Britain during the Iron Age. The first urban dwellings were built in timber and clay, the walls being generally set in continuous foundation-trenches, occasionally resting on a foundation-beam. The method of construction clearly derives from military models. The classic demonstration of such structures is that of the dwellings-cum-workshops on the Watling Street frontage at Verulamium, where building began only a few years after AD 43. At both London and Cirencester, the great majority (perhaps all) of the private houses were timber-framed until well into the second century. As time went on dwarf stone walls were provided. Most of the houses were also small in scale and simple in plan, only ten to twenty metres long and five to ten metres wide, divided into four or five rooms and probably normally of one storey. Painted wall-plaster and simple mosaics appeared in the Flavian period at London and Cirencester, but these amenities were not widespread. Large and sumptuously appointed houses are still unknown in first-century cities and were slow to appear until the mid second century. The British curial class (town councillors) was evidently not quickly converted to urban life, or at least not to the extent that they were prepared to invest in fine residences in the cities. After about AD 150, at a time of rising prosperity, investment in substantial town houses began and more elaborate plans came into vogue. Houses of more than a single range of rooms appeared, often L-shaped, occasionally disposed around three sides of a court. Verandahs and mosaic floors became more common, and roofs were tiled. The larger dwellings might possess twenty or thirty rooms and were clearly designed to house a sizeable household of servants. Generally, these grander dwellings stood alone, apart from the other houses and often with space for gardens or orchards around them. In few cities are there signs of densely packed houses sharing party walls. Nor are there many dwellings closely modelled on the peristyle houses of the Mediterranean provinces. A few had enclosed courts that may have been adorned by formal gardens and statuary, but these were exceptional.

The setting of the larger urban houses within the town plan is of great interest. The more completely examined cities, especially Silchester, Verulamium, Wroxeter and Caerwent, show clearly that the dwellings of the dominant social group generally lay within their own purlieus, sometimes presiding over an entire *insula* (urban block). The number of such residences in any one city was not great. At Caerwent, scarcely more than a dozen such houses appear on the plan, at Silchester about fifteen, at Wroxeter perhaps twenty. Although not all existed at the same time, the distribution of these residences is eloquent of the dominance of relatively small numbers of families within these cities. The same picture is now emerging at Leicester, Exeter, Canterbury and probably Gloucester. In parts of Camulodunum and London much more closely packed houses appear, but at present this appears to be peculiar to these two cities. The implications for urban society in Britain are major, particularly for the period from the later second century to the fourth. A fairly small number of the *curiales* were able or prepared to maintain a large urban residence.

Theatres and amphitheatres are not recorded at most of the major cities and only a few of the recorded buildings are imposing structures. Models for civilian amphitheatres were to hand in the military *ludi*, serving the purposes of both military training and entertainment, which are represented in Britain by the excavated examples at Caerleon and Chester. Urban amphitheatres were usually sited on the margins of a city or outside the walled area, as at Silchester, Cirencester and Dorchester. These were architecturally simple buildings, their seating-banks being no more than dumps of earth revetted in stone. Their economy of construction is seen in its most extreme form at Dorchester, where a Neolithic henge monument was transformed into an earthen amphitheatre in the first century. The London amphitheatre may have been closer to the stone structures of the Continent, but even this was no rival to the great masonry structures of southern Gaul and Italy. In any case, its position close to the fort at Cripplegate probably indicates an origin as a military *ludus*. It is curious that as yet none of the four British *coloniae* has produced evidence of an amphitheatre, though if these were also largely of earth they could easily have been levelled by later building. Familiarity with gladiatorial contests is widely attested on figured pottery and glass and by occasional finds such as a gladiator's bronze helmet found near Bury St Edmunds, and it is known that gladiators were recruited in Britain for display elsewhere. The cupids dressed as gladiators who appear on a mosaic at the Bignor villa in Sussex, although plainly drawn from the common stock of artistic conceits, clearly had some meaning for those who commissioned the work.

The public art once on display in the cities of Britain now exists only in fragments from which a full reconstruction is impossible. The statuary that must once have adorned and enlivened the temples and public squares has largely vanished: what survives may not be fully representative. There are, nevertheless, glimpses of surprising quality. Aside from tombstones, what are lacking are portrait images of the Romano-Britons themselves. Of surviving Imperial portraits, the earliest is a head from a full-size bronze statue of Claudius, found in the river Alde in Suffolk but most probably originally set up in the *colonia* at Camulodunum. This, and a bronze head of Hadrian, also from a life-sized statue, found in the Thames at London, are provincial works of good quality, possibly made by Gaulish artists, but far from outstanding products of the genre. Not until the fourth century does there appear an Imperial portrait of originality and power. This is a head in stone of Constantine I, found in York, where he was hailed as emperor by his troops. The acclaimation of Constantine might have been the occasion for this very piece, for it is a portrait of the ruler in relative youth. Among statues of deities, the finest is a gilded bronze head, all that remains of a cult-statue of Sulis Minerva from the temple at Bath. Also of note is a head of Sarapis in Portland stone from Silchester. This is well over life-size and must have been part of an imposing cult-statue, quite probably the work of an immigrant sculptor. Another fine statue in Portland stone from Silchester is now represented only by fragments. This was a large figure of Tutela, wearing the customary mural crown, which once stood in the central shrine of the basilica.

The provision of defences for cities followed no overall pattern, reflecting the varied origins and histories of the major urban communities. As is graphically reported by Tacitus, the *colonia* at Camulodunum possessed no defences when Boudicca's rebels burst in upon the place in AD 60. An earthwork defence was built after the revolt and, in the earlier second century, a stone wall was added. The colonies founded in the late first century at Lincoln and Gloucester relied in their early years on the existing defences of the earlier legionary bases at these sites. At Lincoln, where good building stone was available in abundance, a stone front was applied to the military rampart about AD 100. Other first-century urban circuits seem to have been rare, and most cities developed for a century or more before receiving defences. Verulamium was enclosed by a bank and ditch in the reign of Claudius or early in that of Nero, while at Silchester the Iron Age defences were superseded by a new earthwork late in the first century. Elsewhere there are few signs of new defences before the mid second century, even at the provincial capital and commercial centre of Londinium. The first concerted efforts to erect urban defences at a number of cities came in the late second century. These were earthwork circuits, comprising a bank and ditch and possibly in some cases a timber palisade. Timber gates were also provided at some cities, including Winchester and Silchester, but at Cirencester and Verulamium monumental gates in stone were striking features of the circuit. The dating of these city defences is not easy, but the final twenty years of the second century seem the likeliest period for them. Their occasion and purpose have been much debated. It is plausible that so widespread a programme of building (for these defences in earthwork were provided to a number of lesser towns as well as cities) was a reaction to a crisis or period of uncertainty, such as certainly prevailed in late-second-century Britain. It seems unlikely that all were strictly contemporary, though they may have had a common origin in the reign of Commodus between about AD 180 and the early 190s. Although they may have been a reaction to crisis, there was nevertheless time and means for some communities to construct imposing gateways in stone.

During the following century, probably in the decades to either side of AD 270, urban defences in stone were either added to existing earthworks or erected on new circuits. As with the earlier defences, not all belong to the same date, though the general occasion to build was probably the devastating invasions of Gaul by barbarian peoples between 250 and 275. In the larger cities the work of constructing stone walls over several kilometres in length must have taken ten or more years, during which time changes in wall-thickness and other modifications will have been introduced, as is clear at Cirencester and Exeter. Interval towers were included at a number of cities, but the design of most of the stone circuits was simple. External towers are not known to have been built before the fourth century, despite the fact that they had been an integral feature of the forts on the Saxon Shore from the 270s onward. The addition of projecting towers to urban defences may date from the time of Constantine and such additions continued until the 370s, being often accompanied by the digging of broad, shallow ditches that would keep attackers at some distance from the front of the wall. Although often described as 'bastions' and viewed as the emplacements for artillery, the towers on the urban circuits in Britain were not well designed to serve as platforms for ballistae or spring-guns, for which solid tower-bases were needed. Nor is it likely that Romano–British communities will have been able to train and maintain the skilled crews that were necessary to operate ballistae. Moreover, it is difficult to believe that the barbarian raiders of Roman Britain in the fourth century would have directed their efforts at walled centres rather than more vulnerable targets in the open countryside.

Few of the decurions and *duoviri* are known to us from the record of inscriptions. An aedile of Petuaria (Brough-on-Humber) presented a stage-front to a theatre in the mid second century, and decurions appear on inscriptions at York and Gloucester. Rather more informative are inscriptions set up by *seviri Augustales*, priests responsible for official religious rites, including the cult of emperors, and usually drawn from the ranks of freedmen. The most interesting case is M. Aurelius Lunaris, who was a *sevir Augustalis* of both York and Lincoln in the earlier third century and who had commercial links with Burdigala (Bordeaux), where he set up a dedicatory inscription in AD 237. He was probably involved in the wine trade between western Gaul and Britain, presumably directly with York and Lincoln. Another *sevir Augustalis* of York was M. Verecundius Diogenes, his cognomen indicating Greek origin. But his home was in the area of Bourges in the Loire basin and he, too, was probably concerned with a direct trade-link between western Gaul and eastern Britain. These brief glimpses of connections between cities in Britain and the adjacent Continent suggest that such links were stronger and more influential than is often supposed. Roman-style organizations within cities certainly existed, and some of these will have had connections with commerce. The appearance of a *collegium* of smiths at Chichester in the first century is worthy of note, while the existence of a *collegium* of *peregrini* (provincial non-citizens) at Silchester, apart from implying the presence of full citizens, also points to a professional or commercial association.

Within the territories of tribes, some elements of the pre-Roman

Celtic order were maintained. The larger tribes contained divisions of territory and population that served the purposes of government and perhaps the raising of armies. These divisions bore the name *pagi* or *curiae*. In some of the tribes of the Continent, the *pagus* could serve as the basis for recruitment into the Roman army, but there is no proof that this occurred in Britain. It is clear, however, that local units of territory were retained in Roman Britain, presumably for administrative and fiscal purposes. Some appear in inscriptions, as does the *Curia Tectoverdorum* in the area of Vindolanda, others in place-names, such as Coria among the Votadini and another Coria among the Damnonii in western Scotland. These are no more than hints, but it is entirely reasonable that Rome should find it convenient to maintain such subdivisions within the larger tribes and those with a scattered population in wild country.

In lowland Britain the centres of *pagi* and *curiae* are to be sought among the minor towns and roadside *vici* of the province, knowledge of which is still not as extensive as it should be. Some of these townships developed into sizeable settlements, with at least some degree of internal planning, as is evident at Kenchester, Alchester and Durobrivae (Water Newton), and were important enough, in the official sphere as well as locally, to be defended in many cases. Most were built loosely to either side of a major roadway and large buildings were rare. A few included private houses of some quality, as is seen at Kenchester, but most of their buildings were modest in plan. Virtually all seem to have contained workshops and other minor commercial buildings, underlining their importance as local market centres, and a considerable number either contained farmsteads or had villas in their near vicinity. Their relationship with the agricultural land around them was very close. There are also a few indications that Imperial officials were stationed in some of these townships. A *beneficiarius* (an officer outstationed to perform various duties) from the governor's staff is recorded at Dorchester-on-Thames, perhaps stationed there to supervise traffic and tolls at the crossing of the Thames. At Irchester (Northamptonshire), a *strator* (remount officer) may have been on duty, assembling horses for official purposes.

The presence of raw materials and their exploitation for industry stimulated the growth of certain towns. Weston under Penyard was concerned with the working of iron from the Forest of Dean, Charterhouse-on-Mendip with the silver and lead of the Mendips. Durobrivae in the Nene valley flourished on the profits of the large pottery industry in the region, with major support from ironworking. Droitwich owed its growth to the deposits of salt there. An interesting group of towns may have originated as local religious centres, later developing other functions as people were attracted to them. Springhead in Kent boasted at least three temples and was clearly a local sanctuary of some import-ance. Nettleton, on the Fosse Way north-east of Bath, possessed a striking octagonal shrine in the third century, dedicated to Apollo Cunomaglos, though other deities were worshipped here, including Diana, Mercury, Rosmerta and Silvanus. Such centres of rural cult are much better known in Gaul, where a theatre or small amphitheatre frequently provided a framework for festival games and other performances. Roman Britain had its counter-parts to these. At Frilford in Berkshire, a Romano-Celtic temple lay within a walled precinct, close to a small, almost circular amphitheatre. A theatre may have been associated with a temple at Wycomb, near Cheltenham, a site lying far from any known Roman road and thus better identified as a rural sanctuary than a minor town.

It is a striking fact that so many of the minor towns, some of them very small indeed, were given defences in the same period as the major cities, the sequence of building following that in the cities quite closely. Thus, earthwork defences were provided at places like Margidunum (Nottinghamshire), Towcester (North-amptonshire) and Irchester (Northamptonshire) late in the second or early in the third century, when there can have been relatively little to defend. This is a further indication of official interest in these places on the major routes, an interest that went beyond mere provision for the Imperial Post. Stone defences went up at many minor towns in the later third century and others were walled early in the fourth. The significance of these places did not decrease as time went on. Rather, they grew in importance as local economic and social centres as well as nodal points within the administrative framework of the province. They may well have taken on some of the functions of the larger urban centres, while a few, including Durobrivae, Rochester and Alchester, could have entered the list of *civitates*, though proof is lacking. The unofficial document known as the Antonine Itinerary, written in the third century but with later changes, includes many of the minor townships, along with cities and forts, with indications of the intervening road-distances, suggesting that they contained official installations such as *mansiones* (halts for rest and accommodation). Structures that may have served this purpose have been excavated at Godmanchester, Chelmsford and Wall. By contrast, important junctions of roads are known at which no Roman settlement of any importance appears to have existed. These include Badbury Rings in Dorset, Old Sarum in Wiltshire and High Cross in Leicestershire. Unwalled settlements, both on roads and remote from them, might often extend over large areas in an unplanned sprawl. These sites are poorly known at present, but their functions were more rural than urban, so far as these can be detected at all.

Those who governed the cities, the decurions who made up the *ordo* or local senate, have left few memorials behind them. Nominally a hundred strong, in a frontier province like Britain the *ordo* might often number considerably fewer. The decurions were drawn from the leading families of the *civitas*, their ownership of property bestowing status and power.

Executive authority lay with four principal magistrates, the two senior of whom were called *duoviri iuredicundo*, the two junior *duoviri aediles*, all elected annually. Every five years the two senior magistrates were chosen with particular care and given the title *duoviri quinquennales*. Their task, which earned those charged with it public esteem, was to supervise adjustments to the property rolls that determined the tax-assessment and to check and regulate other matters relating to the finances of the community. The senior magistrates were responsible for the running of the local courts, or at least for cases involving minor crimes and property below a certain value. Weightier legal matters were decided at the court of the provincial governor or his judicial officer, the *legatus iuridicus*. That court might be convened in provincial assize centres or *conventus*, normally major cities and, perhaps, legionary bases. Cases between Roman citizens were heard in Roman courts. Junior magistrates supervised the maintenance of public buildings and defences, the upkeep of streets and roads, the regulation of markets and the letting of contracts. Election to the ranks of magistrates was the rule in the early Empire; later, co-option was found necessary. A sought-after honour in the first and second centuries, such offices became increasingly burdensome from the later third century onward as central government made ever-greater demands on the energies and pockets of the decurions. Whereas in the early Empire magistrates would celebrate their election by providing buildings, entertainments and gifts to their communities, in the Empire of Diocletian and Constantine many sought to escape the distinction altogether.

At the centre of the duties of magistrates was responsibility for the collection of provincial taxes and their despatch to the procurator, and also the raising of whatever local taxation the *ordo* might determine. The state taxes principally comprised a tax on land (*tributum soli*) and a poll tax (*tributum capitis*), assessed by Imperial officials but locally gathered. Any shortfall might be made a liability on the decurions themselves. The upkeep of the major roads also fell on the urban authorities and in Britain, where cities were relatively few, this must have been a major burden. Over and above the construction and repair of roads, communities were also responsible for the Imperial Post (*cursus publicus*). This was a service of gigs, light carts and wagons for the use of Imperial officials on provincial business. At regular intervals on the major routes there were provided stations where horses could be changed and vehicles repaired (*mutationes*) and *mansiones*. The Antonine Itinerary throws light on the system for much of the Empire. For Britain, sixteen routes are designated in the document, Londinium lying at the hub of a network that linked the main cities and included the principal roads in areas under military control. The provision of horses and the maintenance of *mansiones* will have been no light task for those *civitates* through which heavy traffic passed, for example the Catuvellauni, Atrebates and Brigantes.

The fiscal responsibilities borne by decurions and *duoviri* were thus not of a minor order. The increasing burden will help to explain why it was that the cities of Roman Britain did not develop further than they did. After the later second century, the urban communities appear to have reached a stable condition. Major public works, thereafter, with the notable exception of defences, were undertaken only infrequently; urban growth slowed or ceased altogether. In some places, for instance Caister-by-Norwich, there was contraction. Other forces, of course, were at work, not least the investment of capital by landowners in their own estates, but the downward pressure of the State on the decurial class played perhaps a decisive role in frustrating urban development after AD 200.

CHAPTER FOUR

Rural Settlement and Society

Britain, though a small island, is geographically and geologically one of the most varied provinces of the Roman empire. Any attempt to describe the settlement of the island, in any period of time, must take full account of this fact. As with many other aspects of Roman Britain, rural settlement was as vividly regional a matter as in the medieval centuries. Major distinctions within the island have long been recognized. Sir Cyril Fox's famed construct of Highland and Lowland Zones has long outlived its usefulness, but it did at least underline one of the verities of ancient Britain, which was no doubt fully appreciated by Roman commanders, and others, from the first century onward. The modern student of Roman Britain, with an ever increasing mass of settlement data at his disposal, is likely to be more impressed by localized distinctions and confined ecosystems. Within a fairly limited area like Cornwall and Devon, for example, the variety of soil types and land-forms engendered a correspondingly wide range of rural settlements, including small villas in the east Devon lowlands, rectilinear enclosures in the valleys and the heterogeneous 'rounds' on the hill-slopes. The strongly developing study of landscape archaeology has heightened perceptions of such diversity within relatively small regions and highlighted the need for detailed survey on a scale that has hardly been attempted. The shift from single-site excavation to the study of areas of landscape is now well under way and promises to transform our understanding not only of Roman Britain but, more significantly, of the long continuum in rural settlement from the later first millennium BC to at least the middle of the first millennium AD and probably later.

That brings us to another of the major developments of recent decades in the study of the Romano-British countryside: the general recognition that the centuries of Roman administration were for large tracts of the island a merely arbitrary division of time and must be examined within a time-frame of cultural, economic and technical development that covered a millennium. This does not mean that Roman occupation had little or no impact on the rural settlement of the province, though voices are now heard urging that point. We are still a long way from a full knowledge of the countryside in any area of Roman Britain. Where our knowledge is most extensive, there is abundant evidence of change, sometimes of a radical kind. What is not yet clear is whether that change is due to Roman development of Britain or to internal forces.

LANDSCAPE AND ENVIRONMENT

At the time of the Roman conquest, substantial changes had been under way in the landscape over several centuries, and the pace of development had greatly accelerated after 200 BC. Not only is the number of recorded farmsteads in most parts of Britain markedly greater than for the earlier Iron Age, but the records of pollen spectra and valley sediments indicate a continuing change in vegetation, including widespread clearance of the remaining woodland. For at least two centuries before the conquest a highly developed mixed agriculture had been practised, not only in the South but as far north as the territory of the Brigantes. The farming communities of the later pre-Roman Iron Age were not merely subsistence units. Even before the conquest, exports leaving Britain for the adjacent continent included both grain and cattle, while pre-Roman Iron Age settlements from the middle of the first millennium BC reveal communal storage and processing of grain on a large scale. Equally impressive is the evidence for management of the landscape, including grassland and woodland as well as extensive arable areas, and these practices had a long history before the first millennium BC. The extension of arable farming in the later Iron Age had evidently compelled farmers to cultivate land hitherto marginal, as the presence of certain weed-species indicates. This may reflect a drive to produce more grain under the pressure of a rising population and probably also the increasing demands of tribal leaders. What the archaeological evidence in its sum shows is a relatively heavily cultivated and well-peopled landscape by the first century AD. Some elements in it had been first established two thousand years earlier and had been under more or less continuous modification since then. Other features, such as the growth of large lowland settlements, had made their impact more recently, over the last two centuries BC, and were still developing at the time of the Roman invasion. Technical innovation may also have made some progress in the later pre-Roman Iron Age, notably in improved agricultural implements and in drainage methods. Cultivation by the ard, a light plough, however, seems to have been widespread and the introduction of the heavy plough may not have antedated the Roman conquest. Its widespread use in Britain may not have come until much later, and it may never have reached several upland regions of the province.

One of the major conditioning factors on rural settlement was climate, of which our knowledge is slender and largely inferential. After a fairly severe climatic recession in the first half of the first millennium BC, there was a steady amelioration in conditions over the following five centuries. From the first century BC until the second century AD, the climate of north-western Europe may have been markedly drier and warmer than in the recent past, until cooler, wetter conditions returned in the later third century (a time of marine transgression in the north European coastlands) and continued until the sixth century. If this sequence of climatic change is correct, the Roman conquest and exploitation of Britain occurred at the optimum period, when marginal land could be taken into cultivation, higher upland pastures utilized and animals kept out in the open for longer periods of the year, or even all the year round. The possibility of introducing continental crops, fruit and vegetables was also correspondingly greater. A generally favourable climate might thus have encouraged agricultural development along several routes, even without the added stimulus of Roman administration. But much more detailed work on climatic change is required before this link is accepted, superficially attractive though it is.

The most important single development of the past twenty

years has been the growing emphasis upon the study of areas of landscape through time, rather than upon individual sites of occupation. Naturally, such an approach cannot be confined to the first four centuries AD. The dynamics of landscape development are not constrained by conventional chronological divisions. In most parts of Roman Britain, AD 43 and AD 410 have no more significance for the archaeologist of landscape than they held for the occupiers of the land at those times. Equally, within the Roman period there are evident signs of change and diversity that owe more to local conditions than to official Roman policy or requirement.

In several regions of the province, planned landscapes of some scale and complexity are now known. Among the most extensive areas of planned landscapes, one of the most impressive is an expanse of south Yorkshire and north Nottinghamshire, which is covered by an orderly layout of rectangular fields, often referred to as 'brickwork' fields. In these systems long ditched boundaries, running straight or gently curving for a kilometre or more, mark out narrow strips of ground that are subdivided by cross-ditches into blocks usually measuring fifty to a hundred metres wide. The evidence of date is not impressive, but the bulk of the surface material is Romano-British, with a bias towards the second and third centuries. A pre-Roman Iron Age origin is not entirely excluded but is unlikely. Such large areas of planned landscape clearly are the work of a centralized authority, but it is far from certain what this will have been in this region. No urban centre is close at hand, nor does the fort and *vicus* at Doncaster seem to be a likely candidate as the organizing agency. Villas of any kind are rare in the area, though native sites, both open and enclosed, abound. On present evidence, it seems best to see these ordered landscapes as the product of local enterprise, though an external stimulus is a possibility.

The influence of long-established agricultural practice was heavy on the field systems and other landscape divisions of the Roman province. Over much of lowland Britain, the Chalk downs, Cotswolds and other limestone areas, the characteristic pattern of ditched and banked rectilinear enclosures earlier designated 'Celtic fields' is in evidence. Fields of this general type had emerged by the second millennium BC and they existed until the early medieval centuries. Excavation has recorded prolonged use of some individual systems, over centuries in some cases, with successive recutting of the boundary ditches. Many of the individual fields were small, often measuring less than fifty metres across in any direction, and thus suggesting the use of light ploughs, or ards. On hill-slopes, ploughing over a long period produced terraced fields, or lynchets, and these were distinctive features of the landscape in many parts of southern Britain until recently. Occasionally, very regular field-systems have been identified, for instance at Aldsworth and Eastleach in the Cotswolds, but these are far from common. It is reasonably certain that no area of Roman Britain was subjected to centuriation (the regimented division of urban territories into rectangular blocks separated by tracks, which is most fully preserved in northern Italy and southern Gaul. Numerous attempts to identify centuriated tracts of land in the vicinity of the colonies of Camulodunum, Lincoln and Gloucester have been made since the eighteenth century, but all in vain. Nor have there appeared any distinctive types of field in the vicinity of villas. Series of small closes are known near some villa sites, including Lockington and Cromwell in the Trent valley, raising at least the possibility of an infield–outfield system of agriculture. But no other supporting evidence has been brought forward. Where it has been dated, the introduction of ridge-and-furrow has been shown to be post-Roman.

Villas and their outbuildings are easy to identify and excavate. Much more challenging is the problem posed by the estates that supported them. Archaeologists often gloss over the complexities involved in the ownership of land in the Roman world. Landed estates (*fundi*) were frequently, possibly normally, not unified blocks of land with the villa situated within each block. Although smaller *fundi* did take that form, larger landowners usually owned parcels of land scattered over wide areas, often in several provinces. Archaeologically, such an estate would be impossible to reconstruct. Only the evidence of inscriptions or other literary records would assist. The evidence of the great bronze inscription from Veleia in northern Italy, dating from Trajan's reign, is particularly revealing. On the territory of Veleia, small landed proprietors were numerous on the plain around the city, but in the hills at some distance away, in areas more recently developed, the estates were larger, and in a few cases immense. Not all were owned by citizens of Veleia. Enterprise by the colony of Lucca, 100 kilometres to the south, and by a group of colonists from that city, is recorded, these incomers having bought land near Veleia not long before the inscription was drawn up. That such investment in land by urban authorities could have been made in Roman Britain is clearly to be allowed for. Land ownership was thus a complex mosaic and the full picture has not emerged in Britain. A single villa might be the residence of a local proprietor, or a unit within a local estate, or part of a much larger holding, owned by someone whose main base was far away, possibly in another province altogether. To all this must be added the division of estates and land-blocks as a result of inheritance or confiscation or other changes in family circumstances.

The size of individual blocks of land associated with single villas can only be estimated in approximate terms. The dense concentration of villas in parts of northern Gaul allows an estimate of about 100 to 150 hectares as a unit of land farmed from a single centre. This figure does not seem out of line with the recorded size of the estate of Ausonius in fourth-century Gaul: 250 hectares or 1,000 *iugera*. But many farms must have been much smaller, perhaps between twenty and fifty hectares, and even then not all of this would have been under cultivation at one time.

The extent of Imperial domains in Britain is uncertain, but there are clear indications that several *saltus* (imperially owned estates) did exist. Tacitus records that half the royal lands of the Iceni passed to Nero under the terms of Prasutagus' will, and these presumably remained within the emperor's patrimony. The Fenland, or a large part of it, most probably formed an Imperial *saltus*. Not all such estates were exclusively agricultural in their interests. An inscription found at Combe Down, near Bath, records the restoration of a *principia* (headquarters) by an Imperial freedman and assistant to the procurators in the early third century. In this area, the excellent Bath limestone will have been as attractive a resource as anything offered by cultivation of the land. Combe Down has also produced a lead sealing for an official consignment, labelled P(*rovincia*) BR(*itanniae*) S(*uperioris*).

Other examples of an integrated approach to the study of Roman landscapes are beginning to provide more coherent evidence for the planning and functioning of the Romano-British countryside virtually for the first time. It is increasingly clear that villas (in the commonly accepted sense of that term) need not have played a central role in the organization of landscape in all regions. The extensive work of survey and excavation in the upper Thames valley at Claydon Pike, near Lechlade, reveals a complex of native and Romanized farmsteads, fields, roads, shrines and cemeteries, but no developed villa. This does not mean, of course, that this developed landscape cannot have formed part of a *fundus*. What it does indicate is that the landscape of Britannia was a very much more complex organism than is often assumed. This has long been suggested by the evidence from the major river valleys, where substantial villas are rare or, in some stretches, virtually absent. Along the middle Trent, for example, wide areas of good alluvial land contain very few villas and those that do survive are modest in scale. And yet the valley was densely settled by a wide variety of communities occupying villages, enclosed homesteads, clusters of farms, isolated farmsteads and scattered enclosures. The long-observed division of provincial rural settlement into villas and native farms is here hopelessly inadequate.

Villas dominated the study of rural settlement in Roman Britain for so long that a true assessment of their role is still difficult. Over much of the province, the fully developed Roman *villa rustica* is not represented at all, while in many other regions, even in the fertile lowlands, villas are rare. It is obvious that the growth of villas is closely linked with the development of towns and cities. Where urban centres did not appear, neither did villas. This close relationship reflects the symbiosis between town and country that is at the heart of the social and economic structure of Roman provinces. It is thus easier and more logical to study villa settlement in relation to cities than to other forms of rural settlement. Past studies of Roman Britain have probably overstated the significance of the villa as a rural institution. Less than a thousand villas are known for certain in Britain, of all dates. Quite possibly no more than 600 existed at one time, and that figure must be set against untold thousands of lesser farms and villages.

The earliest villas appear in the south-eastern *civitates* during the reign of Nero, most of the known examples being situated in the vicinity of the emerging cities or close to the coasts facing Gaul. The villa at Eccles in Kent lies only a few hundred metres from the Medway estuary, that at Wingham close to the flats inland from Sandwich Bay – close to the coast in the Roman period. Both of these houses had bathhouses containing mosaics dating from the late Neronian or Flavian periods, while Eccles also possessed a rectangular pool or *nymphaeum*, suggesting at least an architectural link with villas in Gallia Belgica. The coastal plain of Sussex can show at least three villas that had their origins in the first century AD. The great palace at Fishbourne is one, best seen perhaps as an urban villa of the native centre of Noviomagus (Chichester), whether or not it was the residence of Cogidubnus. The villa at Angmering, twenty-four kilometres to the west and four kilometres from the sea, was embellished by a fine bathhouse of Neronian or Flavian date, and, by late in the first century, mosaics that may well have been products of the same group of craftsmen who worked on the Fishbourne residence. At Southwick, near Shoreham Harbour, yet another substantial villa was built late in the first or early in the second century, though its existence was apparently brief. North of the Thames, too, several substantial houses went up before or about AD 100. The villa at Rivenhall, situated to the west of Camulodunum, was a notably ambitious structure, consisting of at least two large buildings of Flavian date, one of which stood on a podium some two metres high. Still more pretentious was the extensive villa at West Mersea, which was probably built about AD 100. This was a loosely planned structure of several separate blocks, looking out over the Blackwater estuary to the sea. Close by stand the remains of a large tumulus or mausoleum set within a cemetery, clearly a monument to one or more members of the owning family. These Essex villas lie within fifteen kilometres of Camulodunum, and thus may be seen as an element in the exploitation of *agri captivi* by veteran colonists. But *incolae* (native inhabitants), who certainly played a part in the growth of the early *colonia*, may also have been involved.

It is predictable that villas would develop early in the vicinity of those cities in which Romanization made significant progress in the decades immediately following the conquest. Such villas are themselves an index of Romanization. To date, the fullest picture has emerged in the area around Verulamium, where a series of villas was established from the reign of Nero onward. Those at Lockleys and Park Street have long been known to provide a glimpse of the spread of Roman standards among the landholding families of the Catuvellauni. More recently, others close to Verulamium have attested the rapid adaptation by the tribal élite to the new order. Some of these houses were relatively modest in scale, as is evident at Northchurch and Boxmoor. But others aimed at refinement at a relatively early date, as is seen at Gadebridge Park (Hertfordshire) by the early Flavian period, where from its origins the early villa possessed separate baths. Even closer to the city, the villa at Gorhambury was an early developer, with timber structures of rectilinear plan emerging by the mid first century and masonry buildings before AD 100, adorned with stucco work, wall-painting and mosaics. This residence clearly belonged to a wealthy member of the first-century community at Verulamium, presumably a member of one of its curial families.

The architectural form of the majority of early villas was simple, most being either rectangular blocks of three or four rooms or else relatively small, winged corridor houses. The latter house-plan originated in Gaul and had been transplanted to Britain by the early Flavian period at the latest, appearing in early examples as an entirely timber structure, as seen at Gorhambury. The verandah linking the main range of rooms provided a degree of privacy, while the projecting chambers added dignity to the façade. In some cases, bath-suites and heated rooms were later provided, though additional accommodation was frequently in the form of separate buildings, often flanking a yard or court, as at Hambleden (Buckinghamshire). Although many winged corridor houses remained unpretentious dwellings, enlargement into spacious residences did occur. At Spoonley Wood (Gloucestershire), the original winged house was transformed into a much larger villa, with three wings arranged around an enclosed court or formal garden. Extensions of an original plan could take many forms. At the Gadebridge Park villa, an early house of three ranges, almost surrounded by a verandah, was later given large projecting heated rooms linked by a portico. This sequence illustrates well the dangers of seeking uniformity in the architectural development of villas. Any number of influences will have been at work, including the taste of the owners, the skills and experience of local builders and the availability of building materials. Courtyard or peristyle villas were not common in Britain, no more than eight being so far known, all of them (Fishbourne apart) dating from the late Empire. Most of these grand residences lay on the territory of the Dobunni, in the Cotswolds.

One of the most revealing excavations of a small villa is that of Barton Court Farm near Abingdon. Here, a succession of three farmsteads lay on a gravel terrace of the river Thames, the first dating from the late Iron Age, the next from the late first century AD and the third from the late third century. At its late-Roman peak, the farmstead was never more than modest, a small house with cellar and verandah, lying within its own ditched close, with a two-roomed dwelling a few yards away. A corn-drying kiln, well-house and infant cemetery were close by, all these lying at one end of a system of small rectangular paddocks. The farming regime followed at Barton Court Farm has been reconstructed in some detail. The crops included spelt, emmer, bread-wheat, barley and flax. Even the damp ground below the river terrace was utilized for arable agriculture in the later Roman period. The animals were dominated by cattle, with sheep, pigs and horses in subsidiary roles. A farming unit of upwards of 150 hectares has been proposed, of which less than half may have been under cultivation at one time. A herd of about a hundred cattle and a flock of two- or three-hundred sheep could have been supported on a block of land of this extent, and eight or ten labourers could have provided an adequate workforce, supplemented by seasonal labour. This small estate may not, of course,

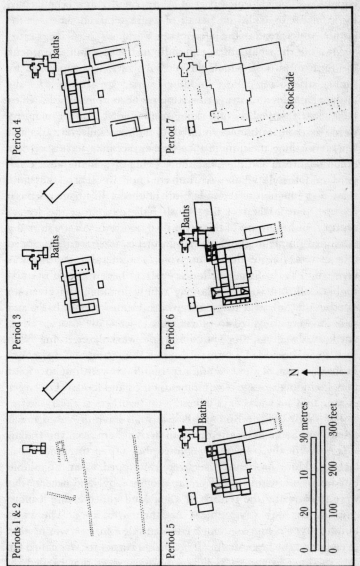

Fig. 2. Gadebridge Park villa

have existed as an entirely independent economic unit. It might equally well have formed part of a larger entity and been farmed by a tenant or bailiff on behalf of a greater landowner, in the fashion widespread in the late Roman world.

Many of the small villas, especially in the east and south, took the form of an aisled hall, the roof of which was supported by timber aisle-posts. These buildings varied greatly in size, the larger examples measuring thirty metres or more in length. Aisled halls clearly served a wide range of functions, but the majority were designed for human habitation, with agricultural tasks and storage facilities as subsidiary roles. Few seem to have served as accommodation for animals, there being a general absence of division for stalling and of drains. They were not, therefore, related in function to the aisled longhouses of Iron Age northern Europe. The earliest of the British halls date from the second century, but most are of the period AD 200–350. Although many remained simple in plan and appointments, some were developed into comfortable residences on which considerable expense was lavished. That at Stroud (Gloucestershire) began as a substantial timber hall, but was later largely rebuilt in stone and given an imposing façade with projecting wings. Heated rooms, baths and mosaics were provided in others. But aisled halls also served as ancillary dwellings, store-buildings and workplaces, being often sited to either side of a farmyard, as at Winterton and Sparsholt. Probably most of these subsidiary buildings were put to mixed uses, including storage of equipment, crops and fodder. On larger estates, they may also have housed estate-workers or *coloni* (serfs).

The origins of the Romano-British halls have provoked much discussion. Some have attempted to derive them from the Italian *villa rustica* or the Iron Age longhouse, but supporting evidence is lacking. More probably, they were developed as an adaptable building type within the Roman province by landowners who were maximizing the returns on their land and creating a more efficient working environment for their workforce. The basic building type is simple, though considerable expertise was needed to construct the larger halls. Great skill in carpentry was called for to roof these structures, skill as sophisticated as that needed by the builders of the great medieval aisled barns. The possible social function of aisled halls, to provide accommodation for both master and man under one roof, is an over-magnified inference from medieval social conditions and has no certain relevance to Roman Britain.

The later development of villas, and thus of *fundi*, was steady but hardly spectacular. Outside the south-eastern *civitates* masonry villas are rare before the early second century, and few attained any great scale before AD 150. This was a period in which the development of urban centres made its most significant progress and the related costs must have been substantially borne by the landed *curiales*. The prevailing impression conveyed by villas of the second and earlier third centuries is of a broad spread of landed wealth that encouraged the growth of a yeoman class, modestly prosperous but only rarely rising above that level of affluence. Villas exemplifying this group include Ditchley (Oxfordshire), Hambleden (Buckinghamshire), Darenth (Kent) and Newton St Loe (Wiltshire).

Extension to the north and west appears to have followed late in the second century and early in the third. In South Wales, villa development in the plain of Glamorgan and Gwent is modest before AD 150 and hardly dramatic in the following half-century. The evidence from the Vale of York is broadly similar, while even in the region between the rivers Trent and Nene the growth of villas is not widely attested much before the mid second century. The emergence of villas in South Wales and Yorkshire is obviously to be related to urban growth in those two regions, and that can hardly have made much progress before the early to mid second century. But in the eastern Midlands, it would be reasonable to expect some repercussions on the occupation of the land following the creation of the *colonia* at Lincoln and the *civitas* at Leicester late in the first century. Such repercussions have not yet appeared.

The Romanization of the small *civitas* of the Silures is well exemplified by the villas of the Glamorgan plain. Some of these, including Llantwit Major and Whitton Lodge, originated in farmsteads of the later Iron Age or early Roman period, but the hostile relations between the Silures and Rome meant that the emergence of residences of Roman style did not occur until well on in the second century. The most extensive of known villas is that at Llantwit Major, but the rather sprawling plan of four ranges around a polygonal court is the product of a long development, extending from the mid second century to the later fourth. The first substantial house was a rectangular block later dignified with a verandah and a suite of baths. The other ranges were later added as prosperity grew. More typical, perhaps, were the small villas at Ely, near Cardiff, and Whitton Lodge. The main dwelling at Ely was of a simple, squarish plan and was later, unusually, surrounded by a banked and ditched earthwork. The site at Whitton Lodge was humbler still. Here, an enclosed farmstead of timber round-houses and raised granaries dating from the later Iron Age was developed into a Roman farmstead of small rectangular buildings in separate units, never brought together into a coherent plan, but nevertheless boasting some of the outward features of Roman life, such as painted walls and hypocausts. The attainment may have been modest, but it is revealing that even at this social level the attempt to furnish such facilities was thought worthwhile.

One area in which both military and civilian interest in the exploitation of land will have been considerable is the Vale of York. This rich tract of country was dominated in the Roman period first by the legionary base at Eboracum, and later by the combination of *castra legionis* and *colonia*. But there was another centre in the Vale and this too must have played some part in its agricultural development: the native town of Isurium Brigantum (Aldborough). Although large areas of this fertile region have not been studied in detail, and much of the Vale is covered by deep silty soils that conceal many early sites, the pattern of Romano-British settlement is beginning to emerge. Recognizably Roman farmsteads and small villas were slow to develop before the second century and, when they did, there was an obvious (and understandable) relationship with York and Aldborough. The Pennine valleys, though reasonably fertile, were not normally the sites of villas; the few occurring owed their presence to special factors. Simple versions of the winged corridor house appeared in the later second century at Beadlam and Dalton Parlours; the latter also has several ancillary buildings grouped around a courtyard, including a small detached bath-suite, presumably for estate workers. Perhaps the most fully known villa is that at Gargrave in the upper Aire valley, an exceptional position explicable because of an outstandingly rich patch of glacial silt. Within a rectangular enclosure lay a winged corridor house, to which a bath was later added, and a second, detached bath-suite. This remote villa reached the peak of its prosperity in the third century, after the stabilization of the northern frontier. The villa-fields survive in part as earthworks at Gargrave. A small series of squarish paddocks lay close to the villa and an unusual set of long, narrow strip-fields further out, the latter presumably for arable purposes. At least forty hectares may have been covered by these fields and ample grazing for cattle and sheep could have been provided by the adjacent moors.

Most of the other Brigantian villas, which extend northward into County Durham, lie on or close to the magnesian limestone belt, which offers a good, workable soil and was widely settled in the Iron Age. No certain evidence relates to ownership of these estates. Native enterprise will account for some, but here and there are indications of other interests. The Calder valley, from Huddersfield to Castleford, has yielded altars dedicated to the tutelary deity of the Brigantes by Roman citizens whose names suggest they were veteran settlers. West of the Pennines, the fort of Bremetannacum (Ribchester) was the administrative centre of an enclave of veterans from the late second century onward, though nothing is known of their occupation of the land.

The pattern of rural development on the territory of the Parisi is broadly similar to that in Brigantia. From simple farmsteads of rectilinear plan set within small rectangular fields, more Romanized units began to emerge from the middle of the second century. The early native farmsteads were often surrounded by strong earthworks, frequently incorporating wide and deep ditches, as though there was the risk of disturbance after Roman units left the tribal territory late in the first century. Good examples of these steadings and early villas are the sites at Rudston, Langton and Settrington. The level of Romanization evinced by these Parisian villas was not high, and a comical naïvety is occasionally in evidence, as in the case of a mosaic in the baths at Rudston showing Venus at her toilette. But the aspiration of such a decorative scene is undeniable and can also be seen in stone sarcophagi found at East Ness and Hood Grange, inscribed by Valerius Vindicianus and Aurelius Severus respectively. The inference that these men represented military families is permissible, and their memorials are eloquent of the continuing links between garrison towns and the rural hinterland. The largest of the Parisian villas, that at Brantingham, by contrast, has links with the native town of Petuaria (Brough-on-Humber). A fourth-century mosaic in this house has as its focal point a bust of a Tyche or presiding spirit of an urban community. Its owner was no doubt a leading figure in the local *curia* and was proud to record the fact.

The third and early fourth centuries saw the apogee of the Romano-British villa, as exploitation of this productive province intensified. If estimates of between 5 million and 7 million for the population of Roman Britain at its peak are roughly correct then such a total could easily have been supported by the productivity of the land, leaving a considerable surplus. Agriculture is likely to have received a marked stimulus during the third century from the rising demands of the state for taxation in kind, while the great inflation after the 230s will also have tended to benefit those producers who had a surplus to dispose of. It is thus entirely understandable that so many villas in Roman Britain seem to have flourished in the third century. Britain was now a secure and prosperous part of the western Empire. Its borders were safe, and the barbarian invasions that devastated Gaul and the Germanies were not visited on the island. The days of prosperity continued into the fourth century for several decades, but about or shortly after the middle of the century there came change. The abandonment of villas is increasingly attested in the second half of the fourth century, for instance at Gadebridge Park and at several sites in Somerset and Wiltshire, while others seem to have run down slowly after about AD 360. The latest stages of rural sites are notoriously vulnerable to later destructive processes, so that the record of the great majority of villas in the fifth century is very poor.

It is a widespread perception that from early in the fifth

century villas declined rapidly and had ceased to play any role in settlement on the land by 450. This was probably true of the residences, but it is a dangerous assumption that villa-estates quickly ceased to retain any significance as territorial units. Some villas did attract incoming Germanic settlers, as is well demonstrated at Orton Longueville (near Peterborough), Shakenoak in Oxfordshire and perhaps Wingham in Kent. A considerable number of villas have produced Anglo-Saxon material of the later fifth and sixth centuries, often a single piece of metalwork or a few sherds of pottery. Too often, this material has been dismissed as the result of 'squatter-occupation' – whatever that is held to mean – and usually it is retrieved from disturbed, later levels on a site and thus has no secure archaeological context. It is frequently forgotten that early Germanic settlers in the Romano-British countryside are unlikely to have possessed much in the way of material goods, and thus their presence will normally have left little mark in the archaeological record.

It is a well-established fact that few of the very large and palatial villas that existed in Gaul and the German provinces developed in Britain. Hardly more than eight grand country houses have been identified and almost all of these date from the late third and early fourth centuries, emerging only after a prolonged period of growth and usually originating in quite modest farmsteads. It is also striking that four of the eight were situated in the Cotswolds of Gloucestershire and west Oxfordshire (Chedworth, Great Witcombe, Woodchester and North Leigh), as though the estates that supported them were exceptionally favoured, or their owners were linked by wealth and status to the uppermost levels of society in *Britannia Prima*. The implication can only be that the number of outstandingly wealthy landowners in Britain was very much smaller than in Gaul or that the wealthiest of the British *curiales* chose not to invest money in great houses, but sought other outlets such as land or portable forms of wealth. For what it is worth (which may not be much), the great bulk of precious metal hoards in late-Roman Britain, both coinage and plate, occur in rural contexts.

The group of Cotswold villas includes the largest of all villas in Britain, the sumptuous palace of Woodchester, near Stroud. First

7. Germanic material AD 400–452

explored by Bradley and Lysons in the eighteenth century, the fourth-century mansion was arranged about a peristyle, no doubt graced with a formal garden. To the rear lay a great court, fifty metres square, which was flanked by at least two large ranges of rooms. A second courtyard abutted this, probably the focus for estate buildings. The great house was splendidly appointed, with numerous mosaic floors, one of which, the largest known in Britain, bore a fine design of Orpheus surrounded by circular friezes of animals. This was the floor of an elegant dining-room, the roof of which was supported by four columns; at the centre a fountain may have played. Elsewhere in the villa there were the

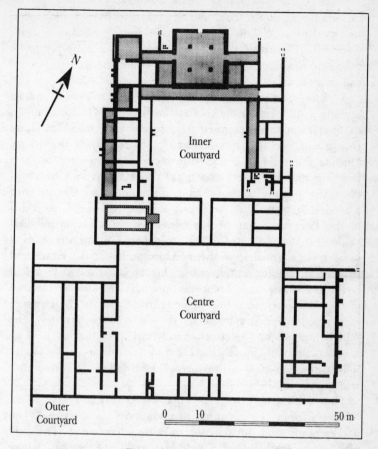

Fig. 3. Woodchester villa

remains of luxurious furnishings. Fragments of perhaps ten statues were found, including a fine figure of Diana Luna and a Cupid and Psyche group, along with pieces of marble veneer for walls, exceptional decoration in all but the richest villas in the province. In the form in which Woodchester is at present known to us the layout is that of a fourth-century villa, probably dating from the early decades of that century. But a much earlier house, originating about AD 100 if not earlier, is suggested by a few finds, and this villa probably was successively enlarged over the following two centuries. Woodchester is barely twenty kilometres from Corinium (Cirencester) and, like Chedworth, is plausibly to be related to the affluent society gathered at the late Roman provincial capital.

A more complete picture of a great rural mansion and its purlieus is afforded by the villa at North Leigh (Oxfordshire). In its final form this comprised a vast courtyard house of many rooms, with servants' quarters and baths occupying two wings. Outside this residential enclosure lay an area devoted to farm buildings and other workaday installations. Excavation has demonstrated that the house began as a simple corridor house with a modest bath-building adjoining it, covering about one third of the later area but plainly connected with the farm. This change in the character of the main house is important, as it indicates the growing wealth and prosperity of the estate and its owners. The beautifully sited villa at Chedworth, in a fold of the Cotswolds near Cirencester, provides yet another instance of the slow emergence from a prosperous farm to the elegance of a gracious country house by the early fourth century. The initial impetus for the creation of wealth provided by agriculture was probably greatly increased by the rise of nearby Corinium to the dignity of a provincial capital following Diocletian's reforms.

The people who owned the villas are largely unknown to us. No more than two or three names survive, and virtually no details of the individuals concerned have remained. The only villa owner recorded in a written source is Faustinus, whose estate lay at or near Scole in Norfolk and is reported in the Antonine Itinerary. Q. Natalius Natalinus, a citizen of probable British origin, included his name in a mosaic at Thruxton (Hampshire) and another citizen, C. Indutius Felix, dedicated an altar to Silvanus at Somerdale (Somerset), presumably on his own estate. This evidence does not take us far. The presumption must be that most villa owners were Britons who found opportunities to build up their estates in the increasing prosperity that attended the Pax Romana. There is neither sign nor likelihood that immigrants came in numbers from the continent to invest in British land, though the occasional incomer may have arrived in the south-east (below, p. 142). The great majority of villas in Britain are moderate in size and pretension. Remarkably few matched the great villas of Gaul, and most of those that did lay within a single region of the province. This points to a fairly even distribution of rural wealth in the third and fourth centuries rather than to the growth of immense landed estates, and it may help to explain the tailing off of urban development after the second century. A solid class of yeomen, of the kind that seems to be in evidence, will scarcely have been able to fulfil the obligations of the curial order to the highest standards.

It would not be surprising if immigration were to be attested in Kent and it is notable that a few villas there do show signs of connection with the adjacent continent. At Darenth (Kent) the villa was fronted by a large courtyard or formal garden containing an ornamental pool. This kind of layout is found at a number of villas in northern Gaul. Another case for consideration is the Lullingstone villa. In the later second century several cult rooms were set up in this house, including a shrine of the nymphs in a basement. At this date, too, the resident family had two fine portrait busts in Greek marble of good quality, obviously imports from some distance. They must be regarded as family portraits of the early to mid second century (for they are certainly not Imperial images) brought to Kent by a migrant, perhaps from Gaul. It is also striking that the largest concentration of walled cemeteries in Britain, a type of burial place well known in Gallia Belgica, is in Kent; at least six have been recorded. The one at Plaxtol contained a barrow-mausoleum: that at Sittingbourne, a monumental tomb; the Lockham one, two monumental structures; and the cemetery at Springhead included a series of graves containing rich objects, amongst which were shoes of purple leather ornamented with gold thread.

Some estates or other large blocks of land may have been bounded by substantial earthworks surviving from much earlier days. The Iron Age earthwork to either side of the river Evenlode in Oxfordshire, known as Grim's Ditch, may well have continued to define a territory in the Roman period. Within its bounds lies an interesting group of at least six villas, including the very large residences at North Leigh and Stonesfield. Another early territorial division still possessed significance in the later Roman period. This was Bokerley Dyke, which still marks one sector of the border between Hampshire and Dorset. The line followed by the Dyke was originally a land boundary in the Bronze Age, well before 1000 BC, and had been extended over a period of a thousand years. It fairly certainly still served a purpose as a boundary during the early Roman centuries, and in the later fourth century it was refurbished over a course of at least five kilometres, protecting a territory to the west, in modern Dorset. This is likely to have been an extensive estate on the good land of Cranborne Chase. Other linear earthworks in southern and eastern Britain, for example in East Anglia and East Yorkshire, may have served similar functions, though few have been examined and dated.

UPLAND SETTLEMENT

Settlement on the uplands of northern and western Britain underwent marked change from early in the first millennium BC. Fieldwork has most fully revealed the sequence in Northumberland, Wales and the uplands bordering the Cumbrian mountains. A range of settlement-types can be identified, though the small, enclosed homestead, built in stone and containing a small number of round-houses, is a virtually constant feature. The picture is fullest in Northumberland, where enclosed homesteads and larger settlements are familiar features of the Iron Age landscape in Roman times, particularly in the valley of the river North Tyne and the lesser valleys that drain the Cheviot hills. Although varied in form, most of these settlements are stone-walled enclosures containing less than six round-houses and with only a single entrance. The surrounding wall is not a fortification, and the siting of most of the settlements, on slopes well below the exposed hilltops, underlines their non-defensive character. The homesteads include small circular and oval sites, with one or two houses adjoining a scooped or level area. These were less common than larger and more nucleated settlements, often roughly oval in plan and consisting of five or six houses. Larger and looser agglomerations are also in evidence, for example at Greaves Ash, where at least thirty stone houses lie in a scatter, suggesting expansion from an original nucleus. So large a complex is rare. In the lowland areas of Northumberland immediately north of Hadrian's Wall, a large number of sites are known, and they all follow a strikingly uniform layout. They are rectangular in plan, often with rounded corners. The houses, usually between three and six in number, were built to the rear of the enclosed area. In front of them were two yards, often cobbled and thus probably serving as stockyards. These settlements did not normally increase in size, as any increase in population seems to have been accommodated by new dwelling-sites. About 200 such rectangular enclosures are now known, most of them probably belonging to the Roman period, a remarkable testimony to the prolonged peace that the Roman frontier brought to this area of Britain, especially in the third and earlier fourth centuries.

In Cumbria both rectilinear and curvilinear enclosures are also in evidence, but there is a wide range of unenclosed settlements, especially on the limestone hills about the Lune and Eden valleys. Some of these sites developed into sizeable nuclei, as is seen at Crosby Ravensworth and Ewe, where over twelve substantial round-houses lie adjacent to small enclosures. Substantial field-systems are also known along these valleys, though their detailed history is still obscure. The lowland areas of Durham and Cleveland contain substantial numbers of Iron Age and Romano-British enclosures, though few have been examined in any depth. The agricultural basis of these communities is far from easy to determine. It is presumed that the Northumbrian upland sites relied upon a largely pastoral economy, for the Cheviot hills can scarcely have supported appreciable crops of grain. Not surprisingly, field systems, although present, are neither frequent nor extensive. Animal bone assemblages are scarce because of highly acidic soil conditions, but such as have been available for study indicate a prevalence of cattle and horses, although there were some sheep, and a certain amount of meat was provided by hunting deer and wild boar. Many querns have been found, indicating that grain, in the form of oats, barley and rye, was available to the inhabitants of these uplands. Presumably, it was acquired by exchange with communities farming the broad valleys to north and south. But the situation of many settlements, at the intersection of high summer pasture and lower slopes suitable for winter grazing and haymaking, underlines the close links with stock-rearing in both Northumberland and Cumbria. The question of the possible relationship between these numerous northern settlements and the provisioning of Roman forts on the frontier and in the northern Pennines is an interesting one. If such a relationship did indeed exist, it has left no discernible trace in the archaeological record. The great majority of the upland settlements reveal little indication of material contact with the Roman frontier forces. By and large, their material culture is uniformly poor, often virtually invisible. Only in a few high-prestige sites such as the hill-fort at Traprain Law is there clear evidence of cultural contacts that resulted in the exchange of surplus crops for Roman imports in some quantity.

Over much of the Welsh hill-country, settlements definitely occupied in the Roman period are far from common, particularly in the central uplands. More surprisingly, the extensive lowlands between the rivers Dyfi and Teifi, bordering Cardigan Bay, also reveal little evidence of native settlement under Rome, though it must be noted that there are numerous hill-forts and other enclosures in this region that have never been examined and that may have remained under occupation. In several parts of Wales, notably in the southern lowlands, there are many small nucleated settlements, appropriate either to extended families or to small family groups. The most fully excavated is the enclosed settlement at Walesland Rath, near Haverfordwest in Pembrokeshire. This was a small but stoutly defended enclosure of only 0.12 hectare, surrounded by a substantial bank and a single ditch, later supplemented by a timber palisade. At least six round-houses existed at a time within the interior and a rectangular house in stone was added in the later Roman period. Similar small enclosures are known elsewhere in west Wales; those which have been excavated date from the later Iron Age and the earlier Roman period. They clearly indicate an occupation of the land mainly by single families and small groups and rarely, if ever, by larger communities, a state of affairs that endured down to modern times. Under the Pax Romana a degree of Roman culture was attained in the planning of buildings and the everyday equipment provided by workshops in the more Romanized parts of the province. But it is unlikely that radical change was made to the social and economic order in this part of western Britain. As in much of upland Britain, life continued without major change into and beyond the medieval kingdoms.

A notable feature of the later Roman period in Wales, undertaken elsewhere in Britain, though probably not on the same scale, was the reoccupation of earlier hill-forts. A few, including Braich y Dinas on Penmaenmawr, were apparently occupied thoughout the Roman centuries. But most cases seem to have involved reoccupation after abandonment. One of the most striking instances is Dinorben, where dwellings of far-from-impoverished peasants were built over the hill-fort defences as well as in the interior. This settlement was by no means short-lived but may have continued throughout most of the third and fourth centuries. Dinorben was not a remote hilltop and it commanded good land in its environs. By contrast, the hill-fort of Tre'r Ceiri occupied a towering and inhospitable height on the Lleyn peninsula of North Wales. Yet here, from the second to at least the early fourth century, a community occupied small round-houses and had access to at least the appurtenances of Roman culture, including agricultural tools, pottery, metalwork and even jewellery. Precisely how this community maintained itself is far from clear. It is possible that Tre'r Ceiri was used mainly in summer by herdsmen tending flocks on high pastures, in more than one sense at the limits of the Roman world.

Aside from the Glamorgan plain, Roman influence is most in evidence in the rich lowland island of Anglesey (Mona; Mam Cymru). Several Iron Age-type settlements from Roman times show clear divergence from the native traditions of upland North Wales. At Din Lligwy, near the north-east coast of the island, a polygonal enclosure surrounded by a solid, stone wall contained a variety of buildings set around a central space, including two round-houses and at least five rectangular buildings, four of which backed onto the perimeter wall. Two of the rectangular structures contained iron-smelting furnaces and other crafts were probably also pursued in these buildings. Much of the datable material found in early excavations at Din Lligwy is of the late-Roman period, mainly of the fourth century, and is more varied than that found in the uplands, including small objects as well as pottery and coins. Din Lligwy is best seen as a developed example of the enclosed hut-groups found in large numbers on Anglesey and on the lower slopes of the mountains of Caernarvonshire and Merioneth. These vary considerably in form but are probably related in their social associations. An excellent example is the enclosed homestead at Cae'r Mynydd in Caernarvonshire, lying at a height of about 200 metres amid terraced fields. This was a roughly oval enclosure, defined by a stone wall between three and four metres thick. Within, two round-houses and a rectangular building abutted the inner face of the wall. A single narrow doorway gave access to the enclosed inner yard. This was clearly a single family steading, but it may not have stood alone as there are several similar sites nearby. A site of related character lay at Caerau, near Clynnog, also in Caernarvonshire. Here a number of farmsteads lay within a field complex, three units surviving out of five or six. The siting of the principal structural elements against or even within the enclosing wall indicates a general similarity with Cae'r Mynydd. The most complex of these dwelling sites is that which incorporates rectangular and sub-rectangular buildings within the structure, as well as a round-house. Irregular in plan, this complex of chambers leading from an internal yard has, superficially at least, much in common with the courtyard houses of west Cornwall. The slight material evidence at Caerau suggests occupation in the second and third centuries. As at Cae'r Mynydd, a striking series of rotary querns indicates access to grain supplies, quite possibly grown by the occupants themselves on the lower slopes.

Several upland areas maintained a surprisingly high population during the Roman period, in several regions as large as they have in modern times. In west Cornwall the granite moors of West Penwith were studded by a variety of enclosed and unenclosed settlements, among which the courtyard-houses are the most distinctive, without close analogy elsewhere in Britain. These were stone-built, roughly oval structures, their stout outer walls bounding a central open yard around which were set a number of chambers, usually including a round-house, a rectangular byre and a small workshop or store. Courtyard houses were solidly built, the outer wall rising to a height of two metres and the central yard usually well provided with drainage. They occur both singly and in small groups, the largest surviving group being that at Chysauster, where no less than ten houses lay to either side of a central street, the whole settlement being surrounded by a field-complex covering 100 hectares. The cumulative dating evidence for courtyard houses indicates that they were mainly if not solely occupied during the Roman period, though some commentators have sought an origin in the Iron Age. Most examples lie out in the open, though occasionally a single house might be enclosed, as at Goldherring. Far more representative of the south-western peninsula as a whole is the earthwork enclosure generally known as the 'round'. Although commonly linked with Cornwall, this form of settlement is also found widely in Devon. Rounds are usually small enclosures, between 0.25 and two hectares, surrounded by a single bank and ditch and sited on a slope a little way below a hill-top or ridge. Morphologically they are extremely varied, ranging from roughly circular or oval to rectilinear or polygonal. Within, buildings are usually confined to a few small oval or round houses, though rectangular structures are also known. The social unit that occupied a round-house was presumably the nuclear family, and the fact that these enclosures are sometimes in loose clusters may point to extended family groups. In the south-west in general, however, community settlements of any size are very rare in the rural landscape.

All over Roman Britain the single farmstead was a prominent component of the rural scene; so prominent, indeed, that earlier generations of commentators (Collingwood among them) believed it was the standard unit of rural settlement. For this reason small community settlements have not yet received the attention due to them. Yet villages and loose agglomerations of farmsteads not easily categorized did exist in many areas and were probably much more important than is often realized. It is far from clear that these villages and farmstead groups have their origins in all cases in the pre-Roman period, for work of appropriate scale has rarely been carried out on them. It is certain, however, that several settlements in eastern England, in Lincolnshire, Northamptonshire and Leicestershire were already nucleated by the first century BC, if not before. The sizeable villages in the Fenland seem to represent development within the Roman period. There are others on the alluvial land of the river valleys that require more study. At Cromwell, Nottinghamshire, for example, an extensive settlement lies on the terrace of the river Trent, with a small villa close by. Further up the Trent valley, at Lockington, Leicestershire, a series of enclosures on either side of a street contain twenty or more round-houses. Here, too, a small villa lies in the vicinity and a link between the two seems highly probable.

The Chalk downs of southern England also supported small, nucleated communities, of which a few have been examined. At Chalton, on the Sussex–Hampshire border, a sizeable village of rectangular houses developed from the late Iron Age down to the early fourth century, covering a ridge-slope for a linear distance of 500 metres. It is likely that this represents an accumulation of settlement over several centuries, but there is no doubt that it was still an extensive communal enterprise. The extensive complex of earthwork enclosures, fields and trackways that lay on the ridge occupied by the hill-fort of Thundersbarrow Hill, near the mouth of the river Adur in Sussex, is even more striking. The Roman village lay immediately outside the hill-fort defences and was clearly a focal point of some importance down to the fourth century. A somewhat similar sequence of settlement is evident at Chisenbury Warren in Wiltshire, where the Romano-British settlement in and around a hill-fort covered at least ten hectares.

Aside from these more or less defined communal settlements, there are numerous cases of loosely scattered hamlets and settlements, the inhabitants of which may have formed social and economic groups that are now difficult to reconstruct. This aspect of the Romano-British countryside is one of the least well understood, and a more detailed survey directed towards a solution of the problem is much needed. The matter is further complicated by the close links that clearly existed between the miscellaneous minor townships of the province and the agrarian landscape. Those townships were in some cases nucleated settlements on major roads, but there also existed in many parts of lowland Britain a heterogeneous series of loosely planned settlements without obvious focus. Some of these may have served as estate-centres, others as independent villages. But in sum they form a potentially important element in the rural settlement of Britannia that is still largely unknown. It is clearly a mistake to treat all such sites as 'small towns', whatever that term is taken to mean. The majority will probably prove to be essentially rural centres with overwhelmingly agricultural interests.

Minor towns, roadside settlements and other such agglomerations possessed central-place functions, in some cases serving as the centres of *pagi*, in others acting as focal points of social and economic activities that involved the rural population in their vicinity. Another form of 'central place' in the Romano-British countryside that also deserves much more attention was the rural shrine. As in Gaul, sanctuaries in rural settings may well have developed functions which, although hallowed by the presiding deities, were nevertheless mundane in character. Under the protection of the god or gods, such places could have served as the sites of fairs and other rural congregations, including those at which men were recruited for seasonal labour. The rural sanctuaries of Britain were generally fairly modest in their architecture and planning, though some showed greater ambition and style. Lydney, in Gloucestershire, west of the Severn estuary, is the most distinguished in terms of its architecture, boasting a fine temple that combines both classical and Celtic elements in its plan, and the most lavish in its amenities, which include a large bath-building and residence for those visiting the shrine. More plausibly related to the surrounding rural population is the sanctuary at Woodeaton in Oxfordshire, between Alchester and Dorchester-on-Thames. Here a square Romano-Celtic temple lay within a large *temenos* (sacred enclosure), within which very large quantities of small votive objects and late Roman coins were

found, the latter presumably representing minor commercial transactions. Occasionally small theatres on the Gaulish model were
provided at these shrines, but no known case rivals the structures
at Ribemont-sur-Ancre and Champlieu. The most imposing of
these British rural theatres is that at the Gosbecks sanctuary, but
this lies only five kilometres from the *colonia* at Camulodunum
and may thus have relied upon urban capital. Gosbecks was a
pre-Roman shrine in origin, as were a number of others, e.g.
Frilford in Berkshire and Thistleton in Leicestershire, so that the
continuance of cult observance here is probable. As places of
tribal or local assembly, not least in the larger *civitates*, these rural
sanctuaries could have possessed considerable significance for a
scattered rural population, whose links with the Romanized urban
centres will have been tenuous or even non-existent.

THE RECLAMATION OF LAND

Several extensive tracts of land in Britain were reclaimed from
fen and marsh during the Roman period for substantially agricultural purposes. The largest and most impressive in terms of the
organization involved was the reclamation of the Fenland around
the Wash, in Lincolnshire, Cambridgeshire and Norfolk, which
appears to have been effected from the later first century onward.
It is now evident that the Fenland was by no means empty of
settlement in the later pre-Roman Iron Age, and the Roman
drainage of the region probably did not occur in a single, massive
programme of work. Rather, the drainage was progressive over
several decades and was not closely coordinated in its planning.
Nevertheless, the digging of the larger drains and channels must
have been supervised by a centralized authority. The linked
system of waterways known as the Car Dyke, extending from
Cambridgeshire to the river Witham at Lincoln, can scarcely
have come into existence by accident. Its primary function seems
to have been that of a wide drain, but that does not preclude its
use as a means of transport over certain stretches.

The forms of settlement found in the Fenland are of unusual

interest. Nucleated farms are prominent, some of these settlements covering several hectares in total. These surely represent clusters of homesteads, grouped together for maximum efficiency in farming methods. Many single farmsteads also existed, however, perhaps indicating the existence of subsidiary holdings. It is striking that villas are very rare within the Fenland itself, although they are found close to its margins, especially to the west. It is sufficiently clear that the development of rural society followed a distinctive course here, dictated by the exigencies of the landscape and possibly an individual pattern of ownership. A substantial area of the southern Fenland may have formed an Imperial *saltus*, administered by a procurator and his staff. A likely centre for this estate lay at Stonea Grange in Cambridgeshire, where a tall, towered structure was the focal point of an unusual site, neither villa nor minor town. Analogies for the tower are found in Italy, not the north-western provinces, thus increasing the likelihood that this was an official *statio*, evidently founded in the reign of Hadrian.

The agricultural basis of the Fenland settlements has been debated since the eighteenth century. Earlier notions that large tracts of the Fens were devoted to growing corn have now been abandoned. The rearing of animals, principally cattle and sheep, has been securely established as a major concern of the settlements so far examined. On present evidence, it seems unlikely that a single, uniform agricultural regime prevailed over the whole region. At the Cat's Water settlement, near Peterborough, mixed farming was the economic basis, with cattle and sheep husbandry the staple. At Maxey near Stamford, sheep rearing for meat and wool continued to play a dominant role well into the Roman period. Aside from agricultural products many Fenland settlements also produced salt as a major sideline. The debris resulting from the boiling of brine is frequently found on sites in the Fens and about their margins, the product being probably as profitable for its Romano-British producers as for those in the medieval centuries. Other aspects of the Fenland economy remain obscure. Use of the fen pastures by transhumant groups with bases elsewhere has been suggested for the later prehistoric period and this could have continued into the Roman period, even on areas belonging to a *saltus*. In short, over the Fenland as a whole, a variety of economic structures probably existed, some long established, others brought into being to serve the needs of Roman administration in the province. All notion of a coherent Fenland economy devoted exclusively to one form of agriculture must be discarded.

Other areas of land were reclaimed in other regions of Roman Britain. Parts of Romney Marsh in Sussex were exploited and had probably earlier been subjected to organized drainage. The lowland to either side of the Severn estuary, in Somerset and Gwent, had also been reclaimed, in part at least, from the later first century onwards and had been used for agriculture and for a variety of industrial purposes, including the smelting of iron and glass-making. Some of the reclaimed area lies close to the base of the legion at Caerleon and the *civitas Silurum* at Caerwent; those two are the most obvious agencies to set this work in train. But elsewhere along the Severn shore we must look to enterprise by the owners of local estates as no large urban centres (with the exception of Gloucester) or military bases lie close to the estuary.

INDUSTRY

It is impossible to exclude industrial working from any account of the Romano-British rural scene, for a large proportion of the industrial complexes of Britannia were in rural situations. Connections with landowners and peasants are obviously to be inferred, though the precise details of the relationship are never clear. A large number of villas, farmsteads and other rural settlements have produced evidence of crafts or industrial working, often in the form of metalworking installations and the like, representing the kind of low-level crafts that peasants traditionally engage in. But there are far more substantial indications of the Romano-British population's involvement with industry. The great pottery industries of the province were mainly in rural locations, not in the vicinity of cities, and the tenurial links, though not closely defined, were presumably with estates and other territorial blocs. Estate production is to be anticipated in any Roman province,

1. Housesteads (Borcovicium); air view

2(a). Head of Claudius from the river Alde; Suffolk

2(b). Cameo of a British bear from South Shields

3. Tombstone of Sextus Valerius Genialis (Cirencester)

4(a). Hoxne spoons

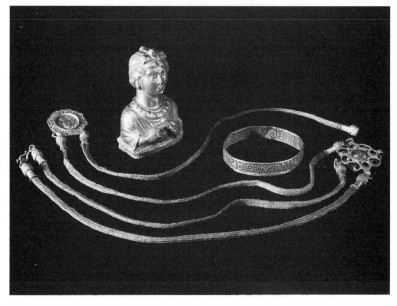

4(b). Hoxne bangle, necklace and bust

5(a). Corbridge Granary

5(b). Corbridge Strongroom

6. Hinton St Mary Mosaic

7. Coin showing Claudius and his Triumphal Arch

8. Relief of Mithras from London

and the fact that Celtic society was land-based makes it all the more plausible that the preconditions for this kind of development existed in Britain.

The largest of the pottery industries of the province, that based on the lower Nene valley, had clear connections with a series of villas, including a very large complex at Castor. But if we take a wider view of industrial sites, it is evident that a high proportion of major production centres lay well away from large urban centres and tended to be associated with minor towns, villas and other rural sites. To a large extent, of course, the extractive industries developed at the point where the raw materials they depended on were concentrated; which was the dominant factor in their location. None of this is particularly surprising or unexpected. Production on rural estates had been a well-established feature of the economy of the provinces from at least the first century BC and even senators, despite a frequently expressed distate for profits drawn from industry and commerce, were actively involved in exploiting the natural resources of their estates, often discreetly veiling the operations behind a screen of freedmen and other agents. Romano-British landowners will not have been slow to exploit the greatly expanded market for manufactured goods from the mid first century onwards. Some such attempt seems to lie behind the manufacture of *terra sigillata* (Samian ware) at Wiggonholt in Sussex during the second century, an ambitious but probably unsuccessful enterprise. The extraction of Purbeck marble and Kimmeridge shale in south Dorset were two much more prosperous undertakings, and both may have been organized from private *fundi*. The making of tiles and bricks from local clays was presumably most easily done on estates in Britain, as in Italy, though the evidence is poor.

ANIMALS

The importance of animals and their secondary products to Roman Britain is clear from the slight literary sources, though we must rely upon the much more broadly based archaeological record for a fully representative picture. It is abundantly clear that during the later Iron Age in southern Britain sheep-rearing was of outstanding importance. On the chalk uplands, on which the faunal remains are often exceptionally well preserved, the bones of sheep and goat frequently amount to about 70 per cent of the total assemblage. This proportion falls in valley and low-land settlements to between a third and a half, so overall sheep husbandry was of prime significance. The value of sheep was obviously based not only on their use as a food source but also as providers of wool, as is well demonstrated by the fact that they were often kept until a relatively advanced age. Pigs also played a major part in late Iron Age husbandry, and this was to continue into the Roman period. The decades immediately follow-ing the conquest in AD 43 witnessed a dramatic change of emphasis in stock-rearing. Cattle dominate the bone-assemblages on both military and civilian sites and this dominance tends to increase throughout the Roman period. It is more marked in military bases and cities than elsewhere, reflecting the increase in the number of consumers, rather than producers, in such centres, but it is a trend that is manifest almost everywhere in the province. Partly, of course, this may have been due to the importance of cattle as draught animals and working beasts on farms, but the predominance of cattle at Roman fort-sites and in cities can only be explained in relation to diet. In such centres it is evident that a substantial proportion of the cattle were female, kept presum-ably for their milk and for breeding purposes. By contrast, sheep were frequently killed when young, for their meat, though on rural sites older animals attest the importance of wool in the economy.

The sheep attested by skeletal remains in Roman Britain were, to a large extent, related to Soay sheep, now represented only in the islands of the Outer Hebrides. This animal is small, rather slender and stands only about 55 cm high at the shoulder. Its fleece is either woolly or hairy and tends to be dark brown in colour. The wool of the important series of textiles found in the late first and early second century fort of Vindolanda bears a close resemblance to the wool produced by Soay sheep. Although these native strains continued into the Roman period, and presumably through it, it is clearly likely that other breeds were imported, especially from northern Gaul, where animals with fleeces of good quality were reared in the first century BC. Indeed, it is possible that such importation into Britain occurred well before AD 43 and that the imported animals were used in selective breeding. Sheep seem to have increased slightly in size during the Roman centuries. It is probable that there was a generally higher interest in wool than meat, so that the high repute enjoyed by British woollen textiles will have been established long before the appearance of the *birrus Britannicus* and the *tapete* in Diocletian's price edict of AD 301. It is notoriously difficult to distinguish the bones of sheep and goat in faunal assemblages, which almost certainly means that the role of goats in the agricultural economy has been underestimated. Their main significance will have been as providers of leather, both for civilian and military markets. It is known that the army used goat leather for tents, uniforms and belts, and the demand must have remained high, while the requirements of the civilian market must have been virtually insatiable.

CROPS

Julius Caesar found appreciable areas of south-eastern Britain given over to the raising of corn in the mid first century BC, and grain was included among the major exports from Britain listed by Strabo half a century later. A slightly warmer and drier climate would have been suitable for both wheat and barley in particular, and the demands of the Roman army and of the growing urban centres would have stimulated the production of grain from an early date. Aside from cereal crops that had long been grown in Britain, rye, oats and flax were either introduced or greatly extended under Roman occupation. There were other introductions among vegetable crops, though we know less about what was grown in later prehistoric Britain. There is evidence that cabbage, lettuce, turnip, carrot, parsnip and celery were all grown in Roman Britain, as were apples, plums, mulberries, cherries and walnuts. There has long been debate about whether or not the vine was cultivated and wine produced. Wine of good quality is made in eastern Britain today and there is no reason why it should not have figured among the products of Roman Britain. The sum of the evidence suggests that it did, though the isolated fragments are not impressive. Grape-pips have been recorded in several places, but these could be imports. A nineteenth-century find at Gloucester is suggestive of wine-pressing, there being reported various parts of the vine and its fruit. More recently, the seeds of the vine have been found at a wide variety of sites in London, Silchester and Doncaster. These are so widespread that they may well have come from plants growing in Britain. Purpose-built structures for the storage of crops are far from common features of agricultural sites in any part of Britain. Substantial granaries on the model of those erected by the army in its forts are rare, the best examples being the buildings at Lullingstone and Horton Kirby, both in Kent. Grain could have been stored in timber bins set within such ancillary structures as aisled halls, possibly after parching in corn-drying installations.

TOMBS AND CEMETERIES

Monumental tombs and cemeteries were notable features of the rural landscape. Here, more than one tradition was at work. Large barrows and other funerary monuments had long figured among the major landmarks of Britain, and monumental tombs, which might combine masonry structures and earthen mounds, had a long history in Italy and were being constructed in Gaul and the Rhineland by the first century AD. Sometimes, as at Nickenich, they included elaborate sculpted ornament. Several of the earthen monuments in Britain might belong to either tradition, for example the three prominent mounds at Badbury Rings, close to the Roman road from Old Sarum to Dorchester, and the large barrow at Knobs Crook in east Dorset, erected over the cremation of a man, whose name may have been Quintus, late in the first century. Several other prominent monuments lie close to roads, following a practice long honoured both in Italy and western Europe, like the Six Hills by Ermine Street at Stevenage. The Bartlow Hills near Great Chesterford seem to bring the native and imported traditions together, for their construction follows late Iron Age models for wealthy graves in this region while their contents are thoroughly Roman. One barrow contained a gold ring, a mark of high social status, glassware and a coin of Hadrian as a fee for Charon. Another contained a folding stool, also a mark of status or office, a bronze lamp, a *patera* (a bowl with a handle) and two flagons, and a glass vessel containing a cocktail of wine and honey, a Roman aperitif named *mulsum*. This was surely the grave of a member of the urban magistracy.

Recognizably closer to the stone mausolea of the western provinces are a number of monuments in south-eastern Britain. At Keston, in Kent, a circular mausoleum, ten metres in diameter and supported by external buttresses, lay in the environs of the villa. Another circular monument, larger and more elaborate in construction, lay at West Mersea in Essex, nearly thirty metres across, stone revetted with an earth filling and braced by radial walls and external buttresses. That sculpture could be used in these monuments is illustrated by a circular tomb within a small cemetery at Harpenden (Hertfordshire), which contained a central niched chamber that had held at least one life-sized statue, presumably of the dead person. Kent has produced an unusually high proportion of the known monumental tombs, presumably reflecting its proximity to Gaul. There are barrow monuments here, too, notably at Holborough, where the grave held a lead coffin ornamented with figures of a satyr and a maenad, a folding stool like that in one of the Bartlow Hills, and the remains of wine and oil used in the funeral feast. Small walled cemeteries were also in use in Kent, as at Springhead and Langley, and elsewhere in the East.

Mausolea associated with specific rural sites are not numerous. Perhaps the most striking is the temple-tomb at the Lullingstone villa, dating from about AD 300. In a burial-pit sunk three metres below a square Romano-Celtic temple lay two inhumations, of which at least one was in a lead coffin and packed in gypsum to preserve the corpse. The grave-goods, furnishings for a feast and a gaming table, were clearly pagan and are thus to be related to a generation earlier than that responsible for the house-church at Lullingstone. The temple-mausoleum may have been commoner in the Romano-British countryside than has so far appeared. A massive example of this type of building existed at Wood Lane End, near Hemel Hempstead (Hertfordshire), possibly rising to more than fifteen metres in height. Beneath the square shrine lay a vault large enough to house at least one burial. These are indications of a burial cult within a Romano-Celtic sanctuary. At Welwyn (Hertfordshire), there is clear proof of a thoroughly Roman burial monument, now destroyed but yielding fragments of a figured marble sarcophagus, a rare find in Britain. The subject of the Welwyn sculpture is not identifiable from the surviving pieces, but the date may be fixed in the earlier third century.

CHAPTER FIVE

Economic Life

The economy of Roman Britain, in common with the economy of the rest of the Empire, was based on the land, its products and the labour of untold thousands of peasants. The contribution of industry to the productivity of Britannia was not negligible but it fell far short of the yield of agriculture and its associated trades. Quantification is impossible but at a reasonable estimate the gross economic product of Britain owed at least 80 per cent to agriculture, while perhaps 90 per cent of the active population worked on the land. This was, then, a relatively primitive economy, though not wholly undeveloped. After the needs of the Roman state were met, in the form of taxation and official exactions, what was left was a confusion of getting and spending. The single most striking characteristic of the provincial economy was its conservatism. Traditional methods of production and manufacture did not alter greatly over the centuries, so productivity remained largely static. In modern terms there was no increase in gross national product. This naturally limited the yield that could be provided by taxes. Emperors had their own military and industrial complexes that served the requirements of the State. There was normally no need for intervention in other areas of economic activity, except the mining of minerals, and little intervention is recorded. Harbour taxes were paid in the major ports and tolls were raised by the cities on roads and rivers. Otherwise, individuals and communities did what they could within broad limits. In a frontier province like Britain, with a formidable military presence, there had to be full regard for the economic needs of the large army, chiefly foodstuffs and *matériel*. Precisely how the military units were supplied is not known in detail but it is likely to have involved a combination of local and long-distance supply. The texts found at Vindolanda, relating to a frontier post in the late first and early second centuries, convey that impression clearly. What they cannot convey is how burdensome, if at all, military supply was to the native communities. It is possible that this burden has been greatly overestimated by modern scholars. After the years of conquest, an occupying army of 40,000 men could probably have been sustained relatively easily by a productive population of 5 to 7 million.

THE WEALTH OF BRITAIN

When the geographer-astronomer Strabo, writing in the early principate of Tiberius (c. AD 17), but recording many things of a generation or two earlier, gives an account of British exports to the continent, he reflects conditions in southern Britain and particularly the goods at the disposal of tribal chiefs and their followers. Corn, cattle, hides and hunting-dogs attest the agriculture and stock-raising of the South. Slaves represent the profit of endemic raiding among the southern tribes. Metals, however, must have come mostly from further afield: silver from the Mendip or Peak deposits; tin from Devon and Cornwall; gold from Wales; iron from the Jurassic ridge, the Weald and the Forest of Dean. The trade in metals implies, as in earlier prehistoric times, that particular connections were more widely developed than they had been in pre-Roman times.

Metals in any province were often almost exclusively State property and formed an important item in the provincial budget. The precious metals came in for special attention, for they could make an immediate and direct contribution to the Imperial treasury.

Only one gold-mine of the Roman period is known in Britain, at Dolau Cothi, near Pumsaint, west of Llandovery in Carmarthenshire. Here the workings were both open-cast and by long, deep adits that followed the veins of gold-bearing pyrites. The galleries were very systematically cut to serve for both drainage and haulage, and in the levels below them wheels for lifting water were installed to drain them, as in the Spanish mines. A panning cradle has also been found in the mine. Contour aqueducts brought water to a number of reservoirs

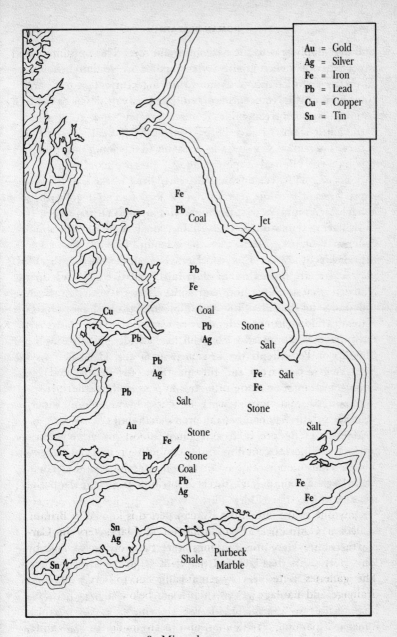

8. Mineral resources

above the workings, for washing the ore after crushing, and perhaps for reducing the softer rock-beds. Not all the surface workings are Roman at Dolau Cothi; gold extraction was carried on here in the Norman period and at intervals down to modern times. Not surprisingly, a Roman fort lay close to the mine, though it seems to have been given up by the early second century. Thereafter, working was probably in the hands of contractors who were allowed a percentage of the profits. Estuarine deposits of gold in Wales could also have been worked, as they have been recently, while it must not be forgotten that gold nuggets have been found in west Cornwall and in south Devon rivers.

Silver was more widely available, along with lead, in sizeable deposits of ore (galena) in the Mendip hills of Somerset, in Flintshire (now in Clwyd), Derbyshire and Northumberland. However, the proportion of silver in the last two fields was so low that it may not have been worth the effort of extraction. But the deposits in the Mendips and Flintshire could have offered a worthwhile yield. The Mendip ore was being worked as early as AD 49, the date of two inscribed lead objects. A later ingot, of Nero's reign, reveals the involvement of the II Legion in the working of the mines and this may have dated from the beginnings in the forties. By AD 60, however, a civilian contractor, C. Nipius Ascanius, was at work here and he is later recorded as active in the Flintshire field after north-east Wales had been annexed. A decade or so later, inscribed ingots from Somerset reveal a Tiberius Claudius Triferna, probably an Imperial freedman, supervising work in the Mendips, and he is later attested in the Derbyshire mines. British lead was well known at the heart of the Empire. The Elder Pliny, writing in the early seventies, reports that the metal was present in such quantity near the surface in Britain that legislation was introduced to control its extraction – an unusual case of official control in the economic field. By the early Flavian period deposits in the Mendips, Flintshire and Derbyshire were all being worked and Pliny was correct in referring to the slight depth at which lead ore was obtainable in Britain. In Derbyshire the veins of lead were reached by digging trenches from the surface rather than sinking shafts, and on the Mendips access was possible directly from ground level, without recourse to underground galleries. The three major fields were evidently soon consigned to private contractors (*conductores*), probably after an initial phase of military supervision. The speed with which this was done may well mean that the main objective of extraction was lead, not silver, and this theory is supported by the fact that the small amount of silver has not been removed from many of the known ingots. Mining companies had emerged by the seventies in Derbyshire and probably in the Mendips. The SOCII LUTUDARENSES or SOCIETAS LUTUDARENSIS worked the Derbyshire deposits from a centre, called perhaps Lutudarum. Dated lead ingots become increasingly rare after Hadrian's reign, and it is probable that in Britain, as elsewhere, a new system of exploitation was brought in. Individual galleries or mines were then leased to individual miners or small groups, the whole enterprise being controlled by an Imperial procurator. This is at any rate in accord with the fact that under Hadrian the Derbyshire ingots bear the Emperor's name alongside the inscription MET[AL-LUM] LUT[UDARENSE] and henceforward there is no mention of civilian contractors.

The mining centres have not in all cases been closely identified and none have been extensively examined. The largest may have been Charterhouse-on-Mendip, where a sizeable planned town with its own amphitheatre can still be traced amid mining remains of several periods. Lutudarum is not certainly located but may have lain in the Wirksworth area, where the greatest concentration of near-surface leadmines occurred.

In the earlier period of Imperial working there is some evidence that Mendip lead was exported. The ingot countermarked by the II Legion was found at St Valéry-sur-Somme, while others have recently been recovered from a wreck off the coast of Brittany, two from the Solent and another from Stockbridge (Hampshire). This suggests a traffic of consignments across the Channel and along the main arterial routes into Gaul or even Italy. It is not likely, however, as the administrative fragmentation of the Empire developed, that this traffic continued briskly.

The earliest stamped ingot from Flintshire is of AD 74, and if the annexation of the area occurred about AD 60, we would expect evidence for rapid exploitation, as in the Mendips. The Italian or Gaulish concessionaire C. Nipius Ascanius cannot be much later, since his countermark appears on a Mendip ingot of AD 59. The centre of the mining operation seems to have been Halkyn Mountain, as in recent times, while the settlement lay at Pentre Ffwrndan, close to Flint, where associated finds suggest an occupation from the later first century to at least the close of the second. There was an elaborate residential centre here, perhaps for a supervising military official. There is also some evidence for third-century exploitation at Meliden, at the northern tip of the Clwyd mountains, at the Talor Goch mine. The ingots from the Flintshire field are stamped DECEANGL, for METALLUM DECEANGLICUM, the name surviving in the medieval district at Tegeingl.

The next dated group of ingots is a small series from West Yorkshire, which also carry the tribal name of the area, in the form BRIG for METALLUM BRIGANTICUM. They are found in the area between Nidderdale and Wharfedale, which was much exploited for its lead in medieval times also. The earliest dated example is of AD 81, exactly ten years after the Roman invasion of the region. Another, from Pateley Bridge during Trajan's reign, is imperfectly recorded. It is probable that this was not the only lead-bearing area worked in Yorkshire. There is a good local tradition of Roman exploitation of the Swaledale deposits, in particular at the Hurst mine; it is connected with an ingot of Hadrian's reign, unfortunately never recorded in detail.

The Derbyshire lead field was one of the largest and most productive in Britain. One of its earliest inscribed ingots bears the name of Tiberius Claudius Triferna, who had been active in the Mendip mines in the seventies. But there is evidence for Imperial working here under Hadrian and the pattern of exploitation was clearly complex. At what stage the *socii Lutudarenses* occur or in what order they came in relation either to the individual lessees or the Imperial working is quite unknown. It may be observed, however, that the *socii* sent their ingots to Petuaria (Brough-on-Humber), either to their own warehouses or to local wholesalers. Yet another aspect of exploitation is the lead ore from stream deposits found at the Roman fort at Navio (Brough-on-Noe), from which the district was in part policed. This may imply a system of collection for which the fort served as central depot. The whole picture in Derbyshire is thus complicated and the relationship of the various elements still obscure.

Hadrianic working of lead is also attested in south-west Shropshire, in the Shelve and Snailbeach areas. Here or in Flintshire the XX Legion took some hand in organizing the mining, since it countermarked an ingot of AD 195 found at Chalon-sur-Saône in central France. Beyond this, however, there is no evidence for later Imperial working, and it may be that the field was turned over to lessees. It is, on the other hand, likely that the small but rich field on the eastern slopes of Plynlimmon, under development during the second century, was always worked by the military.

Military supervision was certainly exercised in the Alston lead mines of south-west Northumberland, which were worked on a small scale in the third century under the second cohort of Nervii. Stamped seals from consignments that reached the fort at Brough-under-Stainmore bear the name of the cohort and the legend METAL(LUM). It is likely that some of the produce also went north-eastwards to Corbridge, where the mineral wax associated with the Alston veins has been found. The fort at Caermote in Cumbria seems to have been a collecting centre for lead from the surrounding fells. Another lead-mining settlement with military connections was at Machen, not far from the legionary base at Caerleon, where both dwellings and remains of workings have been observed. It need hardly be doubted that there were other such ventures in the military zones, since the Imperial government came to develop local resources wherever possible.

If the exploitation of lead may be regarded as of great importance, the copper workings of Britain were also of substantial value in themselves and in relation to the production of bronze, a hard-wearing alloy widely used in the Roman world. The principal deposits of copper lay in northern Shropshire, Caernarvonshire and Anglesey. The Shropshire deposits were centred at Llanymynech, where the cave from which the veins were worked by galleries was apparently inhabited by the miners. Similar conditions appear to have existed in the copper mines of Great Orme's Head in Caernarvonshire, where inhabited caves have also been noted: associated objects date the activity to the third and fourth centuries. This suggests labourers tied to the spot, whether they were slaves or convicts, but it seems that smelting was not carried out near the mine, the ore being carried away for treatment elsewhere. The copper ingots found in Caernarvonshire are stamped with the names of at least two private companies: this could indicate exploitation of the resources by slave-workers, though it is not necessarily true for every mine and for every period. In Anglesey the picture is rather different. The principal mining area was Parys Mountain near Amlwch, though other centres of activity are known, at Aberffraw and Pengarnedd. But the copper ingots in the island are associated with native settlements, as if the ore was gathered by native labour and smelted piecemeal for eventual collection at a central depot. Such economy of effort may well have been an additional recommendation for Roman administrators. The significance of North Wales copper is not to be underestimated. The raw material was distributed not only to other parts of Britain, but also to Gaul, as an ingot discovered at Boubry in Brittany attests. It must be emphasized that these are the most important copper deposits exploited by the Romans in Britain. The mines at Alderley Edge in Cheshire do not appear to have been worked in Roman times, though they were well known to prehistoric and mediaeval man.

The iron deposits of Britain were numerous and abundant, and hardly less productive than the lead mines. Iron was not accounted a valuable metal nor was its output officially restricted, for it is clear that there was always an extensive market for so useful a commodity. Most mining seems to have been in the hands of local workers and there is little evidence of Imperial interest (except in one field) or of organized activity by Imperial agents, as occurred in Gaul and Noricum (modern Austria). The principal deposits exploited lay in the Weald, the Forest of Dean and in the limestone belt of Northamptonshire, though many small and scattered deposits are known to have been worked elsewhere. The Wealden field was being rapidly developed under Claudius and Nero by a guild of iron workers organized in

Roman fashion and based at Chichester in the heart of the realm of the native king Cogidubnus. It is tempting to think that this represents the Romanization of a group of native smiths, who must already have held a special position in the pre-Roman economy. After the end of the native kingdom the exploitation of the iron was varied in character on many sites during the Roman period. Very large quantities of slag and cinders were available for road construction at certain sites, and this might suggest that the *curiales* continued to develop the deposits in succession to the king, using the by-product for road making, another communal concern.

But the direct interest of the provincial government is also attested in at least some of the iron-workings. The eastern side of the Wealden field was under the control of the *classis Britannica* from the later first century until at least the earlier third century. At Bardown a military barracks lay close to the workings, while at Beauport Park a military bathhouse provided essential facilities for those working the ore on an extensive site of some eight hectares. The raw iron was presumably shipped from a harbour close to these workings, probably near Bodiam. Beauport Park may have served as the administrative headquarters for this operation, though the appropriate buildings have still to be discovered.

In the Forest of Dean much working was concentrated at Weston under Penyard (Ariconium), where earlier antiquaries noted an area of eighty hectares covered with slag heaps. Here exploitation can hardly have developed until after the conquest of the Silures in the seventies: the coins indicate activity from the late first century until the fourth, with a marked increase towards the end. The ironstones of Northamptonshire and Lincolnshire and the beds of iron nodules in Norfolk were developed on some scale, especially the Northamptonshire deposits in the region of Corby. Many furnace sites are known here, as at Wakerley and Laxton, shaft furnaces being represented that were capable of yielding a tough form of iron or primitive steel. Similar installations are known in neighbouring Leicestershire, for example at Clipsham, where large slag deposits and workshops remain almost unexplored, and Whitwell, and in south Lincolnshire. The Nene valley near Durobrivae also contained many iron-working sites,

some apparently associated with villas, others with humbler peas-
ant settlements. The furnace sites in the Corby region, though
numerous, have no obvious focus, as though rural dwellers were
exploiting a useful resource that they found on their land and
perhaps providing smelted blooms of iron to local collecting
points. The same may have been the case in Norfolk, where a
variety of localized manufactories are known and where simple
shaft furnaces were in use, for example at Ashwicken. In Yorkshire, large heaps of clinker at West Bierley, near Cleckheaton,
were associated with coins of the late third and early fourth centuries.
Further north still, the military workshops at Corbridge, active in
the third and fourth centuries, were using low-grade smeltings
from native hearths. These blooms were then re-smelted in pud-
dling furnaces ultimately for forging into weapons, implements,
nails and holdfasts produced in the workshops. The source of the
raw material was the Redesdale deposits, just south of the fort at
Habitancum (Risingham).

This picture of a military arsenal is unique in the Roman
world. There must surely have been a far greater degree of
military involvement in the production and collection of iron
than now appears in the record. The legionary fortresses, which
will all have had their *fabricae* (arms manufactory), had endless
requirements for iron, and the *auxilia* will not have been far
behind in their total needs. Excavation in the *vici* of forts frequently produces traces of at least small-scale iron smelting, as
well as evidence for smithing.

Much the most famed of British metals in the days before the
Roman occupation was tin. The vivid accounts by Diodorus
Siculus, of overland packhorse transport of Cornish and Devonian
tin from the Gallic coast to Narbo (Narbonne) in the first century
BC, and of the island emporium of Ictis off the south-western
coast of Britain from which merchants obtained the metal, all
speak of a brisk and flourishing early trade, probably established
considerably before 100 BC. But when the Augustan conquest of
north-western Spain made the Spanish tin deposits available,
commercial interest in British tin declined.

There is certainly little, if any, sign that the tin deposits of
Devon and Cornwall were exploited in the early Roman period.

The rich Spanish deposits remained the principal source of this metal throughout the first two centuries AD; even in the third century, Spanish tin was still regarded as the best available. British tin was not mined but excavated from the course of stream-beds, a process far more labour-intensive than mining underground lodes. This explains why the recorded tin ingots in Britain are so small. Extraction of the stream-tin was, however, pursued more vigorously from the mid third century onwards, after the Spanish mines were damaged in barbarian raids. Stream-workings in Cornwall reveal a larger number of Roman objects from the third and fourth centuries, and a number of tin or tin-alloy vessels of this period are recorded in the south-west. Tin ingots occur, but are very difficult to date. Those of probable Roman date are oval in form, flat on their bases and generally between 5 kilograms and 20 kilograms in weight. Only the rectangular ingot from Carnanton bears stamps, which include helmeted heads suggestive of fourth-century emperors and an inscription, now illegible.

The generally late date of the south-western ingots and other finds is echoed by a group of pewter (tin and lead) ingots found in the Thames at Battersea, six of them bearing the name Sya-grius, others the inscription *Spes in Deo* (hope in God) and the Chi-Rho monogram. Tin was also used in the Imperial coinage from the 260s to the mid fourth century, though not all supplies need have come from Britain. The extraction of tin continued after the end of Roman rule. Early in the seventh century an Alexandrian vessel carrying grain was driven by storms to Britain and there relieved a famine, receiving a cargo of tin in return.

In the following century tin was to form a strikingly high proportion of the metal in which Anglo-Saxon *sceattas* (silver coins) were struck. In Roman Britain the most obvious use of tin was in the pewter alloy from which a wide range of objects were manufactured, chiefly tableware, to provide a substitute for the much more expensive silver vessels. The stone moulds from which pewter platters and shallow bowls were produced have been found across much of southern Britain, from East Anglia to Cornwall, in urban centres such as Silchester and in remote rural spots such as St Just in Cornwall. This was clearly a lively industry, which exported a proportion of its wares to Gaul. Hoards of pewter objects, sometimes of considerable size, for example, the one at Appleshaw (Berkshire), indicate that the material possessed value for its users and was worth hiding away in times of uncertainty.

Coal was also mined in Roman Britain, though it never became, as far as can be seen, an item of export. British coal is mentioned only once in Roman literature, as a curiosity seen upon the altars of Sulis Minerva at Aquae Sulis (Bath). This was presumably the Somerset cannel coal. But coal from Nottinghamshire and Derbyshire has been noted in the Fenland settlements and elsewhere in the East Midlands. Local coal has been found at various sites along Hadrian's Wall, in a smithy at Benwell, at Housesteads and at Corbridge. Its use is dated to the second century at Benwell and Corbridge and to the fourth century at Housesteads and Corbridge. It was also noted in the second century at the Antonine Wall forts at Castlecary and Bar Hill, while less detailed observations attest coal in forts at Risingham, South Shields and Manchester. In industry coal was used for smelting lead at Pentre Ffwrndan, iron and glass at Wilderspool, and iron at Weston under Penyard in the Forest of Dean. It heated hypocausts at Wroxeter and Caerwent, but it must be recognized that wood or charcoal were the fuels more normally employed for this purpose.

The quarrying of high-quality stone for building and for sculpture began at an early date, the Jurassic limestones being especially favoured. Stone from the Cotswolds or Northamptonshire was being used for tomb-monuments at Colchester and London by AD 60 and the qualities of Bath stone were appreciated as early. The Lincolnshire oolite was used widely in the East Midlands and was also transported to London. Kentish ragstone was used in London and the soft greensand of the South-east at Chichester.

The most distinctive British natural product is jet, found only on the North Yorkshire coast at Whitby. This mineral attracted the attention of the third-century writer Solinus, who described it as a substance that could be heated with water, quenched with oil and which became magnetic when rubbed. Jet was widely endowed with almost magical esteem and became a favoured material for ornamental jewellery, much of which was probably manufactured in the *colonia* at York. Hairpins, finger-rings, necklaces and bracelets were made in great variety, some of these ornaments being articulated in minute component pieces. Distaffs, spindle-whorls and other domestic objects were also made. The most interesting items in jet, however, were carved medallions and pendants portraying family groups, betrothed couples and individuals, no doubt to celebrate special occasions, like photographs in a later age. Animal figures were also popular. Whitby is the only source of jet in western Europe known to have been exploited in the Roman period. The jet objects found in the Rhineland (especially at Cologne), and across much of northern Gaul, must therefore represent an export trade from Britain, apparently of the raw material rather than finished pieces. Perhaps lumps of jet were added as a filler to substantial cargoes carried from Britain to the lower Rhine.

The quarrying of good quality stone for building and for sculpture began within fifteen years of the conquest. The excellent oolitic limestone of Northamptonshire, Lincolnshire and the Cotswolds attracted attention as a useful medium for architectural details and such monuments as tombstones. The tomb monument of the procurator Julius Alpinus Classicianus, in London, was carved from stone from one of these sources, as were the earlier legionary tombstones of Longinus and Facilis erected at Camulodunum before AD 60. The qualities of Bath stone were also appreciated at an early date. This fine limestone was later to be used in several cities in the south and in a few of the richer villas. Ragstone from the Maidstone area of Kent was widely used locally, and quantities were shipped to London for use in the city wall. The red sandstone of Cheshire was sent to North Wales, where it was used in the fort at Caernarvon. The availability of workable stone stimulated the development of a range of local crafts, for example the sculpture of the Cotswolds and the making of stone sarcophagi at York and Ancaster (Lincolnshire). Stone for building was to hand in most parts of the province, though flint and brick had to be resorted to in East Anglia and in parts of the South-east. The sites of military quarries are known along the line of Hadrian's Wall, and in a few cases the rock-face still bears inscribed testimony to the work done by soldiers.

Purbeck marble from east Dorset was much prized for various purposes from a surprisingly early date. It was used for mortars, in which a very hard surface was required for pounding, and vessels of this description have been found distributed widely over the province, though more thickly near Purbeck itself. It was also used to make tablets for important inscriptions as far afield as Chichester (the Cogidubnus inscription), Cirencester, Verulamium, Colchester, London and Chester. The variety favoured was greyish-white in colour and formed a particularly handsome speckled background to the vermilion lettering in cinnabar favoured on monumental inscriptions. Panels and mouldings in Purbeck marble were used in public buildings in several cities and in a few villas, and some bathhouses contained lavers of the material. Tabletops and even small items of sculpture were also produced. This stone has been found very far afield, suggesting that it was exported unworked to be finished by craftsmen in many localized workshops. There is certainly no sign, as yet, of a major centre of production in the Isle of Purbeck itself.

Quern stones have not been subjected to large-scale study, but their manufacture and distribution must have constituted a sizeable industry. The army at first imported quantities from the lava deposits in the area of Andernach and Mayen in the Rhineland, but this did not continue long into the second century. Suitable British stones, such as the millstone grit of the Pennines and the puddingstone of Hertfordshire, were exploited later, though few quarries or workshops have been certainly identified. One existed at Wharncliff Rocks near Sheffield, another at Lodsworth on the Sussex greensand. The last-named workshop distributed querns northward as far as the Midlands. A wide variety of local stones was employed in the making of querns and too little attention has been given to this widespread industry. Large mills, such as would have been turned by donkey power, have been recorded only at Canterbury and London. Whetstones are another ubiquitous product, no doubt issuing from many sources. But there were large centralized workshops for these, too, one, located near Stony Stratford (Buckinghamshire), sending its wares over large areas of the Midlands and the South.

Salt had already been extensively worked on the Essex coast

and on the Fenland margins in the pre-Roman Iron Age. To that period and the succeeding Roman centuries belong many of the so-called Red Hills, with their masses of broken clay-lining from furnaces used in the evaporation of brine and from coarse clay vessels used in refining processes. This briquetage is found on many sites in southern Essex, from the Thames to Walton, though surprisingly few locations produce evidence from the later Roman period. Many other salt-making sites are known in Kent, Sussex, Lincolnshire and around the Wash. Geographical sources also mention at least two places called Salinae, where salt springs and brine pits must be a possibility. The first of these is Droitwich, where the salt deposits retained their importance under Anglo-Saxon kings, and the brine baths their attraction for long after that. This was evidently not a spa in the Roman period, however, as the word *Aquae* is not attached to the name. The second site is that at Kinderton, near Middlewich in Cheshire. A further Salinae mentioned by Ptolemy in the canton of the Catuvellauni cannot be certainly identified, but it may have lain close to the Wash. Finally, in the *Digest*, a late-Roman legal code, there may be a reference to *salinae* worked by convicts in the military area of northern Britain. The context suggests the Firth of Forth, where the name Prestonpans commemorates later activity of the same kind. These places cannot have been the only production sites of so indispensable a commodity. Those near the eastern coasts in particular were well placed to export salt to the adjacent Continent, through the agency of the *negotiatores salarii* who reveal themselves at the mouth of the Scheldt.

Britain also won a modest fame for its jewels. British pearls were of some repute, though their duskiness was deprecated. They were found both in rivers and on the seashore and were apparently not gathered from living oysters. Scottish rivers, in particular the Aberdeenshire Dee, have in more recent times produced large examples, up to 2 cm across. Amethysts were also won from an island in the western ocean; this island yielding gems is once mentioned in a geographical source, but without supporting detail. The trade in hunting-dogs also continued, and three breeds at least are known in literature: the Irish wolfhound, seven of which caused a stir in Rome when Symmachus exhibited them; the bulldog, known to Claudian; and a small spaniel described in some detail by Oppian. The favourite dogs of the Nene valley potters, however, were of the greyhound breed and this would indicate a fourth variety at least. The skeletal material reveals a comparable range. Large animals are known, much larger than any recorded for the pre-Roman Iron Age, which were thus probably imported breeds. But there are numerous remains of very small animals, too small to have been working or hunting-dogs. Evidently, house dogs or even lap-dogs had been introduced. Some of the larger dogs are virtually indistinguishable from wolves, themselves denizens of the Romano-British countryside. Bears were also present and were caught for export, mostly for the arena, where, under Domitian, they were already used for lacerating criminals. In the fourth century, when Claudian seeks a characteristic dress for a personification of Britannia, he gives her a bearskin. If he had chosen a sealskin, the conception would have been equally apt, for the pelts of these creatures, in which Britain abounded, were much prized and highly priced in the Roman world. Furs and skins must have formed a significant, though unmeasurable, component of the exports of Britain.

The manufacture of textiles was an important industry, severely under-represented in our sources, mainly for the British market but with some items achieving fame in the Empire at large. The *birrus Britannicus* mentioned in Diocletian's price-edict of AD 301 was a rainproof cloak with a hood, like that worn by Winter on several mosaics, and the *tapete*, a rug or horse-cloth, is the other named garments. On the home market most wool will have been derived from sheep, a little perhaps from goats. A fourth-century panegyrist praises the British flocks laden with fleeces, and there can be little doubt that numerous villa-estates were engaged in wool production. Unfortunately, tangible remains of what was probably one of the major industries of Roman Britain are extremely sparse. Spinning and weaving leave little trace behind them, but were no doubt practised widely. It may be surmised that most of the cloth was produced at myriad local centres in the countryside, with little centralization in the industry except in the weaving-mills (*gynaecia*) which were set up for official purposes in the fourth century, one of which, at Venta (probably Winchester) is recorded in Britain. The fine pair of cropping shears from Great Chesterford (Essex) may have come from a woollen mill, though their function, to give the piece a firm nap, has for long been performed by machinery. Linen is not mentioned anywhere specifically, but its use on a large scale for finely woven shrouds in the York region should be noted. There is no reason why it should not have been made from flax grown in Britain.

One of the most important crafts, of which we still know little, was leather-making. The army's need for leather, for tents as well as jerkins, belts and boots, was insatiable and may have been partly met by exaction from native communities. A depot for leather preparation has been excavated outside the first-century fort at Catterick in North Yorkshire, and there must have been many others in the military zones. Production in civilian centres will also have been widespread, though few indications of working are recorded *in situ*. A manufactory certainly existed at London, as inscribed pieces of leather waste attest, the inscriptions probably being tanners' marks. Another workshop, apparently civilian, was supplying the fort at Caernarvon. Not all leather was produced from the hides of cattle. Goat leather was highly prized, especially for garments, shoes and even army tents.

The natural resources of timber in the island were great and the early decades after the conquest must have seen a rapidly expanding market for dressed timber and an organized industry to supply it. Apart from the voracious appetite of the army for fort-building, the emergent towns were substantially timber-built. The management of woodland had a long pre-Roman history, so that there will have been no dearth of the requisite skills. Aside from the provision of immense quantities of seasoned timber, woodlands would also have been the source of most of the fuel, in the form of charcoal for domestic hearths, bathhouses and industrial kilns and furnaces. These extensive and important activities are inadequately represented in the archaeological record, but they should not be forgotten.

The native pottery industries of Britain were many and varied in their inspiration. High quality wheel-made wares were already widespread in southern Britain before the conquest; in the

Malvern Hills and in the South-east there are indications of centralized Iron Age industries which exported their products over long distances. It is therefore not surprising that several Romano-British industries had roots in the pottery traditions of the pre-Roman period. One of the most remarkable, and successful, was that which turned out vast quantities of black burnished cooking-pots, bowls and other common utensils in south Dorset. In the first century these wares were mainly marketed in the West Country and the South, but later other centres came into operation, in Kent and at Colchester. By the earlier second century the manufacturers had begun to supply the military market in northern Britain, and this lively trade continued into the fourth century. A contract best explains this circumstance, curious in view of the great distance involved: in the military field, inertia can often leave arrangements in place long after all reason for them has been lost.

Pottery making was established early outside the *colonia* at Colchester and continued down to the end of the fourth century. The first-century potters made *mortaria* (mixing bowls usually equipped with a heavy, overhanging rim and with grit studded to its inner surface) and flagons among other wares, reflecting changes in cuisine and table manners. Some workmen or master potters came to Britain from Gaul in pursuit of an expanded market. Such was Quintus Veranius Secundus, a Roman citizen and entrepreneur whose firm stamped *mortaria* with his name at this time. In the second century more ambitious enterprises were set up. Slip-coated wares of some quality were made and exported, and late in the century both plain and decorated Samian ware was being produced by at least fourteen potters who signed their vessels. The venture was evidently not a great success and was not long continued. Other immigrant potters may have been responsible for setting up kilns producing *mortaria* and other wares to the south of Verulamium at Radlett and Brockley Hill in the first century, and the Gaulish manufacturer Quintus Valerius Veranius set up a workshop in Kent, having moved there from Bavai (Belgium).

One of the most distinctively Roman pottery vessels was the *mortarium*. Since some of the earlier manufactories placed name-stamps as trade marks on the rim, these vessels provide invaluable information about the commercial distribution of these products and about the development of the industry. One of the earliest centres producing *mortaria* in Britain was established south of Verulamium about AD 50/55, probably by migrant potters from northern Gaul. The early imports from north-eastern Gaul, especially the products of the firms of Q. Valerius Veranius and Q. Valerius Secundus, quickly stimulated locally based manufacture. As markets developed further north after AD 70, some of the Verulamium potters moved to the area of Mancetter and Hartshill in Warwickshire, along with others, including the firm of G. Attius Marinus, which had earlier been active at Colchester as well as Verulamium. The Hartshill and Mancetter pottery was to grow into an immense manufactory, supplying much of the northern military zone and the Midlands. The manufacturer Sarrius from Mancetter later established a major workshop at Rossington Bridge near Doncaster, no doubt with other entrepreneurs. Meanwhile, another centre of *mortarium* making had been established at Lincoln, from where vessels were transported to the northern frontier region.

Inevitably, the supplying of military bases had a formative influence on the early development of the pottery industry in Britain. Aside from substantial imports of *terra sigillata*, Gallo-Belgic wares were introduced in some quantity from the Marne valley and from the Trier region. These well-made vessels were in part imitations of *terra sigillata* platters and cups, in part continuations of Iron Age beakers and jars. About 15 BC imports into the major *oppida* and high-status settlements in Britain began, and trade was further stimulated by the military presence after AD 43. British workshops certainly existed from the Claudian period and these probably lay in the South-east, possibly near Camulodunum. Other fine wares were first introduced by the army and later produced in Britain to serve the military market. These included slip-coated wares for the table, especially drinking cups, brought in from Lyon, northern Italy and south-eastern Spain; mica-dusted jars from central and northern Gaul; lead-glazed wares from the Allier valley; and wine flagons from a variety of centres in Gaul. All of these stimulated production in Britain by the Flavian period, if not earlier in some cases. That some of this production was specifically for the army is certain, though the precise mechanism of supply is not yet known. Pottery for the early base at Longthorpe was made in the *canabae* (small settlement) outside the fort, perhaps by civilian potters under loose military supervision. The later fortress at Gloucester was supplied with Severn valley ware from a number of sites in the vicinity, while the permanent legionary bases of Chester and Caerleon had their own sources of supply by the early second century. The relationships between civilian and military producers are not well established, but it is likely that influences flowed both ways, offering mutual benefits.

The second century saw the rapid growth of what was to become the largest of the Romano-British industries, that based in the Nene valley west of Durobrivae (Water Newton). Kilns here were excavated in desultory fashion by Edmund Artis in the early nineteenth century, but more recent work reveals how much still remains to be learnt. These potteries turned out a great variety of vessels, both for the table and for kitchen purposes. The slip-coated vessels are the most familiar, among them drinking-cups, beakers and bowls, but much else also came from the Nene valley kilns. It is possible that the stimulus for large-scale production came from eastern Gaul, following the migration of a master-potter, or potters, thence. An extensive market was soon built up in the Midlands and the North. The decorative treatments of the Nene valley wares are among the most varied of any British pottery, and perhaps the most accomplished in the ceramic art of the province. Most appealing are the so-called Hunt Cups, on which dogs chase hares or deer. Human scenes include chariot races, gladiatorial combats and, occasionally, scenes from classical mythology, while sometimes the place of humans or animals is taken by phallic emblems of good luck. The human scenes, though interesting, are seldom successful by classical standards. The very nature of the technique *en barbotine*, by which the figures were traced in wet clay like icing sugar, made it impossible to catch the subtleties of the human form, and denied to the artist the control of outline obtainable by incised technique or by carefully prepared moulds. It would have been wiser to be less ambitious, yet the ambition is of a kind that hardly exists in any other province. Perhaps the most interesting aspect of the attempt is that it should have been thought necessary to attract a market. It reflects, socially speaking, a public gladdened by hunting, racing and stories of divine adventures, even if these activities were not understood in the same terms as they were at the heart of the Empire. But while there was a vivid appeal to the imagination, no attempt was made to imitate the inscribed wares of the Rhineland and northern Gaul. The figured wares in fact formed only a small part of the total output, in which drinking-cups and other table vessels bulked large. The main output dated from the mid second century onward, and production continued well into the fourth.

Several factories were established in the Midlands during the second century, some of them serving military as well as civilian markets. Migrating potters from the region of Verulamium may have started the manufacture of *mortaria* at Hartshill and Mancetter in Warwickshire. Workshops in the vicinity of Lincoln started up about 180 and continued for long after that. Another important regional factory was based in south Derbyshire, serving a market there, but also dispatching vessels later to the northern frontier. In the fourth century the factory at Crambeck in South Yorkshire did much to satisfy the demands of the military market in the North. Further south, there were centres with important regional markets based in Oxfordshire and in Alice Holt forest near Farnham (Surrey). These larger workshops aside, there was a multiplicity of small potteries with a very limited distribution area for their products. Some may have worked for a single community or even a single villa-estate.

Military production, or production under military supervision, is clearly attested in some places and can be argued for elsewhere. The earliest case of production in a works depot is outside the legionary base at Longthorpe near Peterborough, about the middle of the first century. This enterprise is most plausibly explained as one set up by imported potters. The legionary site at Usk in South Wales may also have been supplied by specialists under military direction. The legionary kilns and tileries at Holt on the river Dee helped to supply the needs of the XX Legion at

Chester, and the IX Legion seems to have been involved with the making of pottery, as well as tiles, at Scalesceugh near Carlisle. The Caerleon fortress received supplies of pottery from a source nearby, as did York. And several auxiliary regiments supervised the production of pottery, for instance at Ravenglass and Brampton (Cumbria), Grimscar near Slack (Yorkshire) and Gelligaer in South Wales. But, though military production may have been more common than it appears to have been at present, most garrisons drew the bulk of their supplies from civilian traders, both locally and from a distance.

Few of the large factories lay close to major cities, the notable exception being the Colchester factories. More were close to lesser towns, such as Durobrivae, Mancetter and Brampton, but the majority lay at some distance from any major centre, so that the probability of production on a villa-estate or some other domain must be entertained. This might be confidently suggested for several of the Nene valley kiln groups, since an impressive range of villas occurs in the same area, while the Crambeck workshops and a number of kiln sites in the lower Trent valley may also have lain on estates. Thus, profits of some scale could have been added to the yield of agriculture, especially in the early Empire as the market for pottery was greatly enlarged. Estate production of pottery and tiles was a well-established feature of the Roman provinces, more especially in the late Empire, and British landowners with suitable raw materials to hand will have been alive to the possibilities. Access to river and sea routes was a desideratum, as is underlined by the position of many of the workshops. Seen as a whole, the majority of potteries lay to the south of a line from the Humber to the Bristol Channel. This meant that military supply from the second century onwards involved transport over considerable distances, presumably in fulfilment of contracts struck with the owners of civilian firms.

The organizations that lay behind the manufacture of pottery are poorly understood: they probably varied widely in scale and sophistication. Large contractors, though leaving no trace behind in the record of inscriptions, clearly existed and were able to undertake supply at great distances. Other enterprises, like those in the New Forest and Oxfordshire, supplied a regional market within easy reach of the kiln centres. And there were many smaller concerns with local horizons, representing the work of a single skilled man and a few workmen or slaves. Just how dependent the whole structure of the industry was on the secure order of the province is revealed by the cessation of the larger industries in the late fourth century or within a short time of the administrative collapse early in the fifth.

The New Forest pottery is another, more restrained manufactory, whose period of production lasted from the later third century until the late fourth. The period of greatest output was in the first half of the fourth century. The range of forms is wide; flagons, dishes, bowls, jars, cooking-pots, cases, goblets, and even candlesticks, appear in great quantity and certainly swamp the drinking-cups, though these also abound. Decoration is restricted to simplified running scrolls or conventional triangular patterns, all in white slip, and to repetitive stamped rosettes, demi-rosettes, or ogees. The forms are shapely and sure; the decoration comparatively lifeless. New Forest products are not to be found as far afield as one might have expected, given the proximity of the Channel and several river routes. They were distributed chiefly in southern central England up to the Thames valley, but rarely beyond. The known kilns are sited around the streams Dockens Water, Latchmore Brook and Ditchend Brook north of Linwood, in several small isolated groups with no obvious focus, worked from huts so primitive as to suggest seasonal activity on an estate or on public land. The impression gained by this shifting activity in the woodland is a little like that of charcoal burning, and very different from the well-established kiln-fields of the Nene valley.

Legionary tileries have already been mentioned, but there were many civilian establishments as well. An Imperial tilery existed near Calleva (Silchester) in the reign of Nero, curiously the only one attested in the province. The *colonia* of Glevum (Gloucester) made its own tiles, stamped R(ES) P(UBLICA) G(LEVENSIUM) and sometimes bearing abbreviated names of its *duoviri quinquennales*. These are found not only in the city but on villas and other sites in the region, probably extending well beyond the limits of the urban area. Also based in Gloucestershire was a private company, stamping with variant initials, much employed at Corinium (Cirencester); another such firm was active in the early *colonia* at Lindum (Lincoln). The great building programmes in cities from the later first century onwards must have brought many other tileries into operation that have left no trace behind in the form of stamped products. Some of these concerns were based in the countryside. Decorated roller-stamped tiles from the villa at Ashtead in Surrey are found widely in southern Britain: many of the patterns are plain chevrons but there is a spirited scene of a wolfhound and a stag at bay, and there are some florid patterns with stiff but crowded conventional ornament. This establishment was working from about AD 80 until after the middle of the second century. Another centre producing similar tiles is known at Hartfield in East Sussex, while a third, more localized operation was based in the region of the villas at Plaxtol and Darenth in Kent, where the pattern was formed by the statement '*parietalem Cabriabanus fabricavit*' (Cabriabanus made this wall-tile) repeated. Many commonplace civilian tileries must have existed, especially on estates, though few have been well recorded. Brick, however, was used in most regions for a relatively limited range of purposes in construction, the commonest being in bonding courses in major walls, as voussoirs in windows, doorways and drains, and as pillars in hypocausts.

Glass was produced in a number of places in Britain, including Silchester, London, Caister-by-Norwich and Wilderspool (Lancashire). The range of vessels and containers produced in the province seems to have been rather narrow. None of the elaborately decorated or technically demanding objects, such as the *diatreta* (cage-cups) of northern Gaul, were attempted here. Window glass will have been required in some quantity in towns, and most of this material was made in the island.

Another aspect of Romano-British economic life that is poorly documented is the use of water-powered machinery. It was not a marked feature of Mediterranean civilization because the chief prerequisite, a constant supply of water, was so often lacking. But it was from the Mediterranean world that the undershot water-wheel described by Vitruvius was derived, and it was used in aqueduct overflows for grinding flour and cinnabar at Rome, or for driving the flour-mills at the Barbegal near Arles in southern France. In north-western Europe steady streams were more common, and Ausonius describes mills for flour and for sawing stone on the river Ruwer in the lands around the Moselle. In Britain examples are few but significant. Military use of water-powered mills is evident at three points on Hadrian's Wall, using for the purpose respectively the North Tyne and Irthing rivers and the Haltwhistle Burn. The stone core of the water-wheel's hub can still be seen at the North Tyne mill east of Chesters, and two hub cores of the same kind have come from the river Witham at Lincoln. Iron spindles for power-driven stones are known from Silchester and Great Chesterford (Essex), implying mills near those towns, and a number of villas also possessed water-mills. Leats are known at Woolaston Pill (Gloucestershire) and Fullerton (Hampshire), and large millstones that could only have been driven by water-power have been found at the Chedworth villa. The best recorded mills are two on the Little Stour at Ickham, east of Canterbury. The earlier of these was a timber-framed structure astride a natural water course, which had housed an undershot wheel two metres in diameter. A later mill, of the third and fourth centuries, had been built upstream. This had been served by a mill-race three metres wide, lined with planks, and may have included more than one wheel in simultaneous use. A link with the garrisons of the Saxon Shore forts of Reculver and Richborough seems to be suggested by the military equipment here.

Britain was a productive island. For an indefinite period after the conquest, perhaps a century or so, the province cannot have paid its way. But by the mid second century at the latest, the economic benefits and limitations of the occupation will have been evident. The most significant yields of the province were probably in commodities that are difficult or impossible to study by purely archaeological means: agricultural products, especially grain, wool, meat and leather. But Britain was part of a much wider economic world, not a self-contained entity, and there is considerable evidence for what was imported into the island.

One of the commonest imports to Britain, as to many other parts of the Roman West, was the glossy, red-slipped tableware known as *terra sigillata* or Samian ware. Manufactured in factories situated in northern Italy and, later, in Gaul, this ware is represented by a wide range of plain platters, dishes and cups, and by bowls covered externally with moulded scenes or conventional patterns. The Italian centre of manufacture at the height of its activity in the reign of Augustus lay at Arretium (Arezzo) in Tuscany. Its products, decorated or otherwise, were closely modelled upon metal vessels, of which they were intended to form a cheap, serviceable copy. Early in the first century AD branch workshops were established at Lyon in central Gaul by the large firm of Cn. Ateius, and possibly elsewhere, in order to take full advantage of the enlarged markets on the Rhine. Other factories in southern Gaul, at La Graufesenque, Banassac and Montans, were opened at the same time and quickly rose to dominate the western markets, their products penetrating freely into Italy by the seventies. From southern Gaul production passed steadily to the centre, to the Allier valley near Clermont-Ferrand, and by the beginning of the second century this group of factories, including Lesouz and Les Martres de Veyre, were in the ascendant, dominating the trade with Britain for the next century. A number of workshops were later founded in the Moselle valley and eastwards to the upper Rhine, those at Trier and Rheinzabern despatching wares to Britain. The mass-production methods of the second-century factories reduced the quality of both decoration and finish, so much so that many of the slip-coated wares produced in Britain after 150 were of equal or better quality than the Samian ware. But this did nothing to inhibit import on a huge scale down to the end of the second century. Attempts to set up manufactories in Britain, at Colchester, Pulborough (Sussex) and perhaps in London, came to naught, probably for lack of a suitable illite-bearing clay. The scale of the import from central Gaul was immense. Hardly an inhabited site in the second century fails to yield Samian ware, often in quantity. The army acquired it in bulk, though how this traffic was organized and handled remains uncertain. For the civilian market it came in shiploads, one of which, wrecked in the later second century off Whitstable (Kent), provided in later ages a name for Pudding Pan Rock.

Production of central Gaulish Samian ware came to an abrupt end at the close of the second century, perhaps as a result of the civil war between Septimius Severus and Clodius Albinus, and the confiscations of property which followed. The eastern Gaulish factories continued in production during the third century, but their exports to Britain were not on any great scale. Small quantities of Argonne ware or *Rädchensigillata* came in from north-eastern Gaul in the fourth century, but not evidently as a result of a regular traffic. Much more frequent was the import of the so-called 'Rhenish' slip-ware, some of which is indeed to be attributed to workshops in the Rhineland, though most of it came from the Moselle valley. The vessels were for the table, comprising mainly jugs, beakers and cups. The fabric is thin, with a highly polished dark brown slip-coating, often ornamented in running scrolls or medallions in white slip and also *en barbotine*. Sometimes the shoulder of the vessel carries a terse, colloquial and convivial inscription in white capital letters, such as '*suavis*' (delicious), '*da mi*' (give it to me), '*misce mi*' (mix it for me) or '*vivatis*' (long life to you). The occasional obscenity also obtrudes. A less expected import from the Continent is a small quantity of the coarse Mayen ware from the Eifel kilns, dating from the fourth century. More attractive is the *céramique à l'éponge* from western Gaul which reached southern Britain in similarly small quantity, also in the fourth century.

Mediterranean wine had reached the tables of British chieftains well before the Roman conquest (above, p. 5–6). Imported wine continued to be carried in amphorae from Italy, Spain and Gaul, but it must also be remembered that in the Rhine and Moselle valleys, where wine was produced for export in the second and third centuries, barrels were used, as is revealed by relief sculptures from the Trier region. Barrels of fir found at Silchester and London had no doubt contained wine from that area and from Aquitaine; the wine from the latter was rated by the Italian consumer as second class. It seems certain that M. Aurelius Lunaris, a rich merchant and *sevir Augustalis* of both Lincoln and York, who erected an altar at Bordeaux following a safe sea-passage in AD 237, was one representative of the traders engaged in this traffic, shipping direct to the northern markets, both military and civilian. Lunaris may have been a Briton, but other traders were Gauls. Verecundius Diogenes hailed from Bourges and he too was a member of a group of merchants based at York, presumably importing wine from western Gaul. It should be added that vines were probably grown in southern Britain, vine-stocks being reported from a villa at Boxmoor in Hertfordshire and grape pips from a number of sites. Wine could certainly have been produced in Britain, in a climate somewhat warmer than it is today, but we can form no estimate of its quality. It is not likely to have been memorable.

The liquor that would have outmatched wines for consumption within the province was beer (*cervesa*), a highly popular drink in Britain as in Gaul, and cheaper than wine. In Gaul dark ale is mentioned as being brewed at Trier and there may well have been varieties of brew in Britain, though these are not recorded. A fourth-century panegyrist specifically mentions the twofold use of grain, for bread and beer. Military rations included coarse beer (*posca*), and it is a safe guess that this had a strong appeal to the largely provincial soldiery. Brewing and its associated proc-esses leave little trace behind them. It is, however, highly likely that many of the so-called corn-dryers commonly found on villas and other rural sites were in reality malting-kilns, in which barley was roasted before brewing.

Another of the staple products of Mediterranean agriculture was the olive, its oil being used in the kitchen, in cleansing the body at the bath, and in illumination. The principal area of olive-growing for export in the early Empire lay in southern Spain, along the valley of the Guadalquivir between Cordoba and Seville. From here, oil was despatched in globular amphorae, with small handles close to the neck, to most parts of the West. Fresh olives were also transported in these amphorae: one vessel containing six thousand of the fruit has been found in the estuary of the Thames. At least a certain amount of olive oil was being imported into south-eastern Britain in the late Iron Age, even though it was not until the conquest that the presence of south Spanish amphorae became anything other than rare. By then, the picture is somewhat obscured by the import of fish-sauce (*garum, liquamen, muria*), an incomprehensible delicacy of the early

Empire, produced in the same areas of Spain and exported in amphorae of the same types. The oil was at first mainly directed to the early military bases and the larger townships, but by the second century it was reaching a wider market. Thereafter, the trade fell away, as oil was used less and less for illumination and perhaps in the preparation of food. The characteristic oil-lamps of the first century become scarce after the mid second century in the north-western provinces, suggesting that candles and tallow lamps took their place as a cheaper alternative. Cooking-fats, in which Britain would have been rich, may have taken the place of olive oil for use in the kitchen.

Oysters, though known to Italian epicures of the first century, probably did not travel in quantity, though a gift of fifty oysters was received by a soldier at Vindolanda, perhaps from a source outside Britain. They formed a very large trade within the province. Few Roman sites are without them, even far from the sea coasts, and it is clear that in the taverns and shops outside the fortresses and forts of Britain oysters were the popular fast-food of the day. Mussels are on many sites almost equally numerous, while cockles, scallops, whelks and periwinkles also occur. The Thames estuary and the south-east coast were presumably major sources of seafood, though the Channel coast westwards to Cornwall could also have provided an abundance of shellfish. The land snail was present, and probably consumed, at the Shakenoak villa (Oxfordshire), and the edible frog is known from Silchester. Sea fish are not well represented in the record, mainly because their fragile bones have usually eluded detection. Herring, sea-bream and mullet were caught, as were flounder and plaice, to add to the perch, pike, dace, trout and eel taken from rivers. The sea fish must have been dried, smoked or salted before being transported inland.

The furnishings for the table, in bronze and silver, at first came entirely from overseas. The most costly and the most prized of table services were silver jugs, dishes and cups. These last were being imported, or being presented as gifts to chieftains, before the Roman invasion, as the Welwyn burials reveal. In the province the silver plate which was the pride of every wealthy house in the Roman world came principally from the Mediterranean, though Gaulish silversmiths were becoming important trade rivals by the second century. Some silverware must have been made in Britain, though no candidate for a workshop can be proposed. Surviving pieces follow classical models so closely that it is rarely possible to recognize a provincial copy. Silverware that is certainly local, such as the decorative plaques from shrines or ritual furniture at Barkway and Stony Stratford, also follows the classical repertoire so faithfully as to lose much of the provincial character it might have had. Occasionally the choice of subject, in the Capheaton (Northumberland) pans or *trullei*, suggests a British origin. On those pieces personifications of the deities of sea and river, corn and wine are emblems of trade between Britain and the adjacent provinces. It is possible that silver vessels and other objects were manufactured in Britain, though clear traces of silver-working are rare. Gaul and Italy will have supplied most, or all, of the fine, decorated pieces, including the huge and splendid picture dish from Mildenhall, perhaps from Rome itself, though a number of objects may be from the eastern Mediterranean. The Corbridge *lanx*, a decorated tray which contains repeated references, some obvious, others recondite, to Delos and its cults, is fairly certainly eastern, as perhaps is a nielloed dish in the Mildenhall treasure.

Bronze furnishings were also an important item in any list of imports. Among these figured elaborate table-lamps, candelabra, heating-dishes, strainer-sets for wine, finger-bowls, a wide range of containers and furniture. In the first century the bulk of these objects were imported, but gradually many of them came to be manufactured within the province; and there was an interesting halfway stage during which Italian products were driven out of the market by Gaulish merchandise. This is particularly noticeable in the bronze *trullei* or skillets, used by civilians for heating food and wine, and by the army as mess-tins, which came largely from Campanian firms in the first century, but carry more and more names of Gaulish origin in the second. A major production centre lay near Aquae Granni (Aachen) in Lower Germany.

More exotic imports must also be mentioned. Mediterranean marbles were imported for use in London, Camulodunum, Silchester, Cirencester and Lincoln. The imports to London came chiefly from the eastern Mediterranean, despite the relative accessibility of good material in Italy and Gaul. Perhaps this is to be explained as a result of the energetic activity of well-established distribution networks in the Aegean world. The range of Aegean stones reaching London is impressive: *cipollino* from Euboea, *pavonazetto* from Phrygia, *semesanto* from Skyros, *portasanta* from Chios, and others from Asia Minor. Egypt provided red porphyry from Mons Porphyrites and two other marbles, probably from the eastern desert. The famous white marble from Luni, or Carrara, is naturally represented, along with the bluish-grey *bardiglio* from the same area. Quarries in Aquitaine offered the black and white *marmor celticum* from near St Girens, and the greenish *campan vert* from the Pyrenees. Probably more Gaulish marble reached Britain than at present appears. Egyptian porphyry is further recorded in the cities of Colchester, Silchester and Canterbury, the easily identifiable Carrara marble at Colchester, Silchester, Lincoln, Verulamium and Richborough, *cipollino* at Cirencester, *rosso antico* at Lincoln and *campan vert* at Silchester. It would be wrong to overestimate the significance of such an item as marble, for the traffic can never have been large or regular. But it is interesting to see how its use persisted and how those responsible for the adornment of urban structures tried as best they could to adhere to Mediterranean standards.

Another import was papyrus from Egypt, which must have been in considerable demand, both by official bureaux, military and civil, and by book producers, whose skilled writers copied texts upon rolls. It has been argued that papyrus was imported before the Roman conquest, not in itself implausible but not proven by surviving evidence. It is likely that many official documents, as well as private communications, were recorded in ink on wooden writing tablets, more ephemeral information being impressed in wax by a stylus. The large cache of writing tablets found at Vindolanda is particularly revealing of the form of official records about AD 100, as well as affording fascinating glimpses of private manners in a frontier post. Writing tablets were produced as objects of trade, but those known in Britain were probably made from native timber, especially alder, birch and larch.

Cinnabar (*minium*), an Imperial monopoly, was produced in southern Spain and much used for painting the lettering of monumental inscriptions, in which traces of it are sometimes found. It has now been shown that cinnabar was also widely used as a red pigment in the paint applied to wall-plaster in Britain, so that import of this material, though never very large, takes on a new significance. The trade in incense must have been as large or larger. Cooking spices, notably pepper, ginger and cinnamon, should probably be included in the catalogue, along with perfumes in their glass phials, some from Imperial properties, such as the Judaean balsam groves, in their specially taxed containers, used by the living and for the dead.

Gold-working by jewellers and others was being carried out at London, Verulamium, Cirencester and Chester, as is shown by finds of crucibles, and at Malton (North Yorkshire), as an inscription records. The craft was quite certainly much more widespread, as several gold ornaments reveal individual details of craftsmanship that are the hallmark of a single workshop or group of artisans. The hoard of ornaments found close by the gold-mines at Dolau Cothi points to manufacture close to the source of the metal, at least in the third century. Silver-working, which included the process of cupellation from galena, was carried out at Silchester, remains of the furnaces and of metallic residues having been identified long ago. The building in which some of these remains were recorded has the appearance of a workshop rather than a house, which raises the interesting possibility of a substantial enterprise, though of what kind and how supervised is unknown. Official Roman coins might have provided material for cupellation, here as elsewhere. Several sites have produced clay moulds in which counterfeit coins had been cast, the metal perhaps being provided in part by genuine coins.

Britain had its own enamelled work, especially brooches and other personal ornaments, but these, striking as they often are, can hardly vie with the best work from Gallia Belgica, which belongs to the second and third centuries. Fine enamels had their origin in the pre-Roman Iron Age, but the Roman period objects are far removed from the aristocratic milieu of earlier days. Bright, often garish, brooches and belt-plates had come to the fore in place of the war equipment of Iron Age chiefs. Enamelled bowls, which served as mementos of Hadrian's Wall, bearing a schematic design of the frontier-work together with the names of some of its forts, were more ambitious products. British-made trumpet brooches, with enamel decoration on the bow, are found on the lower Rhine, the Upper German frontier and even occasionally in Italy, but these exports were related to troop-movements involving units that had served in Britain.

A vivid glimpse of the lives of traders active between the mouths of the Rhine and Scheldt and Britain is afforded by the finds of many altars from a shrine of the goddess Nehallenia at Colijnsplaat in the Scheldt estuary. The altars, of which over fifty are known, many of them inscribed, are of fine quality, attesting the handsome profits won from British trade. The merchants themselves came from several parts of Gaul and lower Germany, including Besançon, Trier and Cologne. It is probable that British traders were also engaged, one man hailing from one of the British towns called Venta. A few recorded the commodities in which they traded: salt, pottery and fish-sauce. No doubt other goods travelled the same route. Nehallenia had another sanctuary on the island of Walcheren near Domburg, and here too a trader in pottery with British interests dedicated a statue to the goddess *ob merces recte conservatas* ('for goods preserved in good order'). Other traders with Britain were based further inland, at Cologne for instance, and probably in northern Gaul, where pottery and jet of British origin is found.

A survey of the economic life of a Roman province must include some account of the coinage, though it is vital to remember that the use of currency varied greatly according to the social and economic standing of individual communities. This much is evident from the series of coins found on different kinds of site. Coinage circulated freely in military bases and cities but saw far less use in rural settlements: while in the upland areas of the northern and western Britain coinage may not have penetrated at all beyond the forts and *vici*.

For up to a century before the conquest the southern British tribes had used coinage for a steadily expanding range of purposes, so that by AD 43 a market economy existed, at least in embryo, from the South-east to Dorset and the Severn basin, and north to the Trent. A gold and silver currency was in use over most of these parts of Britain; bronze was confined to the south-east. Roman coinage was not normally imported, even to those areas engaged in cross-Channel trading. The Roman conquest brought a rapid transformation to the currency system, chiefly through the agency of the army, though pre-Roman coinages were not deliberately driven out of circulation. On the contrary, the silver coins of the Iceni circulated freely down to at least AD 60, and issues of the Dobunni and Durotriges are also commonly found in deposits well after AD 43. But the economic significance of army units, affluent and accustomed to paying for goods and services in coin, will have been immense from the very beginning of Roman occupation, and the coin-using habit quickly spread to civilian communities. Early military and civilian users alike faced difficulty in acquiring bronze coinage in adequate quantity, as the central government did not despatch any sizeable bulk of coin to Britain after the invasion and had in any case tried to withdraw from circulation the issues of Claudius' predecessor Gaius. In consequence, a huge number of bronze asses and dupondii were struck in imitation of the early issues of Claudius at provincial centres and were obviously connived at, or even initiated by, the military authorities. As Nero struck no bronze coinage for the first ten years of his reign, these provincial issues of Claudius went on circulating until the mid sixties or even later. No great flood of gold and silver coin entered Britain for nearly thirty years after the conquest. The Flavian advance in the north and the contemporary development of urban life, industry and commerce drew more high-value currency into the province. By this date, too, British silver and gold will have made its own contribution to the Imperial finances. Precious metal hoards of the first hundred years of Roman Britain are not common, implying a fairly stable economic base. Aurei went on circulating for decades after they were issued, as did the base denarii of Mark Antony. The coinage reform of Trajan that led to a finer silver currency tended to extend the earlier, lighter pieces in circulation, though no great problems beset the coinage as a whole until after the middle of the second century. The large brass sestertius took on an enhanced role in the currency, as inflationary pressures began to make their presence felt. The origins of a steep economic decline can be traced in the 160s, when Marcus Aurelius debased the silver coinage in order to support vastly increased military spending, forcing the denarius into an exposed position in the currency. The downward spiral of debasement and inflation that followed was to continue without check for the next half-century. Gold coinage was now of such high value that it was taken out of circulation by hoarders. Large hoards of silver and sestertii were commonly deposited and the volume of lesser denominations was greatly reduced. Some alleviation of the latter problem was provided in Britain by the issue of the Britannia asses of Antoninus Pius in 155, quite possibly from a temporary mint in Britain, as these coins are so common in the island and virtually unrecorded elsewhere. The interconnected evils of inflation and debasement continued to beset the currency from the later reign of Marcus Aurelius. The weight and purity of the denarius fell in a series of steps until the coin contained only half its weight in silver. Greatly increased military spending by Septimius Severus exacerbated the decline of the silver coinage, the debasement inevitably driving earlier, purer issues out of circulation. In 215 Caracalla's issue of a new silver coin, the antoninianus, with a value of two denarii, was not in principle illogical, but the fact that each coin contained considerably less silver than two denarii of the time merely added a fresh twist to the spiral. The denarius was driven out of the monetary system and, after an interruption between 222 and 238, replaced by ever more debased antoniniani. By the mid third century the value of the ostensible silver currency had collapsed to less than 10 per cent of its face value. Gold coinage was struck in small quantities but was clearly too high in value to enter free circulation. Even the large bronze denominations were barely worth minting. As a medium for issuing and receiving payment, coinage was greatly reduced in its usefulness. The resultant difficulties for military pay and taxation must have been acute.

Reform when it came in the reign of Aurelian was ineffective. The attempt to issue coins of standard weight and purity, but not improved in either respect over those of the preceding decades, and at a high tariff, failed within ten years. Aurelian's reformed coinage is rare in Britain, either because it did not enter the island in quantity, or because it was restruck by later rulers. The shortfall in currency, in Britain as in Gaul, was made good by immense quantities of base copies, mostly of issues of the Gaulish emperors, especially those of Tetricus. These radiate copies (or 'barbarous radiates') flowed from many provincial sources between 273 and 286, some of them close to their prototypes, many grotesquely garbled in their design and inscriptions. The usurpation of Carausius in 286 ended this chaotic state of affairs. Carausius, and Allectus, issued a base coinage related to that of Aurelian, but added a silver issue of high purity and a gold series for official payments. The restoration of Britain to the central Empire roughly coincided with the major coinage reform of Diocletian (296). A high-quality silver coin, the argenteus, had been issued from 293 and this was followed by a bronze issue with a silver content of about 3 per cent (follis). The follis is not commonly found in Britain and seems not to have enjoyed wide popularity in the western provinces generally, probably because it was too large for everyday use and was over-tariffed in relation to silver and gold. Several of the earlier issues of folles reveal deliberate clipping by their users. A mint producing these coins was active in Britain for at least a short time after 296, presumably to strike coinage for Constantius' forces.

Diocletian's currency system lasted barely a decade. By 305 the follis was reduced in size; the silver argenteus was discontinued in 308; in 310 the gold coinage was reduced in weight and a new gold piece, the solidus, was issued, assisted by the large amount of gold released from temple treasuries after 312. The mint of London was retained by Constantine until 324, but was then abandoned and never again refounded. The coinage of Constantine's reign reveals a return to a trimetallic system of gold, silver and bronze, with an especial emphasis upon silver from 325. The issue of both gold and silver coins to a high standard of purity continued down to the end of the fourth century, ensuring payments to Imperial officials and the army, as well as the collection of taxes. But the base coinage (billon) proved problematic and vulnerable to the ravages of inflation. By 348, a reform of these small denominations was needed, three new types of coin being issued, all bearing the legend FEL(IX) TEMP(ORUM) REPARATIO ('the restoration of happy times'), in celebration of the eleven hundredth anniversary of the foundation of Rome. There was to be no happy restoration of the billon coinage. Debasement rapidly followed and by 360 billon had degenerated into a token currency, greatly enlarged by locally struck copies. This wretched coinage in bronze, and the inflation of which it was a major symptom, continued down to the end of Roman Britain, alongside the relatively stable gold and silver issues. After about 380, the amount of coin in circulation fell away sharply, the bulk of the bronze coinage coming from mints in Gaul from 388 to 395. Silver coinage, however, was still relatively abundant, as is seen in a striking series of hoards dating from the late fourth and early fifth centuries. After the mints of Gaul closed in 395, coinage still reached Britain from Rome and Aquileia, but this supply was not to last for long. By 402 the last substantial body of coin had been received for official purposes, although a small quantity of gold and silver issued by Constantine III did reach Britain, probably before 410, as did a few silver coins dating to the 420s. Many of the silver siliquae of the late fourth and early fifth centuries had their edges clipped, thus providing a modest, though evidently still worthwhile, source of precious metal. Among the latest gold and silver coins to enter Britain were those which were buried in the great hoard at Hoxne in Suffolk early in the fifth century. By about 425, coinage had ceased to play any part in the economic life of Britain and it was not to be revived until the late seventh century, in very different circumstances. Like so much else in the economic fabric of Roman Britain the demise of the currency was rapid and without any legacy to the following age.

CHAPTER SIX

Religious Life

At the time that Britain was brought within the orbit of Rome
there had recently been major developments within the official
cults of the Roman State. The worship of the Capitoline Triad of
Jupiter, Juno and Minerva had long been a dominant feature in
State ceremonial and cult. Jupiter Capitolinus was not merely
the supreme god of Heaven, but also the god who protected the
State. As the bounds of the State widened to embrace most of
western Europe, the provincial aristocracy played an increasingly
important role in the Capitoline cult. The *coloniae* of Caesar and
Augustus normally included a *Capitolium* among their public
buildings, a focus of loyalty without overt political colouring. In
his long reign, Augustus skilfully, though cautiously, identified
himself and his family with the religion of the State; an easy
matter in the eastern provinces, with their long history of ruler-
cults, but one requiring careful handling within a well-defined
context in the western lands. The cult of the emperor was linked
with that of the goddess Roma and deification during the lifetime
of a ruler was avoided or played down as far as possible. Much
safer was worship of the spirit of the emperor, his numen or
genius, or of his entire family, the *domus divina*. The peoples of the
western provinces proved not unwilling to accord divine honours
to their emperor, though the political dimensions of the cult must
always have been in the ascendant over direct, personal
involvement.

The first appearance of the cult of an emperor in Britain was
not auspicious. The temple of the deified Claudius at Camulodunum, possibly preceded by the provision of an altar of the cult,
placed a heavy burden of expense upon the leading figures
among the Trinovantes and thus contributed to the resentment
which burst forth in the great revolt of AD 60. The location of the
cult centre at Camulodunum followed Roman practice elsewhere
in the west. Lyon, one of the oldest *coloniae* of the three Gauls and

the leading city of those provinces, had been chosen as the site of the altar of Rome and Augustus; and the Roman coinage had proclaimed the fact as one of its main messages. On the lower Rhine, the *colonia* at Cologne emerged as the principal Roman city in that frontier region and was thus the obvious site for the Imperial cult and its altar.

Claudian policy in the encouragement of emperor worship in the provinces was restrained; that of Nero swung to the other extreme later in his reign. The Flavian emperors sprang from a relatively obscure family, and thus may have been prompted to appear among the company of gods and enjoy their favour. Certainly, the new rulers showed no hesitation in accepting divine honours. The inscription set up in Chichester at the behest of Cogidubnus, recording the dedication of a temple to Neptune and Minerva, also sought the 'well-being of the divine (i.e. Imperial) house'. Other direct glimpses of the cult of emperors in Britain are not numerous, but such worship will have been centred in the cities and legionary bases, and the former have produced few inscriptions of any kind. Such a centre certainly existed at London, where the province of Britannia set up a temple or altar to the numen of an unknown emperor. This dedication suggests that a provincial Council existed in Britain, as in Gaul, and was based in London, one of its main functions being the organization of an annual festival celebrating the divinity of the ruling emperor, as well as providing a link between the provincial notables and the monarch. The cult of emperors followed no smooth and even history. After the Flavians, Trajan resisted a personalized cult. So did Hadrian early on, but then he bent to the will of his eastern subjects. Antoninus Pius associated himself with various deities (Victoria, Fortuna, Pax), but was not averse to divine honours. Marcus Aurelius was less enthusiastic, while Commodus saw himself as the Roman Hercules, the new founder of Rome. Few of these fluctuations are revealed in the evidence from Britain. A statue base dedicated to Nero survived later condemnation at Chichester. At Brough-on-Humber, a magistrate of the *vicus* of Petuaria dedicated a stage building to the divine house of Antoninus Pius and to the Imperial numina. The organization of the cult in the province followed established practice elsewhere. A college of six priests, *seviri Augustales*, usually freedmen engaged in commerce, supervised the cult and paid for many of the appropriate games and festivals from their own resources, and in addition might underwrite the provision or repair of public amenities. *Seviri Augustales* are recorded for both York and Lincoln. One trader, M. Aurelius Lunaris, was a *sevir* of both cities in the earlier third century; his commercial interests linked eastern Britain and western Gaul and had clearly provided him with wealth and prestige. Other groups of *seviri* presumably existed at the other *coloniae* and perhaps at other cities. Finds of sculpture add a little detail. A fine late-Augustan or early Tiberian marble head of a young man, quite possibly Germanicus, reported to have been found at Bosham, if not imported in modern times, may have been housed in a shrine to the *domus divina* at the heart of the realm of Cogidubnus. The famous bronze head of Claudius, found in the River Alde in Suffolk but originally probably from Camulodunum, is unlikely to have belonged to a cult statue. More plausibly, it had stood in a building or open space within the early *colonia* and had been broken and carried off in AD 60. On the other hand, the bronze head of Hadrian found in the Thames at London Bridge could have come from a cult statue in a shrine devoted to Imperial worship. The limestone head of a mid-third-century ruler, also from London, could have been linked to an emperor cult, but equally well might have stood in a public place.

Worship of the old, established deities of the Roman state is attested by a range of evidence surprising for so remote a province, which belies the common conception that religious observance was largely Celtic in its inspiration. Neither is such honour to Roman gods confined to the cities and military bases. Mars, Victoria, Hercules, Neptune, Apollo, Asclepius, Mercury, Vulcan, Fortuna, Diana, Minerva and Ceres, as well as Jupiter and his spouse Juno, are all represented in Britain, along with Abundantia, Bellona, the Fates and a variety of tutelary and territorial deities. A high proportion of dedications were, of course, made in urban and military contexts, but by no means all. At Lincoln, Mercury and Apollo were honoured in corporate worship by two of the constituent *vici* of the city, perhaps as patrons. In the same city there is another reminder of the prevalence of corporate worship in a dedication to the Parcae (the Fates) and the Imperial numina by the treasurer of a burial guild. The worship of Jupiter Optimus Maximus is attested in most parts of the province and in almost every milieu, but is most common in forts and their associated *vici*. In most contexts, too, Roman deities are found closely associated or even identified with Celtic gods, sometimes gods with a specific and localized significance. Hercules appears at Silchester in association with Saegonius or Segomo, Mars with Medocius at Camulodunum, Mars with Braciaca at Bakewell, and Mercury with Andescocioucos at Camulodunum. Some Celtic deities were introduced from Gaul and identified with a Roman counterpart, often Mars. Mars Loucetius appears at Bath, Mars Lenus at Caerwent, in the latter case connected with Mars Ocellus Vellaunus, a local god. British deities, often known from a single inscription, abound and occur in virtually all social contexts, either on their own or, more commonly, in association with a Roman god. Arciaco occurs alone at York, Maponus Apollo at Ribchester and Callirius Silvanus at Camulodunum. The outstanding case of association between a god linked to a specific location and a Roman deity, however, is that between Sulis and Minerva at the hot spring at Bath (Aquae Sulis). Virtually nothing is known for certain about Sulis; there is even ambiguity about the gender of the god. But though the precise relationship between Celtic godling and Minerva may have been unsure, those who developed the cult were intent on creating a cult centre that was as Roman as it could possibly be. This is clear not only in the magnificent buildings provided at Bath, but in such details as the presence of a haruspex, who was concerned with divination, an ancient and thoroughly Italian strain in Roman religion.

There were a variety of imports from the adjacent provinces of Gaul and Germany. Among the most prominent of these were the Matres or Matronae of northern Gaul and the Rhineland, a triad of fertility goddesses usually shown with fruit or loaves in their laps, and occasionally children. Their cult was widely adopted in Britain and its devotees have left behind several notable sculptures, for example at Cirencester and Ancaster, and dedications, such as the gilded silver patera found at Backworth, Northumberland. In the northern frontier area, a striking number of altars were erected to the Matres Campestres, 'mother-god-desses of the camp', a cult perhaps carried there by auxiliaries from Gaul. There were other introductions of native gods from the Rhine frontier lands. The Frisii brought Mars Thincsus and his female companions the Alaisiagae to Housesteads, the Suebi their goddess Garmangabis to Lanchester. Another cult of prob-able German origin was that of Hvitir, also found on the northern frontier, and so outlandish that some of its devotees Latinized the name to *di veteres*, the old gods. Finally, another regiment of Germans at Old Penrith honoured the Unseni Fersomari, clearly an import but otherwise unknown.

The cults of Egyptian gods are represented by a small number of finds, chiefly sculpture and statuettes, and are not likely to have made a major impression on the religious life of the province. Possibly the earliest in date is a reference to a shrine of Isis in a graffito on a first-century wine flagon found in Southwark across the Thames from Londinium. A port site like Londinium is likelier than most to have housed an Isiac community and it is not surprising that three other objects, all showing busts of the goddess, have been recorded here. Perhaps the most influential of Egyptian deities in the western provinces was Serapis, the god of fertility and plenty. The emperor Severus was a devotee and went so far as to associate himself with the deity. This may help to explain the existence of a temple of Serapis in the *colonia* at York, attested by a dedicatory inscription recording construction by the commander of the VI legion, virtually certainly in the years about AD 200 and thus within the reign of Severus and, possibly, during his residence at York. Further north, at the fort of Kirkby Thore in Cumbria, Serapis was linked with Jupiter on an altar, although this does not imply the existence of a temple here. A head of Serapis from Silchester is a better pointer to a shrine and once again the date may be Severan.

The cults worshipped in cities are not fully revealed to us, as the record of inscriptions from urban centres is limited. In the native centres an unadulterated acceptance of purely Roman cults was rare. The city itself might be represented, as at Silchester, by a Genius or Tutela with a mural crown. Also at Silchester there are traces of a cult of Mars, not necessarily a war-god in a Celtic setting. Hercules appears too, but equated with the Celtic Segomo. At Cirencester the famous and charming group of the Matres represents a cult of Celtic mother-goddesses, usually depicted in triplicate to indicate their power.

There are only a few signs of the wider diffusion of Roman deities as the provincials themselves became Roman citizens. Cirencester has yielded the base of a column to Jupiter Optimus Maximus, restored by a fourth-century governor who wished to pay homage to the 'old religion', quite probably in the face of an advancing Christianity. This monument type is particularly well known in the Rhineland. Chichester has produced an earlier dedication of similar type. This form of the cult of Jupiter is an interesting one, since it brings Britain into a north-western European circle of belief in a rider-god who trod down the powers of the Underworld under his feet and was early identified with Jupiter. Neptune and Minerva were honoured by a temple at Chichester, as patron deities of the manufacture and seaborne traffic of a guild of ironworkers, but this was exceptional by virtue of its early date and the rapid Romanization of the realm of Cogidubnus. Thoroughly classical statuettes of Mars (from the Foss Dyke and at Barkway), Mercury and Venus (at Verulamium), Bacchus (Spoonley Wood) and Jupiter (West Stoke, Sussex) suggest that the cults of such gods were more widespread than the roll of inscriptions and sculpture reveals. Alongside this evidence must be set the fact that Celtic cults were taken up by Roman officers. A transport officer to the governor of Britain dedicated a shrine to the Italian Matres, thus extending the power of those goddesses to his homeland.

It is tempting to suppose that native Celtic cults continued to attract worshippers without interruption until long after the conquest. Although there are numerous indications that Celtic deities retained their power, it is a far from easy matter to isolate and identify Celtic gods whose representation has been untouched by Roman conventions. There is a seeming abundance of evidence for Celtic cult and practice in the form of inscriptions, stone sculptures, bronze figurines and a variety of votive finds, but the great bulk of the evidence available to us is Roman in date and character; none of it can be safely back-projected into the Iron Age. There are other difficulties and limitations in distinguishing Celtic from Roman provincial in the sphere of religion. In certain fundamental matters Roman belief and practice sprang from the same Indo-European roots as the religion of the Celts and had not diverged greatly from that mainstream over several centuries. This is particularly true of the deities of nature and fertility and their sanctuaries. The native cults of Britain are thus accurately described as Romano-Celtic even when there is no obvious relationship between a Celtic and a Roman deity. *Interpretatio Romana* was frequently overt, as in the case of Sulis Minerva or Mars Lenus; but it could also operate in less obvious ways.

By no means all Celtic deities worshipped in Britain were confined to the island. Several were the subjects of widespread cults in western Europe, especially in Gaul. The Matres or Matronae, honoured in northern Gaul and the Rhineland, appear widely in Britain, both in towns and military bases. They most probably owed their introduction to Britain to auxiliary troops and traders, but it is certain that the cult of these protective maternal powers appealed to a wide spectrum of Romano-Britons precisely because they reflected a deep-seated human need. Another triad that linked Britain with Gaul and Germany was the *genii cucullati*, shown as hooded dwarf-like figures, occasionally in attendance on a mother-goddess. These, too, are found in the North, and in the West of the province, around Cirencester and Bath. At Bath their worship may be linked with the healing spring rather than the forces of fertility. The Celtic goddess Epona and her horses, another fertility deity with connections with the Underworld, is only occasionally represented in Britain and is yet another import from northern Gaul. Sucellus and his consort Nantosvelta, also with attributes suggesting fertility and prosperity, appear occasionally in Britain, perhaps introduced by immigrants from Gaul. The forces of the Underworld are represented by the stag-horned god Cernunnos, in a relief at Cirencester accompanied by two snakes with ram's horns, themselves chthonic creatures.

Celtic gods native to Britain are known in some numbers, but are often little more than names. One of the most influential was Nodens, not shown in human form but represented by the dog, another creature of the Underworld, most strikingly at the sanctuary at Lydney (Gloucestershire). At this healing shrine Nodens extended his care over those who sought his aid, assisted by his totem, a dog, as did Aesculapius in the Mediterranean world. Aside from gods of natural forces, it is no surprise that the Celts in Britain should have honoured gods of war and the virtues of fighting. Several native gods appear in this guise, including Belatucadrus and Cocidius on the western side of Hadrian's Wall, both of these identified with Mars. Mars Alator was worshipped at Barkway (Hertfordshire), Mars Ocellus at Caerwent. It may at first sight seem strange that the worship of native war-gods was permitted so freely. But Roman tolerance of native cults was very generous and in any case the virtues of the warrior were worth cultivating if they were turned to the service of Rome. Other Celtic deities are no more than names (Cuda at Daglingworth, Antenociticus at Benwell, Viridius at Ancaster) and were presumably usually the presiding spirits of places or natural features. Other gods and cults are revealed by sculpture and figurines. In eastern Britain between the Humber and the Thames there occur reliefs and figurines of an armed rider-god, occasionally shown in combat with a monster. The god is unnamed, but was evidently a force that conquered harmful powers. The forces of darkness again appear in a bronze showing a voracious wolf-like creature devouring a man, from the temple at Woodeaton.

Many Romano-British shrines were architecturally simple in plan, comprising a central square *cella*, lofty and tower-like, surrounded on all sides by a square or rectangular ambulatory. This Romano-Celtic temple type is found over much of Gaul and the German provinces and extended eastward to the Celtic lands on the middle Danube. Surviving examples in Gaul indicate that the *cella* might rise to a height of twenty metres, though most of the British structures were probably no more than half this in height. Although common in rural contexts, this form of shrine was also constructed in cities, as is clear at Verulamium, Caerwent and Silchester. Architectural embellishment was rare, though a few had porches or antechambers. But the larger examples must have been striking features in the landscape, the tall *cellae* being visible from some distance. Within, the altars, cult-images, offerings and other shrine-furniture would have created their own impression of sanctity and awe. The origins of the square Roman temple-plan lie in the pre-Roman Celtic world. In Britain, the most convincing instance of an Iron Age shrine is a building at Heathrow, west of London, which consists of a rectangular *cella* set within a rectangular enclosure or ambulatory. Other Iron Age shrines lie beneath later Roman buildings. This is the case at Hayling Island, where a circular Iron Age shrine was succeeded by a well-built masonry shrine in the later first century AD. In the later temple, even a soldier in the IX legion could record a dedication. The temple site at Lancing (Sussex) lay on a site of ancient sanctity reaching back a thousand years before the coming of Rome. At Farley Heath and Harlow, considerable quantities of Iron Age coins point to pre-Roman use of these sites, presumably at shrines or in sacred spaces such as groves, known to have played a significant part in Celtic rites. The structures of Iron Age shrines are otherwise poorly recorded, but pre-Roman buildings certainly existed at Frilford and at Worth (Kent).

Circular and polygonal temples also existed in Roman Britain. Some of these were modest structures, as at Brigstock and Colley Weston (Northamptonshire), but certain of the most ambitious buildings in the province fall into this broad category. The most striking examples are those at Weycock Hill (Berkshire), Nettleton (Wiltshire) and Pagan's Hill (Somerset). The superstructure of these buildings is not easily reconstructed, but the same basic relationship between *cella* and ambulatory was preserved. At Pagan's Hill the outer wall was buttressed, which should indicate that it was solid. Within, the *cella* was defined by a ring of columns, the plan recalling the architecture of mausolea. Weycock Hill was probably a similar structure, but it rested on a substantial podium.

One of the most intriguing temples in the province was the so-called Arthur's O'on, which stood, almost intact, 4 kilometres north of the Antonine Wall near Falkirk until it was demolished in 1743. Antiquarian drawings record a corbelled dome rising to a height of 7 metres above a circular base 8 metres in diameter.

Close analogies to Arthur's O'on are unknown. The high quality of its workmanship clearly points to construction by the army and its position strongly suggests some official purpose or occasion. It may well have been a temple which also served as a *tropaeum*, commemorating the victory of Lollius Urbicus that preceded the building of the Antonine Wall. Such a shrine might have been dedicated to Victory, or Victory linked with Mars, or the numen of the emperor.

Several shrines or groups of shrines lay deep in the countryside, remote from towns and roads. These are highly likely to have had social and economic, as well as religious, functions. At Woodeaton (Oxfordshire) the temple lay within a large walled *temenos* in which were found large numbers of votive objects and coins. A subsidiary, but important, role of such a site may have been as a fair or other assembly that drew the scattered population together. At a few places communal buildings were provided near the shrine. Frilford (Berkshire) boasted a theatre or small amphitheatre, much in the manner of the well-known rural sanctuaries of Gaul at such sites as Champlieu and Sanxay.

Several of the rural shrines of southern Britain were architecturally ambitious, and sumptuous in their internal decoration, but often only the plans of the building are left as evidence of devotion and heavy capital outlay. The elaborate octagonal temples at Weycock (Berkshire) and Pagan's Hill (Somerset), and the sanctuaries at Jordon's Hill (Dorset) and Woodeaton (Oxfordshire), have not afforded any precise indication of the deity worshipped in them. In some cases, however, there are hints of complexity that is not betrayed by the surviving relief sculpture. At Uley (Gloucestershire) for example, curse tablets are addressed both to Mars-Silvanus and to Mars-Mercury, while the bulk of small offerings, and a fine cult-statue, point to the worship of Mercury. It is thus unwise to attempt to identify the presiding deity or deities from a limited series of finds. The point is underlined by the finds from Lamyatt Beacon (Somerset). The relief sculpture indicates a cult of Mars, and this is supported by the deposition of votive weaponry. But finds of antlers hint at the worship of a fertility god, such as the Celtic Cernunnos, and further complications are introduced by brooches in the form of horsemen. It is highly likely that many visitors to Romano-Celtic shrines were not certain about the identity or concerns of the resident deities, hence the dedications to *dis cultoribus* ('to the gods who dwell here') or *sive deo sive deae* ('to the god or goddess').

Other sacred places of the Celts possessed no temples or other permanent structures. Greek and Roman writers were aware that the European Celts worshipped in groves or woods sanctified by the presence of gods; certain place-names in Britain reveal the existence of such sanctuaries in the island by the inclusion of the element *nemeton*, meaning 'sacred grove'. Vernemetum on the Fosse Way in Leicestershire is one such name; Aquae Arnemetiae (Buxton) is another. But the most interesting, and enduring, of the *nemeton* names are found in central Devon, where several villages and hamlets still preserve the memory of a major Celtic holy place: e.g. Nymet Rowland, Broadnymet, King's Nympton. The broad spread of these place-names should mean that a sizeable area was held in reverence, possibly about the confluence of the rivers Mole and Taw, rather than a single spot. But what is particularly striking about the Devon *nemeton* is that memory of its name was preserved throughout the Roman centuries and down to the present day.

By far the grandest religious complex lay, not in a major city, but at the small town of Aquae Sulis (Bath), the site of a famous hot spring, already known and perhaps revered by the Iron Age inhabitants of the region. The presiding deity was Sulis, with whom Minerva was associated, apparently at an early date. Although often described as a spa, Aquae Sulis was first and foremost a religous centre, the residence of a healing deity to whom many visitors had recourse, some of them from far away. Like Aachen and Baden-Baden in the German provinces, Bath was visited by soldiers and veterans from the provincial army, perhaps in some cases for rest and recuperation after strenuous service. The buildings established on the site were magnificent, among the finest that are known in Roman Britain. A fine Classical temple dominated the centre of the town, confronted it may be by a theatre, now beneath Bath Abbey. The first form of the temple is strikingly early in date, of the late sixties or early seventies AD, at which date also the spring within the temple precinct was enclosed by a polygonal reservoir. The great suite of baths fed by the spring was an imposing structure, though simple in plan, recalling legionary *thermae* of the period and thus hinting at the employment of military engineers. Some of the craftsmen, however, came not from the legions but from northern Gaul, as is revealed by the sculpted ornament. The place is rich in sculpture, altars and offerings. The splendidly restrained and serene bust of Minerva in gilded bronze, probably the main cult-image, was found by chance in the eighteenth century. Recent excavation of the pool has yielded up a rich collection of coins and small items thrown in by worshippers; one of the least expected objects is part of a ballista (siege catapult). The finest piece of sculpture came from the pediment of the temple: a male water-god endowed with the qualities of Medusa, flanked by Tritons. Few other sculptures in Roman Britain approach the vigour and power of the Bath pediment.

The other sacred spring-cum-spa was Aquae Arnemetiae (Buxton) in the Peak District. There is all too little evidence of the Roman structures here, though there is a reliable statement that lead-lined baths, associated with Roman buildings, were seen here in the late seventeenth century and further remains a century later, all close to St Anne's Well. St Anne herself may, indeed, be the Christian version of Arnemetia, the patron goddess of the spring, whose Celtic name means 'she who dwells near the sacred grove (*nemeton*)'. Like Bath, the site had been under military occupation in its early days, when its tepid waters were presumably first observed. But unlike Bath it always remained on the fringe of the military area, in this resembling such places as Aquae Mattiacorum (Wiesbaden) and Aquae Granni (Aachen), which lay immediately behind the military zone of Roman Germany. The social pleasures of such places counted for at least as much as their religious and curative qualities, and they were pleasant resorts for soldiers and officials on leave or civilians on holiday.

The civilian world had its regulated and calendared observances, but these are obscured both by lack of direct evidence and by the large number of private, sporadic and occasional dedications. The military world also displays an abundance of dedications of the latter class, but there was so large a number of regiments, each with its official cults, that the chance of survival is greater and the picture so much the more complete. In Britain the class of soldiery about whose worship there is the least evidence is that of the legionaries, quartered for most of the period at the three great fortresses, Caerleon, Chester and York. Between them these fortresses afford a fleeting glimpse of official religion. A dedication to the legionary standards at Chester and the fragmentary doorposts of a subsidiary shrine in the administrative offices of the headquarters at Caerleon are almost all that remain of the wealth of official dedications that such buildings elsewhere have produced in more favourable conditions. A rich altar dedicated by a *tribunus militum* to the *genius loci* for the safety and welfare of two emperors in the early third century, a clerk's dedication to Minerva and a senior centurion's altar to Jupiter Tanarus are the outstanding individual dedications from Chester, and the York fortress yields no better results. Only at sites where legionaries are out-stationed do reflections of the cults of their bases appear. At Corbridge, for example, the elaborate furnishings of a third-century headquarters commemorate, first, the standard of the detachment, with a decorative reference to the public festival of the Rosaliae, when the standards were garlanded with roses for worship, and secondly, the worship of Hercules, which was inextricably connected with the cult of the Emperor and the duties and labours of his army. Statues of the Capitoline deities, a remarkable decorative panel and pediment from a shrine of Dea Roma, and also statues of the genius or guardian deity who presided over the individual unit or its station have survived. At Newstead a centurion commanding a detachment in garrison dedicated in the headquarters an altar to Jupiter Optimus Maximus, the god who had so successfully guided the destiny of Rome for centuries. An out-stationed soldier on special duties at Dorchester-on-Thames dedicated an altar and the screens round it to the same god, reverenced in the office or post of which he had charge. The eagle of Jupiter crowned the legionary standard and so often crowned it with Victory. The goddess Victoria thus came to be associated with each legion, and a silver arm, torn from a half-scale statue of the Victory of the VI Legion at York, found far from its shrine in Lancashire, demonstrates how costly the more portable offerings might be. Amid this array of official deities, the emperors had their place, both on the decorative plaques of the standards and in the regimental shrine, where the statue of the reigning emperor occupied a prominent position.

The auxiliary regiments, recruited from non-Roman provincials for the most part, provide in Britain a wider field. Their regimental shrines apparently did not house dedications to Jupiter, but contained altars to the guardian deity of the emperor and of the regimental standards, or to the emperor's discipline, 'the Empire's strongest bond', as a Roman once called it. Most of them contained a life-sized statue of the reigning emperor, of which fragments have occasionally been found, as at Carvoran, or its great base, as at Bewcastle. When emperors multiplied, as in the fourth century, their statues might have to be placed at the approach to the sanctuary, as at Risingham or Brough-by-Bainbridge, or the shrine itself might be enlarged, as at Corbridge. In addition there were the standards to be housed, and in order that the chapels might display effectively all that they contained they were often equipped with raised platforms (*suggestus*) inside and open fronts marked by low decorative screens behind which the holy things might be seen.

But if Jupiter found no place in the regimental shrine, he and the appropriate associated deities had their recognized place upon the parade-ground, where the commander of the regiment, acting on its behalf and in its presence, took the annual vows for the welfare and safety of the State on the first day of January and for the Empire and emperor two days later. Here, year-in year-out, new altars to Jupiter Optimus Maximus, the guardian deity of the Roman State, were erected and the old ones solemnly and reverently buried below ground. Few of these buried groups of altars have been discovered, for even in Roman times they left no indication of their presence above ground. But a remarkable group from Maryport (Alauna, in Cumbria) and chance finds at Birdoswald belong to this category, and other groups may still await discovery at other forts. The Maryport series, though manifestly incomplete, forms an excellent representative example and deserves brief description. The most numerous class is formed by dedications to Jupiter Optimus Maximus, plainly representing the annual vows and offered both by the commander personally and by the unit corporately. Normally Jupiter holds the field alone, but he is occasionally and significantly coupled with the Augustan numen both by commander and regiment. One commander dedicated a building or a tribunal, a parade-ground platform, to Jupiter Capitolinus for the welfare of Antoninus Pius. The repetition of dedications and dedicators, related to the annual renewal of vows, is frequent; five officers recur three or four times upon different stones, and the units dedicating corporately are repeated many times also. In addition to the altars of Jupiter, there are altars to Mars, with the highly significant qualification of *Militaris*, to distinguish him from non-military types of this god. Victoria Augusta (Imperial Victory) is another complementary dedication of which a duplicate is extant. Plainly the series is incomplete, but it gives a highly interesting and important picture of the annual ceremonies. A vivid literary record of the same thing is furnished by the so-called *Feriale Duranum*, a calendar of official festivals (*feriae*) of the Twentieth Cohort of Palmyrenes from Dura Europos on the Euphrates, dated to soon after AD 225. The altars belong to a special occasion, but the calendar reveals how every week brought its own religious celebrations that it was the duty of the regiment to observe and that linked its traditions with the public worship of the Roman State. That other festivals not covered by the surviving portions of the *Feriale* were duly kept is shown by the Papcastle (Derventio, Cumbria) dedication dated 19 October, the *Armilustrium*. The third-century altar from Housesteads, set up to 'gods and goddesses according to the interpretation of the oracle of the Clarian Apollo', is a particularly interesting case, in which an oracular instruction was implemented by Imperial order throughout the whole Empire.

The parade-grounds themselves leave little visible trace except on hilly sites, where they happen to be cut and levelled. A fine example of this kind occurs at Hardknott (Cumbria) and another at Tomen-y-mur (Gwynedd), while that at Maryport itself was destroyed in the nineteenth century. All were levelled areas, about 100 metres square, suitable either for squad drill or a general parade. Traces of a tribunal in the centre of one side have been noted at Hardknott and Maryport. They had their own deities, the Campestres, mother-goddesses in origin and no doubt imported by the Celtic regiments. The Campestres are normally associated with cavalry. At Benwell (Condercum) they were worshipped together with the *genius alae*. There must also be reckoned the deities disturbed by the reconstruction of a deserted fort, as at Newstead, where Diana and Silvanus, patrons of the wild who had taken temporary possession of the site, were honoured by the commander of the new garrison. Sometimes an officer arriving in a new land would dedicate personally a whole series of altars to deities of local significance, as did the centurion M. Cocceius Firmus at Auchendavy on the Antonine Wall, who included an offering to the genius of the British land. Such personal dedication might also be made on completion of a term of office.

Within the fortress or fort most buildings had their presiding deity or genius. The commander in his own house worshipped the *genius praetorii* among the household gods (*lares*); a Greek tablet at York mentions the gods of the governor's *praetorium*. The military clerks, working in the unit's record-office, or the pay-clerks in the regimental bank, erected altars to Minerva. Each of the *centuriae* into which an infantry regiment was divided, or each *turma* of a cavalry unit, had its genius presiding over the barrack-block, a deity sometimes rendered in classical convention and sometimes descending to a comfortable everyday level. In the stables, Epona, a Celtic horse goddess, might find her place, as at Carvoran. The fort bathhouse came within the purview of Fortuna, because naked man was particularly vulnerable to the powers of evil and required protection, but also because she might be invoked during games of chance played in the communal rooms. Sometimes this Fortuna is called Augusta, at other times Conservatrix, always with the intention of emphasizing her power. At Birdoswald she is portrayed in person, graciously enthroned, with her particular emblems or attributes at her feet.

Outside the fort and beyond the range of the parade-ground an auxiliary unit might worship collectively the gods of its homeland, brought with it from overseas. At Vinovia (Binchester,

County Durham) the *ala Vettonum* from north-east Spain was worshipping the Matres Ollototae *sive transmarinae*, a slightly inaccurate interpretation of the Celtic word, which actually means 'of the foreigners'. A famous case is that of the Tungrians at Blatobulgium (Birrens, Dumfries), who brought with them from eastern Belgium their god Mercury and their goddesses Viradechthis and Harimella. The Dea Hammia, brought to Carvoran by Syrian archers, is another case, matched by Virgo Caelestis or Dea Syria, to whom a famous metrical hymn was dedicated by the commander of the garrison. Mogons was introduced from the middle Rhine by the Vangiones at Risingham, the Matres Alateivae from the lower Rhine by Gallo-Germans at Cramond. Apollo Anextlomarus from eastern Gaul appears at South Shields and the Gallic god of Victory with his storks at Chesterholm and Risingham. Other important introductions of the same kind were effected in northern Britain during the third century by the irregular levies from the Germanic fringes of the Empire. The Frisians from beyond the lower Rhine in Holland brought to Housesteads Mars Thincsus and his attendant female godlings, the Alaisiagae, four of whose names, each more outlandish than the last, are preserved. A second irregular unit, the *numerus Hnaudifridi*, called after its native chief, also participated in the cult. But whatever may be thought of the names of deities and dedicators, the barbarisms are purged when representations are required. Thincsus emerges as Mars in armour, with attendant goose, while amorino-like figures with wreaths and palms hover like Victories, though unlike Victory, they remain naked; similarly, the dedications are in Latin. The education in Roman ways and Roman equivalents that would eventually turn these folk or their sons into Roman citizens had thus begun. At Longovicium (Lanchester, County Durham) the Suebi were worshipping their goddess Garmangabis. The Germans at Voreda (Old Penrith, Cumbria) imported the Unseni Fersomari, perhaps the most uncouth-sounding group that has been recorded. This permission to outlanders to retain their homeland cults has sometimes been interpreted as barbarization of Roman religion; but the *interpretatio Romana* by which barbarian cults were accepted, formulated and shaped to Roman convention is no less important. So also is the frequent association of the dedications with the Augustan numen, stressing an Imperial loyalty. It was a Roman Empire and a Roman pantheon in which these deities took their place. How long such transplants survived in their new homes is unknown.

A more ambiguous northern cult, associated with both the army and civilians, has left numerous dedications in the central and western areas of the Hadrian's Wall zone. The name of the deity concerned is variously spelt and seems to have started as something like Hvitir; but it ends often as a plural in the form Vitires or Vetires, so that the dedicators might be thought to have intended their humble altars, none of which bears a sculpted relief, for the *di veteres*, 'the old gods'. Hvitir, with its initial aspirate, suggests a German origin and this is not forbidden by the equation at Netherby with Hercules or with Mogons. But to link the cult with German irregular troops would be rash without further evidence.

The spread and penetration of Christianity in Romano-British society are very difficult to assess. Written references to British bishops attending the councils of Arles (AD 314), Nicaea (AD 325), Sardica (AD 343) and Ariminum (AD 349) are sufficient proof of an organized Church, but its material remains are relatively slight, although in some cases of striking interest. The scarcity of urban churches is notable, only the small building near the centre of Silchester having claims that most would accept as strong, if not overwhelming. If it was indeed the principal church in the fourth-century city, then its small size is telling, for it can have housed scarcely more than forty worshippers at a time. Elsewhere, older secular buildings may, of course, have been converted into churches in the reign of Constantine, but if so no material evidence proclaims their new function. Cemetery churches and *cellae memoriae* will certainly have existed, as in Gaul and Germany, and a building within a late Roman cemetery at Icklingham (Suffolk) may fall into the former category. A *cella memoriae* may be confidently expected at St Albans, burial-place of the most distinguished British martyr. Burials are known here, beneath the medieval minster, but as yet no structure of late-Roman date has been located. A *baptisterium* of a type well known in Gaul lies within the walls of the Saxon Shore fort at Richborough, close to the masonry piers of a substantial structure that was apparently a late addition to the fort. This may be a church, but final proof seems unattainable.

More convincing as a Christian building is a basilica set within a late-Roman cemetery outside the walls of Camulodunum and apparently contemporary with the burials. This looks more like a cemetery-church on the Gaulish model than anything else yet recorded in Britain.

House-churches or private chapels in wealthy rural residences reveal themselves less ambiguously. The most famous is the chamber in the villa at Lullingstone (Kent) decorated with fine wall-paintings depicting *orantes*, early Christian figures in an attitude of prayer. The fine mosaic from Frampton (Dorset) with the Chi-Rho monogram embodied in the design and the still finer contemporary mosaic from Hinton St Mary in the same county, displaying in its central roundel a calm-featured portrait of a young man, are reminders that leading members of the *curiales* will, many of them, have embraced the new faith with no more or less fervour than members of the Imperial court, and for similar reasons. Among objects certainly to be associated with Christian observance the most striking are the mainly silver vessels and mounts that comprised the hoard found at Durobrivae. This is without doubt a cache of church plate, the earliest by far known from any part of the Roman Empire. Aside from its early date, fourth century and probably no later than 350, one of the less predictable features of the treasure are the Eastern resonances of the inscriptions on two of the vessels. The contacts of Romano-British Christian communities may thus have been much wider than is commonly assumed. Christian symbols or formulae on portable objects, or graffiti on structures, prove little more than the existence of an atmosphere or climate not unfavourable to the religion adopted by emperors and thus can tell us nothing about the extent of Christian observance.

It is difficult to believe that a majority of the inhabitants of Britain had embraced Christianity, even by the late fourth century, and just as compelling as the evidence for the Christian faith in the more affluent social groups are the indications of active paganism in the final decades of the province. At least fifteen pagan shrines still had their devotees in the later fourth century. Most of these were in rural locations, several lying on hilltops within old hill-forts, as at Maiden Castle, Lydney, Chanctonbury Ring and Uley. To judge from the coin finds, several of these late shrines, including Woodeaton, Frilford, Lamyatt Beacon, Brean Down and Cold Kitchen Hill, continued to attract worshippers down to the early fifth century, if not later. There are other clear signs of adherence to pagan cults at this late date. A hoard of gold and silver objects found at Thetford (Norfolk), buried between 375 and 400, contained silver spoons bearing the name of the Italian deity Faunus, a rare appearance of this god in the West. This collection of fine objects indicates the persistence of a local pagan cult down to the time when, in the reign of Theodosius, pagan shrines were being closed down and their ceremonies declared illegal.

Many of the western cults so far described were at a stage in which worship took the form of corporate vows rather than individual allegiances. The eastern cults had a more developed basis of appeal and called for greater individual response. One of the most popular, especially in higher social circles, was that of Jupiter Dolichenus, the god of Doliche whose high seat was in Syria Commagene, and who, with his consort Juno Regina, made animal creation his footstool and the firmament of heaven his kingdom. He required for his worship a special form of temple, the Eastern house-type with many rooms, of which the existence in Britain is attested by various inscriptions. No British example has, however, yet been identified on the ground and excavated, although a fine sculptured frieze from such a building exists at Corbridge. His orders and advice were interpreted by the priest in charge of the temple, and it was no doubt his capacity to furnish responses to the perplexed that won for Dolichenus his popularity. To the army his appeal was also that of a powerful war-god and a great worker in iron for the sinews of war. In Britain his worship first occurred in the mid second century, reaching a peak in the third. For a few years, indeed, the Emperor Alexander Severus (AD 222–35) and his Empress-Mother Julia Mamaea were actually identified with Dolichenus

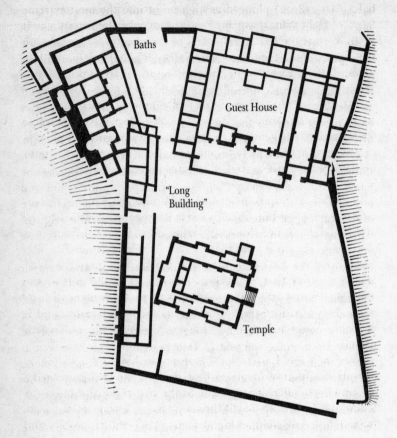

Fig. 4. Lydney religious site

and his consort and worshipped in that guise in regimental headquarters, of which a relic seems to exist in a statue at Chesters. Less popular in the West was the cult of Jupiter Heliopolitanus, whose mighty temple at Heliopolis (Baalbek) still proclaims the wealth and influence of the cult in the Syrian world to which it belonged. There is no doubt that the Roman world was disgusted by the zeal with which the Syrian-born Emperor Elagabalus (AD 218–22) plunged as high priest into the most extreme forms of Heliopolitan worship, and this may be the reason why it failed to rival the less orgiastic cult of Dolichenus. Sometimes, on the other hand, the direct association of an emperor with a particular cult seems to be the sole reason for its appearance in Britain. The connection of Severus with Serapis is the likeliest explanation of the occurrence of a temple at York and of a Kirkby Thore (Cumbria) dedication. It is certainly responsible for a Castlesteads gem, which shows him in this guise. A parallel case is the compliment to his empress, Julia Domna, as Caelestis by the inclusion of this epithet, in word and representation, in the personification of Brigantia.

But it was a mistaken identification with the Emperor Commodus and the public obliteration of his memory that led to the mutilation of a fine legionary dedication to Sol Invictus, at Corbridge, set up in AD 162–3. This form of sun-worship also came from the East but is rare in Britain, except when later associated with that of Mithras. Rarer still is the cult of the Tyrian Hercules and his consort Astarte at Corbridge, with its altars dedicated in Greek. This was served by a priestess and is probably connected with the known presence here of Eastern traders.

None of these Eastern cults appears to have been so highly organized as that of Mithras, the god of Persian and Zoroastrian origin whose cult reached Rome in the first century BC and the Rhineland before AD 100. Mithras was a god who exacted from the individual worshipper high standards of conduct, probity and courage, in exchange for ultimate revelation and union. Knowledge of the mysteries, with their sacred symbolism, precepts and ritual food and drink, was attained by grades of initiation, in which physical and psychological ordeals were included. For these reasons the cult was secret and it excluded women. It can be well understood how its tenets might appeal to a good soldier or an upright merchant; but to suppose that it had a wide appeal would be wrong. It asked too much effort, both spiritual and intellectual, in a climate where little was required. Dedications to Mithras were habitually made by officers and frequently by commanders, while in the military area the temples to the god were so small that they can never have held more than a dozen or, at most, a score of worshippers. The only temple yet known for certain in a city is the fine example in London, where a legionary veteran occurs among the wealthy merchant worshippers, whose means and taste impelled them to import splendid sculptures from the Greek Mediterranean. Wherever they were erected, the temples always conformed to a standard type, in which the essential elements were the sanctuary, a long narrow nave flanked by single low solid benches facing out into it and an outer room screened off from the nave. The interior was normally shrouded in darkness, as befitted a deity born in a cave. Some of his continental shrines were contained within natural caves. The heyday of the cult in the western provinces was undoubtedly the third and early fourth centuries and it is to this period that the excavated examples on Hadrian's Wall and in Wales belong. Four have been excavated in the military zone, at Caernarvon, Housesteads, Carrawburgh and Rudchester, the last being the largest and Carrawburgh the best-preserved. Interesting points emerge from comparisons between these buildings. At Rudchester and Carrawburgh the dedications were made by commanders of the regiment, who either introduced the cult or acted as its chief ministrants. At Housesteads the dedicators were a legionary centurion and a legionary seconded to special duties by the governor. It is evident that there was no long or regular succession of men capable of organizing the elaborate ritual, and both at Carrawburgh and at Housesteads there were indications of intermittent use of the building divided by periods of abandonment, when it was deserted but in no sense desecrated. The three temples on Hadrian's Wall suffered destruction late in the third century or early in the fourth, the desecration of Carrawburgh being evidently deliberate, the site being thereafter used as a rubbish dump for animal refuse. This looks like the work of a Christian commandant; for certain aspects of Mithraism, and especially the ritual meal, were regarded by Christians as a diabolical mockery of the Christian sacraments.

The different aspects of the cult are worth note. At Rudchester the accent is upon the sun-god who was the companion and advisor of Mithras, except on one altar, of which the sculpted reliefs refer to two of the different grades. At Carrawburgh the emphasis is upon Mithras himself. In one period of use, stress was also placed upon initiation by ordeal, a cist for temporary entombment being provided. Revelation was later stressed and a remarkable altar depicts the god as he is described in an Egyptian liturgy at the moment of his manifestation in glory, his sun-ray crown being pierced for illumination from behind. Comparable use of a sudden lighting effect was made at Housesteads, where Mithras is given the title *saecularis* and is so portrayed, as lord of ages, in a pierced background of radiance enclosed by the signs of the Zodiac. It is possible that the different representational emphasis corresponds to differences in ritual, but in all the shrines, Mithras and his two attendant gods of light and dark, Cautes and Cautopates, are present, and at both Carrawburgh and Housesteads there is evidence for the existence of the central bull-killing relief, representing the conquest of wild nature by Mithras and his release of the vital forces from which sprang the good things of the earth. Whatever the variations in emphasis or presentation, it seems certain that the central tenets remained the same. One widespread misconception about the ritual should be removed. Although Mithras slew the bull to release the vital power of the blood, his worshippers neither bathed nor were baptized in it. There is no evidence whatever for this practice, which belonged to the worship not of Mithras but of Cybele.

So complicated a ritual and theology explains why the cult of Mithras appealed to few, yet its personal appeal secured those few, often influential, initiates at many points. In addition to the three known temples, there is further evidence for the cult on or near Hadrian's Wall at Castlesteads, Carlisle, Newcastle, Wallsend and High Rochester, while the legionary fortresses at York, Chester and Caerleon have also yielded evidence for the cult and almost certainly had temples for it. The London *mithraeum*, with its numerous associated deities and magnificent furnishings, is linked with Eastern merchants of some substance as well as with a veteran, perhaps from the garrison of the provincial capital, quartered in the north-west, or Cripplegate quarter of the Roman city. The London temple is the earliest to Mithras so far known in Britain, dating from the late second century.

Of other mystery religions there is little trace in military contexts, though Corbridge has yielded some fragments of sculpture suggestive of the worship of Cybele. Here, as in the cult of Hercules and Astarte, such dedications may be due to immigrant traders rather than to military men. Christianity has yielded virtually no trace among the ranks of the army at all, though a Gnostic gem from a signet ring at Castlesteads may suggest the existence of a stray eclectic believer, just as there will have been stray Christians.

Other cults and mysteries are more surprising visitors to Britain. In the fourth century the owner of the villa at Brading on the Isle of Wight had an interest in the ideas of Gnosticism, a theosophical cult which had parted company with Christianity in the second century, but which still retained a belief in the revelation of hidden knowledge and in the redemption of the soul. The mosaic floors in the Brading villa reveal an astonishing series of mythological scenes, in which images of redemption and security provided by the gods are set against images of rejection and flight. Who was responsible for introducing these ideas into Britain must remain as mysterious as the images themselves, but there is no doubt that he came from some distance, quite possibly in the service of the emperor. There may, perhaps, be a deliberate emphasis in the Brading mosaics on pagan myth at the very time when active defence of paganism was needed and this may be reflected in other fourth-century mosaics in Britain, including the pavement showing the Dido and Aeneas legend at Low Ham (Somerset) and the Orpheus and Apollo design in the cult-room at Littlecote (Wiltshire).

These are brief but precious glimpses of the intellectual life of Roman Britain in its latter days. Yet another is afforded by one of the finest works of art to have come from Roman Britain, the lanx, or rectangular dish, found in the Tyne near Corbridge in 1735 and almost certainly part of a sizeable hoard. This was a picture-dish intended for display and of a quality which marks it as a product of a Mediterranean workshop. Its scenes contain a wealth of references to the worship of Apollo and related cults on the island of Delos, the scene of a famous sacrifice by the apostate emperor Julian. It is not beyond all possibility that the Corbridge lanx not only dates to Julian's brief reign but also refers to his visit to Delos *en route* to his Persian campaign and death.

The use of magic to summon aid from the infernal powers, or to placate them, was widespread in the Roman world and is well represented in Britain, in the form of apotropaic amulets and, above all, of curse tablets, inscribed sheets of lead which were consigned to the ground or to water, carrying to the powers below imprecations on others for offences or injuries received. Some curses were not specific, merely naming a person or persons, but others were occasioned by particular acts, such as thefts, crossings in love, insults, abductions and assaults. A fascinating series of 130 lead curse tablets has been recovered from the sacred spring at Bath, one of the largest groups yet recorded in the entire Roman Empire. More than half of the Bath curses were responses to the theft of such items as cloaks, blankets, bathing dresses, rings, bracelets, gloves, money and a ploughshare. Of the rest, many are lists of names of people against whom the aid of the presiding god was invoked. A few, however, were more sophisticated. One is a sanction against perjury, accompanying a solemn oath sworn at the sacred spring on a particular day by a number of people. Anyone who had committed perjury on that occasion would pay for the offence to the goddess Sulis.

The religious life of the province was thus remarkably diverse, but from the Roman point of view there was rationality in the diversity. In Roman eyes the most important worship was that by the citizen body, corporately and individually. One of the reasons given for the extension of the citizenship in 213, not entirely cynically, was that there should thus be created more citizens to worship the gods, to whom the welfare and salvation of the State was due. While the evidence for regular calendared observances by Roman citizens in the British *coloniae* is weak, it is not absent; there is enough to make it certain that the requirements were regularly followed. The army, on the other hand, presents a strikingly orderly picture and its most remarkable side is not so much the Roman citizen army, of the legions, but the army of the auxiliary troops. While these men were not Roman citizens, they had nevertheless taken an oath of loyalty to emperor and State, and their commanders were educated and wealthy

Roman citizens. Such units worshipped the Roman military gods corporately on the parade-ground, and annual vows were paid both by the unit and by its commandant. But the matter did not end there: the military gods had their special festivals throughout the year, while members of the Imperial House, living and deified, were similarly honoured. All these feasts were fully and regularly observed, together with the more purely military functions, like the *Rosaliae signorum* or the *armilustrium*. The troops could not take their part in such festivals without learning something of what they meant, either by observation or such actual instruction as might come from an intelligent commander, with the effect that slowly but surely these conscripts from frontier lands, and increasingly from Britain itself, learnt the import of Roman religion and felt their way towards conscious and responsible membership of the Roman State. Until AD 213 Roman citizenship was granted to them on retirement after their twenty-five years' service: after then, if they were born free within the Empire, it was theirs already and, although the old outward forms which distinguished the traditions of such regiments from those of the legions seem to have survived, they would take part in their traditional calendared festivals with a sense of still more immediate relevance.

The arrangements made for levies from the borders of the Empire or beyond, who supplemented the auxiliaries from the second century onwards, are less evident. It is clear that these troops were permitted to establish their own native cults and that the dedications of such cults were usually coupled with vows to the Augustan numen. Roman loyalties were thus linked to memories of the homeland from the first. But it cannot be doubted that such troops also shared in at least the annual vows and the logical course would certainly have been to associate them, however distantly, with the general run of important festivals. They were destined ultimately to become citizens of the Empire and the sole question would be how rapidly understanding and sympathy in relation to its cults might be induced. It may well be that the first generation of men in such levies did not progress far beyond expressions of loyalty to the Imperial House. But in addition to this, it is important to observe how a Roman guise or interpretation is accorded to their native deities from the first, for this is in reality another and perhaps more subtle way of educating the worshipper.

Through the association of their own cults with the expression of reverence for the emperor's numen the imported levies were in fact brought into line with the natives of the province in general. It is clear that the opportunity of combining worship with a declaration of loyalty was regularly taken by provincials and it may be presumed that it was expected of them. Otherwise there was evidently a wide diversity of cults, many of them harking back to pre-Roman days. It is difficult, however, to estimate whether such deities as the Matres were indigenous to the province or whether they were introduced to Britain by Gauls during the Roman occupation. If such imports are eliminated, then the cults of Roman Britain would appear to be considerably more localized than those of Gaul, or at least there is an absence of generally worshipped deities. This may well be true, for it would reflect the notable lack of political cohesion and cultural unity which permitted so rapid an acquisition of the province in the first place, and defeated the first attempt to introduce a religious focus of loyalty at Camulodunum.

Bibliography

GENERAL

General works on Roman Britain are now legion and only a short
selection is given here.

The two best full-scale histories of the province are S. S. Frere's
Britannia. A History of Roman Britain (3rd edn, 1987) and P. Salway's
Roman Britain (1981). An excellent illustrated treatment is Salway's
Oxford Illustrated History of Roman Britain (1993). A compact history is M.
Todd, *Roman Britain* (5th imp. 1993) and a survey of the past thirty
years' work is contained in M. Todd (ed.), *Research on Roman Britain
1960–1989* (1989). The geography and structure of Roman Britain is
covered by the Ordnance Survey's *Map of Roman Britain* (4th edn 1978)
and by A. L. F. Rivet and C. Smith, *The Place-Names of Roman Britain*
(1979). An invaluable guide to political geography, though now requiring revision, is Rivet's *Town and Country in Roman Britain* (2nd edn 1963).
A conspectus of the archaeological evidence is offered by R. G. Collingwood & I. A. Richmond, *The Archaeology of Roman Britain* (2nd edn
1969), though this is increasingly out of date. Inscriptions, a vital source
of information on many subjects, are collected in R. G. Collingwood and
R. P. Wright, *The Roman Inscriptions of Britain I* (1965); *II* (1990) – later
parts of *II* are edited by S. S. Frere and R. S. O. Tomlin. An essential
study of the holders of official posts is A. R. Birley, *The Fasti of Roman
Britain* (1981). The same author's *The People of Roman Britain* (1979) is a
fascinating account of the provincial population. M. Millett's *The Romani-
sation of Roman Britain* (1990) is a provocative view of a complex subject.
L. Allason-Jones' *Women in Roman Britain* (1989) is an excellent short
study of a neglected subject. The Roman army in Britain lacks a
comprehensive treatment. P. Holder, *The Roman Army in Britain* (1982)
provides an introduction. On art, two works by J. M. C. Toynbee are
fundamental: *Art in Roman Britain* (1963) and *Art in Britain under the
Romans* (1965). I. D. Margary's *Roman Roads in Britain* (3rd edn 1973) is
important on the infrastructure of the province. S. S. Frere and J. K. St
Joseph, *Roman Britain from the Air* (1983) is highly informative on the
topography of many sites.

BRITAIN BEFORE THE CONQUEST

Basic on the environmental background is M. Jones, *England before Domesday* (1986). Iron Age cultures are fully discussed in B. Cunliffe, *Iron Age Communities in Britain* (3rd edn 1991) and D. W. Harding, *The Iron Age in Lowland Britain* (1974). A contentious view of *oppida* is presented by J. Collis, *Oppida. Earliest Towns north of the Alps* (1984). Among many major site-excavations, the following are of particular note: B. Cunliffe, *Danebury. An Iron Age Hill-fort in Hampshire. Excavations 1969–78* [1984]; B. Cunliffe and C. Poole, *Danebury ... The Excavations 1979–88* (1991); B. Cunliffe, *Hengistbury Head, Dorset. The Prehistoric and Roman Settlement* (1987); C. F. C. Hawkes & M. R. Hull, *Camulodunum* (1947); R. E. M. Wheeler, *Maiden Castle, Dorset* (1943); E. M. Clifford, *Bagendon: a Belgic Oppidum* (1961); G. J. Wainwright, *Gussage All Saints. An Iron Age settlement in Dorset* (1979); G. Bersu, ('Excavations at Little Woodbury...'), (*Proceedings of the Prehistoric Society* 6 (1940), 30–111; C. Partridge, *Skeleton Green* (1981). I. M. Stead, *The Arras Culture* (1979) is an invaluable regional study. A. L. F. Rivet (ed.), *The Iron Age in Northern Britain* (1966) contains several important studies on Scotland. On Caesar's invasions, C. F. C. Hawkes, 'Britain and Julius Caesar', *Proceedings of the British Academy* 63 (1977), 125–92 is challenging. S. Macready & F. H. Thompson (eds.), *Cross-Channel Trade between Gaul and Britain in the pre-Roman Iron Age* contains several important studies. Full treatments of their subjects are S. Piggott, *The Druids* (1968) and C. Fox, *Pattern and Purpose. A survey of Early Celtic Art in Britain* (1958).

MILITARY HISTORY

Numerous sites throw light on the period immediately following the invasion, among them: B. Cunliffe, *Richborough V* (1968); I. A. Richmond, *Hod Hill II* (1968); B. Cunliffe, *Excavations at Fishbourne, 1961–69* (1971); J. Wacher and A. MacWhirr, *Early Roman Occupation at Cirencester* (1982); H. R. Hurst, *Kingsholm* (1985); S. S. Frere & J. K. St Joseph, 'The Roman Fortress at Longthorpe', *Britannia* 5 (1974), 1–129; W. H. Manning, *Usk. The Fortress Excavations, 1968–71* (1981). The events surrounding the great revolt of AD 60 are discussed in G. Webster, *Boudica* (1978). The occupation of the North is covered by a multitude of works, including: W. S. Hanson, *Agricola and the Conquest of the North* (1987);.

G. S. Maxwell, *The Romans in Scotland* (1989); O. G. S. Crawford, *Topography of Roman Scotland north of the Antonine Wall* (1949); L. F. Pitts and J. K. St Joseph, *Inchtuthil: the Roman Legionary Fortress* (1985); J. Curle, *A Roman Frontier Post and its People: the Fort of Newstead in the Parish of Melrose* (1911); I. A. Richmond & J. McIntyre, 'The Agricolan Fort at Fendoch', *Proceedings of the Society of Antiquaries of Scotland* 73 (1938/9), 110–54; G. S. Maxwell, 'New Frontiers: the Roman fort at Doune and its possible significance', *Britannia* 15 (1984), 217–23. Early studies of Roman works in the North are still invaluable, e.g. A. Gordon, *Itinerarium Septentrionale* (1726) and W. Roy, *Military Antiquities of the Romans in North Britain* (1793). For Wales, V. E. Nash-Williams, *The Roman Frontier in Wales* (2nd edn 1969). One first-century fort has been completely excavated: A. H. A. Hogg, 'Pen Llystyn. A Roman Fort and Other Remains', *Archaeological Journal* 125 (1969), 101–92.

The northern frontiers are well served by general works, notably Ordnance Survey, *Map of Hadrian's Wall* (2nd edn 1975); D. J. Breeze and B. Dobson, *Hadrian's Wall* (1976); D. J. Breeze, *The Northern Frontiers of Roman Britain* (1982); C. E. Stevens, *The Building of Hadrian's Wall* (1966); E. Birley, *Research on Hadrian's Wall* (1961). On the native population in the frontier regions: I. A. Richmond (ed.), *Roman and Native in North Britain* (1958); P. Salway, *The Frontier People of Roman Britain* (1965). Of the numerous fort-excavations, two may be mentioned: P. T. Bidwell, *The Roman Fort at Vindolanda* (1985); M. C. Bishop & J. N. Dore, *Corbridge. Excavations of the Roman Fort and Town, 1947–80* (1989). The frontier in Scotland has seen important work in the past twenty years. The major work of G. Macdonald, *The Roman Wall in Scotland* (2nd edn 1934), is still a vital work of reference. W. S. Hanson & G. S. Maxwell, *Rome's North-West Frontier: The Antonine Wall* (2nd edn 1987) is an excellent short treatment. Two forts with long histories are: A. S. Robertson, *Birrens [Blatobulgium]* (1975) and S. S. Frere and J. J. Wilkes, *Strageath* (1989).

A general account of the coastal defences is S. Johnson, *The Roman Forts of the Saxon Shore* (1976); some of the related problems are addressed in D. E. Johnston (ed.), *The Saxon Shore* (1977). Among individual sites, the following are important: B. Cunliffe, *Richborough V* (1968); B. Cunliffe, *Excavations at Portchester I* (1975); S. Johnson, *Burgh Castle* (1983), and B. Philp, *The Excavation of the Roman Forts at Dover* (1981). On events in the historical record: N. Shiel, *The Episode of Carausius and Allectus* (1977); J. C. Mann, 'The Northern Frontier after AD 369', *Glasgow Archaeological Journal* 3 (1974), 40–42; S. Esmonde-Cleary, *The Ending of Roman Britain* (1989).

URBAN LIFE

There is no up-to-date study of the cities. J. S. Wacher, *The Towns of Roman Britain* (1975) is dated in part. B. Burnham and J. S. Wacher, *The Small Towns of Roman Britain* (1990) is a good survey of an important subject. S. Esmonde-Cleary, *Extra-mural Areas of Romano-British Towns* (1987) deals with a vital and still little-known topic. F. Grew and B. Hobley (eds.), *Roman Urban Topography in Britain and the Western Roman Empire* (1985) contains several useful papers. On the origins and early phases of cities, G. Webster (ed.), *Fortress into City* (1988). I. A. Richmond, 'The Four Coloniae of Roman Britain', *Archeological Journal* 103 (1946), 57–84 is still worth attention. On individual sites, the following are important studies: P. Crummy, *Excavations at Lion Walk, Balkerne Lane and Middleborough, Colchester* (1984); B. R. K. Niblett, *Sheepen: An early Roman Industrial Site at Camulodunum* (1985); D. Fishwick, 'Templum Divo Claudio Constitutum', *Britannia* 3 (1972), 164–81. M. Jones, *The Defences of the Upper Enclosure [Lincoln]* (1980); F. H. Thompson and J. B. Whitwell, 'The Gates of Roman Lincoln', *Archaeologia* 104 (1973), 129–207; H. R. Hurst, *Gloucester. The Roman and Later Defences* (1985); Royal Commission on Historical Monuments (England), *Eboracum, Roman York* (1962); P. Marsden, *Roman London* (1980); R. Merrifield, *London, City of the Romans* (1983); G. Milne, *The Port of Roman London* (1985); P. Marsden, *The Roman Forum Site in London* (1987). Verulamium and Silchester still provide the fullest picture of Romano-British cities: R. E. M. and T. V. Wheeler, *Verulamium. A Belgic and Two Roman Cities*: (1936); S. S. Frere, *Verulamium Excavations I* (1972); *II* (1983); G. C. Boon, *Silchester. The Roman Town of Calleva* (2nd edn 1974); M. G. Fulford, *Silchester Defences* (1984); J. P. Bushe-Fox, *Excavations on the Site of the Roman Town at Wroxeter I* (1913); *II* (1914); *III* (1916); D. Atkinson, *Excavations at Wroxeter, 1923–27* (1942). Major public buildings are dealt with by S. S. Frere, 'The Roman theatre at Canterbury', *Britannia* 1 (1970), 83–113; M. Hebditch and J. E. Mellor, 'The Forum and Basilica of Roman Leicester', *Britannia* 4 (1973), 1–83; P. T. Bidwell, *The Legionary Bath-house and Basilica and Forum at Exeter* (1979). Urban housing is not as fully known as it deserves to be. Frere, *Verulamium I* contains important material, as does A. MacWhirr, *Houses in Roman Cirencester* (1982). The remarkable buildings at Bath have been studied in outstanding publications by B. Cunliffe, *Roman Bath* (1969) and *The Temple of Sulis Minerva at Bath. The Site* (1984). The documents from the sacred spring here are striking records of urban life: R. S. O. Tomlin, *Tabellae Sulis* (1988).

Urban cemeteries are still poorly recorded. The best are L. P. Wenham, *The Romano-British Cemetery at Trentholme Drive, York* (1968); A. MacWhirr et al., *Romano-British Cemeteries at Cirencester* (1982); G. C. Clarke, *Pre-Roman and Roman Winchester: the Roman Cemetery at Lankhills* (1976).

RURAL SETTLEMENT AND SOCIETY

There are few general treatments of this increasingly complicated field of study. Most of the papers in C. Thomas (ed.), *Rural Settlement in Roman Britain* are badly dated. More recent, but not always reliable, is R. Hingley, *Rural Settlement in Roman Britain* (1989). Several contributions in D. Miles (ed.), *The Romano-British Countryside* (1982) are very useful. For the North, J. C. Chapman and H. Mytum (eds.), *Settlement in North Britain 1000 BC to AD 1000* (1983) contains much of value. Villas are well covered by A. L. F. Rivet (ed.), *The Roman Villa in Britain* (1969); M. Todd, *Studies in the Romano-British Villa* (1978); J. Percival, *The Roman Villa* (1976). Several studies of individual *civitates* contain useful accounts of rural settlement, e.g. B. Cunliffe, *The Regni* (1973); N. Higham and B. Jones, *The Carvetii* (1985); B. Hartley and L. Fitts, *The Brigantes* (1988); M. Todd, *The Coritani* (2nd edn 1991). Other important regional surveys are: J. P. Wild, 'Roman Settlement in the lower Nene valley', *Archaeological Journal* 131 (1974), 140–70; C. F. C. Hawkes, 'Britons, Romans and Saxons round Salisbury and in Cranborne Chase', *Archaeological Journal* 104 (1948), 27–81; G. Jobey, 'Hillforts and Settlements in Northumberland', *Archaeologia Aeliana 4th Series* 43 (1965), 21–64; L. Macinnes, 'Brochs and the Roman Occupation of Lowland Scotland', *Proceedings of the Society of Antiquaries of Scotland* 114 (1984), 235–49; C. W. Phillips (ed.), *The Fenland in Roman Times* (1969). Villa excavations are abundant and only the more informative are listed here: S. Lysons, *Roman Antiquities at Woodchester* (1797); G. Clarke, 'The Roman Villa at Woodchester', *Britannia* 13 (1982), 197–228; S. S. Frere, 'The Bignor Villa', *Britannia* 13 (1982), 135–96; D. S. Neal, *The Excavation of the Roman Villa in Gadebridge Park* (1974); D. S. Neal, *Gorhambury* (1989); W. J. and K. A. Rodwell, *Rivenhall* (1986); I. M. Stead, *Excavations at Winterton Roman Villa . . .* (1976); G. W. Meates, *The Roman Villa at Lullingstone I* (1979), *II* (1988); M. G. Jarrett & S. Wrathmell, *Whitton* (1981). The study of floor mosaics has long been a British speciality: W. Fowler, *Engravings of the Principal Mosaic Pavements . . .* (1804); S. Lysons, *Reliquiae Britannico-Romanae I* (1813); *II* (1817); *III* (1817); T. Morgan, *Romano-British*

Mosaic Pavements (1886); Prof. Buckman & C. H. Newmarch, *Remains of Roman Art in Cirencester . . . Ancient Corinium* (1850); A. Rainey, *Mosaics in Roman Britain* (1873).

Humble rural settlements and their field-systems have been well studied in Britain. H. C. Bowen, *Ancient Fields* (1961) is a basic text. A small selection of sites is here listed to illustrate regional variety. H. E. O'N. Hencken, 'An Excavation . . . at Chysauster, Cornwall', *Archaeologia* 83 (1933), 237–84; G. J. Wainwright, 'The Excavation of a Fortified Settlement at Walesland Rath, Pembrokeshire', *Britannia* 2 (1971), 48–108; R. Leech, 'Excavation of a Romano-British farmstead and cemetery at Bradley Hill, Somerset', *Britannia* 12 (1981), 177–252; D. A. Jackson and T. M. Ambrose, 'Excavation at Wakerley, Northants', *Britannia* 9 (1978), 115–242; D. F. Mackreth, 'Excavation of an Iron Age and Roman Enclosure at Werrington, Cambridgeshire', *Britannia* 19 (1988), 59–151; N. J. Higham and G. D. B. Jones, 'Frontiers, forts and farmers: Cumbrian aerial survey 1974', *Archaeological Journal* 132 (1975), 16–53.

ECONOMIC LIFE

Metals and Mining: P. R. Lewis & G. D. B. Jones, 'The Dolau Cothi Gold Mines I: the Surface Evidence', *Antiquaries Journal* 49 (1969), 244–72; J. W. Gough, *The Mines of Mendip* (1930); G. C. Whittick, 'Roman Lead-mining on Mendip and in North Wales', *Britannia* 13 (1982), 113–23; K. S. Painter, 'Two Roman Silver Ingots from Kent', *Archaeologia Cantiana* 97 (1981), 201–7; O. Davies, 'The Copper Mines on Great Orme's Head', *Archaeologia Cambrensis* 100 (1948), 61–6; R. D. Penhalurick, *Tin in Antiquity* (1986); H. Cleere & D. W. Crossley, *The Iron Industry of the Weald* (1985); W. H. Manning, *Catalogue of the Romano-British Ironwork in the Museum of Antiquities, Newcastle upon Tyne* (1976); S. Rees, *Agricultural Implements in Prehistoric and Roman Britain* (1979).

Other minerals and organic materials: A. J. Lawson, 'Shale and Jet Objects from Silchester', *Archaeologia*, 105 (1976), 241–75; J. Liverside, *Furniture in Roman Britain* (1955); J. P. Wild, *Textile Manufacture in the Northern Roman Provinces* (1970); M. J. Rhodes, 'Inscriptions on Leather Waste from Roman London', *Britannia* 18 (1987), 173–81.

Glass: T. May, *Warrington's Roman Remains* (1904); C. Isings, *Roman Glass from Dated Finds* (1959).

Pottery: M. H. Callender, *Roman Amphorae* (1965); D. P. S. Peacock, *Pottery in the Roman World* (1982); V. G. Swan, *The Pottery Kilns of Roman*

Britain (1984); W. F. Grimes, *The Pottery and Tilery of the XXth Legion at Holt* (1930); G. B. Dannell and J. P. Wild, *Longthorpe II: the Military Works Depot* (1987).

Pottery production centres: E. T. Artis, *The Durobrivae of Antoninus* . . . [1828]; C. J. Young, *Oxfordshire Roman Pottery* (1977); M. G. Fulford, *New Forest Roman Pottery* (1975); P. R. Wilson (ed.), *The Crambeck Roman Pottery Industry*; P. V. Webster, 'Severn Valley Ware', *Transactions of the Bristol and Gloucester Archaeological Society*, 94 (1976), 18–46.

Pottery imports: C. M. Johns, *Arretine and Samian Pottery* (1971); M. Fulford and J. Bird, 'Imported Pottery from Germany in the late Roman Period', *Britannia* 6 (1975), 171–81; B. Richardson and P. A. Tyers, 'North Gaulish Pottery in Britain', *Britannia* 15 (1984), 133–41.

Organisation of trade: P. Stuart and J. E. Bogaers, *Deae Nehalleniae* (1971); J. du Plat Taylor and H. Cleere (eds.), *Roman Shipping and Trade: Britain and the Rhine Provinces* (1978).

RELIGIOUS LIFE

The best general treatment is M. Henig, *Religion in Roman Britain* (1984). On structures, M. J. T. Lewis, *Temples in Roman Britain* is useful, as is W. J. Rodwell (ed.), *Temples, Churches and Religion in Roman Britain* (1980). Individual shrines of particular importance include: W. J. Wedlake, *The Excavation of the Shrine of Apollo at Nettleton, Wiltshire* (1982); R. E. M. and T. V. Wheeler, *Report on the Excavations of the Prehistoric, Roman and Post-Roman Site in Lydney Park, Gloucs.* (1932); N. E. France and B. M. Gobel, *The Romano-British Temple at Harlow, Essex* (1983); R. G. Goodchild & J. R. Kirk, 'The Romano-Celtic Temple at Woodeaton', *Oxoniensia* 19 (1954), 15–37. The eastern mystery cults are fully discussed in E. and J. R. Harris, *The Oriental Cults in Roman Britain* (1965). Among *mithraea* are the following: I. A. Richmond et al., 'The Temple of Mithras at Carrawburgh', *Archaeologia Aeliana* 4th Series 29 (1951), 1–92; G. C. Boon, 'A Temple of Mithras at Caernarvon-*Segontium*', *Archaeologia Cambrensis* 109 (1960), 136–72; W. F. Grimes, *The Excavation of Roman and Medieval London* (1968). A classic account of religious observance in the army is I. A. Richmond, 'Roman Legionaries at Corbridge, their Supply-base, Temples and Religious Cults', *Archaeologia Aeliana* 4th Series 21 (1943), 127–224. Early Christianity is excellently and judiciously discussed by H. Williams, *Christianity in Early Britain* (1912). More speculative is C. Thomas, *Christianity in Roman Britain* (1981). Several papers in M. W. Barley and R. P. C. Hanson (eds.), *Christianity in Britain 300–700* (1968) are worth attention. For structures and objects: S. S. Frere, 'The Silchester Church: the Excavations by Sir Ian Richmond in 1961', *Archaeologia* 105 (1975), 277–302; P. D. C. Brown, 'The Church at Richborough', *Britannia* 2 (1971), 225–31; C. J. Guy, 'Roman Circular Lead Tanks in Britain', *Britannia* 12 (1981), 271–6; C. Johns and T. W. Potter, *The Thetford Treasure* (1983). On the Church in fifth-century Britain, E. A. Thompson, *St Germanus of Auxerre and the End of Roman Britain* (1984).

Index

PLACES

Albion 1
Alchester 82, 84
Aldborough 71, 100
Ancaster: Anglo-Saxon cemetery
   52; Iron Age settlement 58;
   town 58
Anglesey 25, 30, 111–12; Roman
   attack on 25
Angmering 59, 94
Aquae Arnemetiae (Buxton) 74,
   172, 173
Aquae Sulis (Bath): baths 61, 74–
   5, 165, 172–3; coal 136; cult
   statue 79, 173; *genii cucullati*, 168;
   sculpture 172; springs 61, 74,
   165, 172
Ardoch 41
Arras, medallion 46

Backworth: patera 166
Badbury Rings: burial-mounds
   122; settlement 84
Bagendon 60
Bardown: iron-workings 133
Bartlow Hills: burial mounds
   123
Barton Court Farm 96–8
Beadlam 100
Beauport Park: iron-workings 133
Benwell 177
Bertha 41
Bewcastle 38

Bignor 78
Binchester 72
Birdoswald 48, 54, 175, 177
Birrens 39, 42
Brading 186
Braich y Dinas 111
Brampton 36
Brancaster 45
Brean Down 181
Bremetannacum 101
Bridgeness 40
Brigstock 170
Bochastle 34
Brough-on-Humber 29; aedile
   81, 163; Humber crossing 71;
   lead ingots 130–31; port 73;
   theatre 81, 163
Brough-on-Noe 42

Caerau 112
Caer Gybi 49–50
Caerleon: amphitheatre 78;
   dedications 174; legionary base
   29, 35, 37, 73, 118, 131, 174
Cae'r Mynydd 112
Caernarvon: fort 49; mithraeum
   184
Caerwent 64, 69, 76, 118,
   169
Caister-by-Norwich: Anglo-Saxon
   cemetery 52; city 69, 86; water-
   supply 76

Caister-by-Yarmouth   73

Calderdale: inscriptions 71–2, 101; veterans 101

Cambridge   58

Camulodunum   5, 7, 8, 21, 22, 26, 56; cemetery 180; church(?) 180; *colonia* 56, 57, 61, 79, 91, 94–5, 116, 143, 162–3, 189; marble 154; pottery industry 142; temple of deified Claudius 162, 189

Canterbury   60–61; in fifth century 52; plan 67; theatre 61

Cardean   35

Cardiff   46

Carlisle: fort 35, 36, 39, 50; town 54, 72

Carpow   44

Carrawburgh: mithraeum 184

Carvoran   36, 175

Castleford   29

Cat's Water   117

Catterick   72

Chanctonbury Ring: temple 181

Charterhouse-on-Mendip: lead-mining 83, 129

Chartres: sculptor 75

Chedworth   103, 106

Chelmsford   84

Chester: amphitheatre 78; dedications 174; gold-working 156; legionary base 29, 30, 31, 35, 37, 73, 174

Chesterholm: fort 36–7, 50, 54; headquarters 49; *vicus* 72, 82; writing tablets 36–8

Chesters: fort 47; *vicus* 72

Chichester   9, 58–9, 67, 81; Cogidubnus inscription 163

Chisenbury Warren   114

Chysauster   113

Cirencester   60, 67, 106; amphitheatre 78; Cernunnos 168; defences 80; gates 80; *genii cucullati* 168; gold-working 156; houses 76–7; Jupiter column 167; marble 154–5; Matronae 165; water-supply 76

Claydon Pike   93

Clipsham   133

Cold Kitchen Hill: temple 181

Colijnsplaat: altars 157; merchants 157

Colley Weston: temples 170

Cologne   137

Combe Down   92, 93

Corbridge   175, 181, 183; coal 136; fort 35–37, 50, 54; lanx 186–7; *vicus* 72; workshops 134

Corby   133–4

Coria   82

Cranborne Chase   108

Cromwell: settlement 114; villa 91, 114

Crosby Ravensworth   109

Dalginross   34

Dalswinton   35

Dalton Parlours   100

Darenth   99, 107

Din Lligwy   111–12

Dinorben   111

Ditchley   99

Doncaster   29

Dorchester (Dorset)   70; amphitheatre 78; aqueduct 76

Dorchester-on-Thames   58, 82, 174

Doune   31

Dover: fort 45; port 73

Droitwich   83, 139

Durno 33
Durobrivae 82, 83, 84; hoard 180;
    pottery industry 83

Eccles 94
Elslack 46
Ewe Close 109
Exeter: baths 60; city 58, 60, 67,
    72; defences 80; houses 77;
    legionary base 24, 27, 58

Farley Heath 170
Fendoch 34, 35
Fishbourne 24, 59, 94, 96
Forden Gaer 49
Frampton 180
Frilford: amphitheatre 83, 171;
    temple 83, 116, 170, 171, 181

Gadebridge Park 95, 96, 102
Gargrave 101
Glenlochar 35
Gloucester: colonia 57, 72, 91;
    decurion 81; defences 79;
    legionary base 57; plan 67;
    tiles 147
Godmanchester 84
Goldherring 113
Gorhambury 95
Gosbecks 116
Greatchesters 47
Great Witcombe 103
Greaves Ash 109

Halton Chesters 48
Hambleden 95, 99
Ham Hill 23
Hardknott 176, 177
Harlow 170
Harpenden 123
Heathrow 170

Hembury 23
Hengistbury Head 5, 6, 73
High Cross 84
High Rochester 35
Hinton St Mary 180
Hod Hill 23
Holborough 123
Horton Kirby 122
Housesteads: headquarters 48; fort
    47; Frisii at 166; mithraeum
    184; restoration 48; vicus 72
Hoxne 161

Icklingham: cella memoriae 179;
    cemetery 179
Ictis 5, 134
Ilchester 70
Inchtuthil 35
Inverquharity 34
Irchester 58, 82; defences 83;
    strator 82
Ireland 32

Kenchester 82
Keston 123
Kingsholm 25, 27
Kinvaston 25
Knobs Crook 122

Lake Farm 24
Lamyatt Beacon 171–2, 181
Lancaster 46
Lanchester 166
Langton 101
Laxton 133
Leicester: Anglo-Saxon cemetery
    52; baths 60, 63; city 60;
    development 63, 99; fort 58;
    forum 63; Iron Age settlement
    58; Jewry Wall 63; macellum 63;
    plan 67

Leighton 25
Leintwardine 49
Lexden 8
Lincoln: aqueduct 75; *castellum aquae* 75; *colonia* 57, 63, 71, 72–3, 91, 99, 164; defences 80; fifth century 52; Iron Age settlement 58; marble 154–5; *sevir Augustalis* 81, 164; *vici* 164–5
Littlecote: cult-room 186; mosaic 186; villa 186
Llantwit Major 99–100
Llyn Cerrig Bach 3
Lockham 107
Lockington: settlement 114; villa 91, 114
Lockleys 95
London 26, 37, 61–2, 67, 72, 85; amphitheatre 78; defences 80; demolition 66; exports 61–2; gold-working 156; Imperial cult 163; imports 61–2, 74; Isis cult 166; legal status 62; marble 154–5; mint 160; mithraeum 184, 185; port 61–2, 73–4; temple 184, 185
Lullingstone: granary 122; house-church 180; temple-mausoleum 124; villa 107
Lutudarum 129
Lydney 115, 169
Lympne 45
Lyons 43

Maiden Castle 23
Malling 34
Malton: fort 29, 50, 71; gold-working 156
Margidunum 83
Maryport 175, 176
Massalia 1

Maxey 117
Mona (Anglesey) 25, 30
Mons Graupius 33, 34
Mount Batten 5, 73
Mucking 52

Netherby 39
Nettleton 83, 170
Newbrough 36
Newcastle 38
Newstead 31, 35, 174, 177
Newton Kyme 46
Newton St Loe 99
North Leigh 103, 106, 108

Old Carlisle 72
Old Kilpatrick 40
Old Penrith 72
Old Sarum 84
Orkneys 34
Orton Longueville 103
Osmanthorpe 27

Pagan's Hill 170, 171
Papcastle 176
Park Street 95
Piercebridge: fort 46, 50; *vicus* 72
Plaxtol 107
Poole 73
Portchester 45

Reculver 45
Richborough 21, 45, 73, 179–80
Rivenhall 94
Rochester 84
Romney Marsh 118
Rossington Bridge 27–8
Rudchester 48, 184
Rudston: mosaic 101–2; villa 101

St Albans: *cella memoriae* 179; cemetery 179

Sea Mills 73

Settrington 100

Shakenoak 103

Silchester 9, 52, 60, 64, 66, 67–9; amphitheatre 67, 78; basilica 66; baths 68, 69; church (?) 69, 179; *collegium* 64, 81; *curia* 69; defences 79–80; forum 67, 68; gates 80; Hercules cult 64, 167; Iron Age coinage 67; Iron Age *oppidum* 67; *mansio* 69; marble 68, 154–5; Mars cult 167; mint 67; plan 68–9; private houses 68–9; Sarapis cult 79; tiles 147; Tutela 68, 79, 166–7; water supply 76

South Cadbury 23

Southwick 59, 94

Sparsholt 98

Springhead 83, 107, 123

Spoonley Wood 96

Stanwix 39

Stonea Grange 117

Stonesfield 107

Strageath 35, 41

Stroud 98

Templeborough 27

Thetford 181

Thundersbarrow Hill 114

Towcester 83

Traprain Law 110

Tre'r Ceiri 111

Uley: curse tablets 171; temple 171, 181

Usk 25, 27

Veleia 91–2

Vernemetum 172

Verulamium 5, 26, 52, 58, 60, 64–6, 95; defences 79; economic life 66; fire 66; gates 80; gold-working 156; monumental arch 66; mosaics 66; pottery industry 143, 145; shops 66; temple 65, 169; theatre 67; urban houses 65, 76, 77; villas 95

Wakerley 133

Walcheren: merchants 157; shrine 157

Walesland Rath 110

Wall 25, 84

Wallsend 38, 47

Wapping 45

Welwyn: burial 6; monument 124

West Bierley 134

West Mersea: mausoleum 123; villa 94

West Stow 52

Weston under Penyard 83, 133

Weycock Hill 170, 171

Whilton Lodge 99–100

Whitby 137

Winchester 60, 67; defences 80; gates 80; Iron Age settlement 58; plan 67

Wingham 94, 103

Winterton 98

Woodeaton 115, 169, 171, 181

Wood Lane End 124

Woodchester 103, 103–6

Worth 170

Wroxeter: aqueduct 75–6; baths 62–3, 66; city 58, 60; development 62; fire 63; forum 60, 62, 66; houses 76; legionary base 27, 58, 62; *macellum* 63; timber buildings 66

Wycomb 83

York: *colonia* 71, 100, 164;
   Constantius, death at 47;
   Constantius, renovation by 46;
   decurion 81; dedications 174,
   177; jet 137; legionary base
29, 31, 37, 44, 50, 71, 100,
174; provincial capital 49;
sculpture 79; Sarapis cult 166,
183; *sevir Augustalis* 81, 164;
shrouds 141

SUBJECTS

Abundantia 164
Adminius 20
aisled halls 98–9
agriculture 3, 45, 102, 109–10,
   121–2, 149
Alaisiagae 166, 178
ala Petriana 39
Alexander Severus 181
Alfenus Senecio 43
Allectus 46, 160
Alpinus Classicianus, J. 27, 61,
   137
amethysts 139
amphitheatres 78
Andescocioucos 165
animals 3–4, 88, 96, 109–10, 117,
   119–21, 149
Antenociticus 169
Antonine Itinerary 84, 85
Antonine Wall 40–42, 42, 171;
   ditch 40; evacuation 42;
   'expansions' 41; final
   abandonment 42; fortlets 40, 41;
   garrison 41; reoccupation 42
Antoninus Pius 40, 60, 159, 163,
   176
Apollo 164, 165, 176
Apollo Nextlomarus 178
Apollo Cunomaglos 83
aqueducts 75–6
Arciaco 165

ard 89
areani 47
argenteus 160
Argonne ware 151
Armilustrium 176, 188
Arthur's O'on 170–71
Asclepius 164
Atecotti 50
Atrebates 7, 8, 9, 69, 85
Attius Marinus, G. 143
Augustus 8, 9, 18, 19
Aurelian 159, 160
Aurelius Lunaris, M. 81, 151

Bacchus 167
ballistae 81
barrels 151
Batavians 36
bears 140
Bede 38
Belatucadrus 169
Belgae 9
Bellona 164
beneficiarius consularis 83
birrus Britannicus 121, 140
Bokerley Dyke 108
Boudicca 26, 79
Braciaca 165
Brigantes 2, 15, 24, 28, 30, 31,
   70–71, 85, 88
Brigantia 183

Britannia: coin-type 41
bronze vessels 153–4

Caledonii 32, 33, 34, 40, 44
Calgacus 2, 31
Callirius 165
Calpurnius Agricola 43
Campestres 177
Cantiaci 1, 9
Capitolium 162
Caracalla 44, 159
Caratacus 2, 21, 24, 28
Carausius 46, 48, 160
Car Dyke 116
Cartimandua 2, 15, 24, 28–9
Carvetii 70
Cassius Dio 21, 44
castellum aquae 75
Cassivellaunus 17–18
Catuvellauni 7, 8, 9, 85
Ceres 164
Cernunnos 168, 171
chariots 3
Christianity 179–80
Cinhil 54
cinnabar 138, 148, 156
citizenship 188
classis Britannica 45, 46, 133
Claudian 140
Claudius 2, 9, 20–21, 56, 59,
    79, 164; portrait 79; temple
    56
Claudius Paulinus, T. 70
Claudius Triferna, T. 128, 130
client-king 59
climate 3, 89
Clodius Albinus 43
coal 136
coastal fortlets 49
Cocceius Firmus, M. 177
Cocidius 169

Cogidubnus 21, 58, 59, 60, 68,
    70, 133, 138, 164
coinage: British 6–7, 9, 11, 13,
    157–8; Claudian 159; Gaulish 6;
    hoards 46, 158, 161;
    Roman 157–61
collegium 59, 81, 132–3
coloniae 57, 78, 79
Commius 6, 8–9, 67
Commodus 43, 80, 163, 183
Constans 47
Constantine I 47, 80, 85, 160;
    Britannicus Maximus 47; coinage
    160; portrait 79
Constantine III 51–2; coinage
    161
Constantius Chlorus 46, 160
conventus 84
copper 131–2
Corieltauvi 2, 12
Cornovii 12
courtyard houses 113
cropping-shears 141
crops 110, 121–2, 149
Cuda 169
Cunobelin 5, 7, 8, 20, 21, 56
curia 82
Curia Tectoverdorum 82
curse-tablets 187
Cybele 185, 186

Damnonii 82
Dea Hammia 178
Dea Roma 174
Deceangli 12, 23
Demetae 11–12
Demetrius of Tarsus 32
Diana 164, 177
Diana Luna 105
Didius Gallus 21
Diocletian 47, 85, 106, 121, 160

Diodorus Siculus 134
Dobunni 11, 96, 158
Domitian 30, 32, 34
druids 25
Dubnovellaunus 7, 9
Dumnonii 10
duoviri aediles 84; *iuredicundo* 84;
  quinquennales 84
Durotriges 10–11, 23, 70, 158
dux Britanniarum 48

Elagabalus 182–3
enamels 156–7
Epona 168, 177
Eppillus 5, 9, 68
exploratores 47

Fates, the 164, 165
Faunus 181
Faustinus 106
Fenland 92, 116–18
Feriale Duranum 176
field army 48, 53
fields 4, 90–91, 109; 'brickwork'
  90
fish 153
fish-sauce 152–3, 157
fleet 32, 46
follis 160
Forth–Clyde line 40
Fortuna 164, 177
Franks 45
Frisii 166, 178

Gaius 20
Galba 21
Gallic Chronicle 51
Garmangabis 166
genii cucullati 168
Geta 44
Gildas 51

gladiators 78
glass-making 118, 148
Gnosticism 186
gold 126, 128, 156; mine 126,
  128, 156; working 156
grain 88–9
Gratian 51
Grim's Ditch 107
gypsum 123

Hadrian 36, 38, 60, 62, 65, 79,
  129, 163, 164
Hadrian's Wall 38–44; coins 53;
  end of occupation 50, 54;
  fortlets 38; garrison 39, 47, 49;
  invaded 42; milecastles 38, 49;
  purpose 39; restoration: by
  Constantius 46–7; by Severus 43;
  by Theodosius 48; turrets 38, 49
hanging-bowls 53
Harimella 178
haruspex 165
Hercules 164, 165; Saegonius
  (Segomo) 64, 165
hill-forts 5, 10, 12, 15
Honorius 50, 51; letter to
  civitates 51
Horace 19
hunt-cups 144
hunting dogs 126, 139, 140
Hvitir 166, 179

Iceni 2, 13, 25, 26, 69, 158
Imperial cult 56, 81, 163, 175
Imperial post (*cursus publicus*) 83,
  85
imports 5, 6, 81, 149–56, 157
Indutius Felix, C. 106
iron 83, 118, 126, 132–4
Isis 166
Iulius Agricola, Gn. 28, 30–34, 60

Iulius Frontinus, S. 28–30

jet 74, 136–7
Julia Domna 44, 183
Julian 186–7
Julius Caesar 1, 6, 8, 9, 16–18,
   20, 121, 162
Julius Verus 41
Juno 162, 164; Regina 181
Jupiter 162, 164, 167, 175, 176;
   Dolichenus 181, 183;
   Heliopolitanus 182–3; Tanaris
   174
Jupiter Optimus Maximus 165,
   167, 174, 175, 176

Kimmeridge shale 119
kingship: Iron Age 1, 2

land-ownership 92–3
landscape 88–90
lanx, Corbridge 154
lead 74, 83, 126, 128–31,
leather 121, 141
legatus iuridicus 84
legions: II Augusta 20, 24, 26,
   29, 57, 70, 128, 129; II Adiutrix
   29, 35; VI 174–5; IX Hispana
   20, 26, 27, 28, 29, 57, 146; XIV
   Gemina 20, 27, 28; XX 20, 27,
   28, 30, 34, 145; in conquest
   20–23; at Nijmegen 36;
   vexillations 36
limitanei 53
Lollius Urbicus 40, 171
Loucetius 165

Maeatae 43, 44
Magnentius 48
Magnus Maximus 49, 50
Mandubracius 18

mansio 84
Maponus 165
marble 107, 124, 138, 154–5
Marcus 51
Marcus Aurelius 159
Mars 164, 165, 167, 171, 176;
   Alator 169; Braciaca 165; Lenus
   64, 165, 168; Loucetius 165;
   Medocius 165; Ocellus
   Vellaunus 169; Thincsus 166,
   178
Matres 165, 166, 167, 168, 189;
   Alateivae 178; Ollotatae 178
Matronae 165–6, 168
mausolea 107, 123–4
Mayen ware 151
Medocius 165
Mercury 164, 165, 167, 171
metalwork 7, 53, 153–4
mills 138
minerals 1, 20, 126–32
Minerva 162, 163, 164, 165, 167,
   174, 177
Mithras 62, 183–5; saecularis 185
Mogons 178, 179
mosaics 101–2, 104, 106
mulsum 123

Nantosvelta 168
Natalius Natalinus, Q. 106
negotiatores salarii 139, 157
Nehallenia 157
nemeton 172, 173
Neptune 163, 164, 167
Nero 26, 28, 59, 62, 68, 79,
   92, 94, 95, 162, 163
New Forest: pottery industry
   52–3, 146–7
Nipius Ascanius, C. 128,
   130
Nodens 169

Novantae   15–16, 32, 35
numerus Hnaufridi   178

Ocellus Vellaunus   165
oil lamps   152
olive oil   73, 152–3
oppida   5, 11
Ordovices   2, 12, 24, 29, 30
Orpheus   104
Ostorius Scapula   21, 24, 28, 56
Otho   28
oysters   153

Padern Pesrut   54
pagus   82–3, 115
papyrus   155
parade-grounds   176–7
Parisi   14–15, 70–71, 101
Paul, 'the Chain'   48
pearls   139
Pescennius Niger   43
Petilius Cerealis, Q.   26, 28–30, 31, 71
pewter   135–6; ingots 135; moulds 135
Picts   46, 47, 48, 49, 54
Plautius, Aulus   20–21
Pliny, Elder   128
pottery industry   52–3, 119, 141–7; Colchester 142; Derbyshire 145; Dorset 142; East Yorkshire 52; Iron Age 141–2; Holt 145; Gaul 142–5; Longthorpe 144; military production 145–6; mortaria 142–3; Nene Valley 52, 119, 140, 144, 146; New Forest 51–2, 146–7; Oxfordshire 52, 145, 146; Rossington Bridge 143; Severn Valley 144; terra sigillata 119, 143; Verulamium 145;

Warwickshire 143, 145, 146; Wiggonholt, 119
Prasutagus   13, 26, 92
Pudding Pan Rock   150
Purbeck marble   119, 138
Pytheas   1, 5

querns   138

Regni (Regini)   58
Rhenish ware   151
rosaliae signorum   188
'rounds'   87, 113

Saegonius   165
salinae   139
salt   83, 117, 138–9, 157
saltus   92, 117
sanctuaries   115–16
Sarapis   166, 183
sarcophagus   102, 124
Sarrius   143
Saxon Shore   45, 48, 53
Saxons   45, 48, 51–2; pottery 52
sceattas   135
Scotti   50
sculpture   78–9
seals   140
Selgovae   15–16, 32, 35
Seneca   26
seviri Augustales   81, 164
Septimius Severus   43, 159; division of Britain 45; invasion of Scotland 43
sheep   120–21
Silvanus   106
Silures   2, 11, 24, 29, 70
silver   6, 10, 83, 126, 128, 156; Derbyshire 129; Flintshire 128, 129–30; Mendips 128,

129; Northumberland 128; vessels 6, 8, 153–4, 186
slaves 126
socii Lutudarenses 128–9
Solinus 136
Sol Invictus 183
Stanegate 36
Stilicho 50, 53
stone 137; Bath 137; Cotswolds 137; Lincolnshire 137; Kent 137
Strabo 1, 8, 126
subsidies 40
Sucellus 168
Suebi 178
Suetonius 70
Suetonius Paullinus 25, 27, 28, 30
Sulis Minerva: cult 74, 165, 168; cult-statue 79
Sulpicia Lepidinia 36

Tacitus 2, 18, 24, 33, 60, 65, 79, 92
tapete 121, 140
taxes 125
temples 169–73
terra sigillata 149–50
territorium 57
Tetricus 160
theatres 78
Theodosius: *comes* 48, 49; restoration of Britain 49
Three Gauls: tribute yield 55
tiles 145–6, 147–8; Ashtead 148; Gloucester 147; legionary 147; Plaxtol 148
timber 141
tin 1, 5, 10, 126, 134–5
Tincommius 8, 9, 67
Titus 30

Togodumnus 21
tombs 122–4
Trajan 158
Trebellius Maximus 28
tributum capitis 85
tributum soli 85
Trinovantes 7, 9, 18, 26, 56
Tyne–Solway line 31, 36

Ulpius Marcellus 43
Unseni Fersomari 166, 178
urban defences 79–81
urban government 55–8, 60–61
urban housing 76–8
usurpers 48, 50–51

Valentia 49
Valentinian 48
Valerius Veranius, Q. 142, 143
vegetables 121
Venus 167
Venutius 28, 29
Veranius Secundus, Q. 142, 143
Verecundius Diogenes, M. 81, 152
Verica 5, 9, 20, 23, 59
Vespasian 21, 23, 30, 59, 60, 162
Vettius Bolanus 28, 29, 30
Victoria 164, 171, 174, 176
vicus 72
villages 113–14
villas 93–106
vines 122, 151–2
Viridius 169
Virius Lupus 43
Virodechthis 178
Vitellius 28
Vocontii 70
Votadini 15, 40, 82
Vulcan 164

walled cemeteries 107, 123
warfare 2–3
water mills 148–9
weaving mills 140
whetstones 138
wine 5, 8, 73, 122, 151–2

wool 140–41
writing tablets: London 62;
    Vindolanda 36–7, 125,
    155

Zosimus 51

READ MORE IN PENGUIN

In every corner of the world, on every subject under the sun, Penguin represents quality and variety – the very best in publishing today.

For complete information about books available from Penguin – including Puffins, Penguin Classics and Arkana – and how to order them, write to us at the appropriate address below. Please note that for copyright reasons the selection of books varies from country to country.

In the United Kingdom: Please write to *Dept. JC, Penguin Books Ltd, FREEPOST, West Drayton, Middlesex UB7 0BR.*

If you have any difficulty in obtaining a title, please send your order with the correct money, plus ten per cent for postage and packaging, to *PO Box No. 11, West Drayton, Middlesex UB7 0BR*

In the United States: Please write to *Consumer Sales, Penguin USA, P.O. Box 999, Dept. 17109, Bergenfield, New Jersey 07621-0120.* VISA and MasterCard holders call 1-800-253-6476 to order all Penguin titles

In Canada: Please write to *Penguin Books Canada Ltd, 10 Alcorn Avenue, Suite 300, Toronto, Ontario M4V 3B2*

In Australia: Please write to *Penguin Books Australia Ltd, P.O. Box 257, Ringwood, Victoria 3134*

In New Zealand: Please write to *Penguin Books (NZ) Ltd, Private Bag 102902, North Shore Mail Centre, Auckland 10*

In India: Please write to *Penguin Books India Pvt Ltd, 706 Eros Apartments, 56 Nehru Place, New Delhi 110 019*

In the Netherlands: Please write to *Penguin Books Netherlands bv, Postbus 3507, NL-1001 AH Amsterdam*

In Germany: Please write to *Penguin Books Deutschland GmbH, Metzlerstrasse 26, 60594 Frankfurt am Main*

In Spain: Please write to *Penguin Books S. A., Bravo Murillo 19, 1° B, 28015 Madrid*

In Italy: Please write to *Penguin Italia s.r.l., Via Felice Casati 20, I-20124 Milano*

In France: Please write to *Penguin France S. A., 17 rue Lejeune, F-31000 Toulouse*

In Japan: Please write to *Penguin Books Japan, Ishikiribashi Building, 2-5-4, Suido, Bunkyo-ku, Tokyo 112*

In Greece: Please write to *Penguin Hellas Ltd, Dimocritou 3, GR-106 71 Athens*

In South Africa: Please write to *Longman Penguin Southern Africa (Pty) Ltd, Private Bag X08, Bertsham 2013*

READ MORE IN PENGUIN

HISTORY

A History of Wales   John Davies

'Outstanding ... Dr Davies casts a coolly appraising eye upon myths, false premises and silver linings ... He is impartial. He grasps the story of his country with immense confidence and tells it in vigorous and lucid prose ... Its scope is unique. It is the history Wales needed' – *Daily Telegraph*

Daily Life in Ancient Rome   Jerome Carcopino

This classic study, which includes a bibliography and notes by Professor Rowell, describes the streets, houses and multi-storeyed apartments of the city of over a million inhabitants, the social classes from senators to slaves, and the Roman family and the position of women, causing *The Times Literary Supplement* to hail it as a 'thorough, lively and readable book'.

The Anglo-Saxons   Edited by James Campbell

'For anyone who wishes to understand the broad sweep of English history, Anglo-Saxon society is an important and fascinating subject. And Campbell's is an important and fascinating book. It is also a finely produced and, at times, a very beautiful book' – *London Review of Books*

Customs in Common   E. P. Thompson

Eighteenth-century Britain saw a profound distancing between the culture of the patricians and the plebs. E. P. Thompson explains why in this series of brilliant essays on the customs of the working people, which, he argues, emerged as a culture of resistance towards an innovative market economy. 'One of the most eloquent, powerful and independent voices of our time' – *Observer*

The Habsburg Monarchy 1809–1918   A J P Taylor

Dissolved in 1918, the Habsburg Empire 'had a unique character, out of time and out of place'. Scholarly and vividly accessible, this 'very good book indeed' (*Spectator*) elucidates the problems always inherent in the attempt to give peace, stability and a common loyalty to a heterogeneous population.